Spring Web Services 2 Cookbook

Over 60 recipes providing comprehensive coverage of practical real-life implementations of Spring-WS

Hamidreza Sattari

Shameer Kunjumohamed

BIRMINGHAM - MUMBAI

Spring Web Services 2 Cookbook

First published: February 2012

Production Reference: 1130212

Published by Packt Publishing Ltd.
Livery Place
35 Livery Street
Birmingham B3 2PB, UK.

ISBN 978-1-84951-582-5

www.packtpub.com

Cover Image by Asher Wishkerman (wishkerman@hotmail.com)

Credits

Authors

Hamidreza Sattari

Shameer Kunjumohamed

Reviewers

Biju Kunjummen

Bhavani P Polimetla

Daniel Vaughan

Acquisition Editor

Sanjay Rajan

Lead Technical Editor

Chris Rodrigues

Technical Editors

Manasi Poonthottam

Lubna Shaikh

Sakina Kaydawala

Copy Editor

Leonard D'Silva

Project Coordinator

Shubhanjan Chatterjee

Proofreader

Elinor Perry-Smith

Indexer

Hemangini Bari

Graphics

Manu Joseph

Production Coordinator

Aparna Bhagat

Cover Work

Aparna Bhagat

About the Authors

Hamidreza Sattari started software development in 2002 and has been involved in several areas of Software Engineering, from programming to architecture as well as management. His area of interest has been integration among the software applications.

Hamidreza Sattari earned his Master's degree in Software Engineering in 2008 from Herriot Watt University, UK, and his Bachelor's degree in 1994 in Electrical Engineering (Electronics) from Tehran Azad University, Iran. In recent years, his research area of interest has been scientific data mining using algorithms and statistical techniques in pattern recognition, estimation, and machine learning. He maintains the blog justdeveloped.blogspot.com.

First, I should thank the open source community that is too large to name. Definitely without using the products, ideas, articles, and web log of this community, I would have never been able to write this book. Besides, I would like to thank my friend, Shameer P.K., for his cooperation in writing this book.

Shameer Kunjumohamed is a software architect, specialized in enterprise application integrations and SOA. He is well-versed in J2EE and Microsoft .NET platforms. He is interested in various mobile platforms, including Android, Blackberry, and other cross-platform mobile frameworks that are in the market these days.

After graduating from Calicut University, India, in 2000, Shameer handled different roles in software engineering. He earned his Master's degree in Software Engineering from Heriot Watt University of UK (Dubai campus) in 2009. He has worked for Wellogic ME, at Dubai Internet City. At present, he works as a Solutions Architect in Dubai, UAE, and is a guest lecturer at Heriot Watt University for Post Graduate students in Information Technology.

He maintains the blog `http://justcompiled.blogspot.com`.

I would like to thank a number of people who encouraged me to write this book and reviewed my blog (`http://justcompiled.blogspot.com`), which was a route to this book. I thank my wife Shehida, and my daughters Shireen and Shahreen, who were supporting me and bearing with me when I was busy writing the chapters. It was their precious time I was utilizing for this book. Also, I would like to thank my friend, Hamidreza Sattari, who is a great friend and colleague; without his support and hard work, I wouldn't have taken up this challenge. I extend my thanks to all those who contributed to my knowledge and passion towards technology to make me capable of writing this book.

About the Reviewers

Biju Kunjummen is a Senior Software Developer with Johnson Controls Inc. and works on an Enterprise Java-based Web application, with focus on integration using the open source stack—Core Spring, Spring Integration, Spring Web-Services, and Apache Active MQ.

He has been in the Software Industry since 1998, with focus on Enterprise applications across the Finance and Healthcare domains.

> I would like to thank my wife, Athira, and daughter, Sara, for their patience during the review process.

Bhavani P Polimetla is learning and working in the IT Industry since 1990. He graduated with Bachelor of Computer Science and Master of Computer Applications degrees from Andhra University, India. He worked on standalone Swing applications to Grid computing and the N-tire architecture. He has worked with the world's top-class clients including three from Fortune 50 companies. At present, he is working as an independent Java consultant in Atlanta, Georgia, USA.

To demonstrate his skills, he completed more than 25 certifications in the spectrum of J2EE, Database, and Project Management subjects. He also achieved many awards for many of his projects. He spends his free time performing social service activities. More information is available at his website www.polimetla.com.

Daniel Vaughan has been a commercial software developer since the late 1990s, and over the recent years, has increasingly specialized in Java-based web applications. He has worked with startups through to multinational organizations, either as a part of small agile teams or in consulting roles.

He is currently privileged to be a Software Engineer at the European Bioinformatics Institute in Cambridge, UK, where he works with a large amount of data and tries to understand the magical world of biology.

Daniel is also the author of *Ext GWT: The Beginner's Guide* and can be found at http://www.danielvaughan.com.

www.PacktPub.com

Support files, eBooks, discount offers, and more

You might want to visit www.PacktPub.com for support files and downloads related to your book.

Did you know that Packt offers eBook versions of every book published, with PDF and ePub files available? You can upgrade to the eBook version at www.PacktPub.com and as a print book customer, you are entitled to a discount on the eBook copy. Get in touch with us at service@packtpub.com for more details.

At www.PacktPub.com, you can also read a collection of free technical articles, sign up for a range of free newsletters and receive exclusive discounts and offers on Packt books and eBooks.

http://PacktLib.PacktPub.com

Do you need instant solutions to your IT questions? PacktLib is Packt's online digital book library. Here, you can access, read and search across Packt's entire library of books.

Why Subscribe?

- ▸ Fully searchable across every book published by Packt
- ▸ Copy and paste, print and bookmark content
- ▸ On demand and accessible via web browser

Free Access for Packt account holders

If you have an account with Packt at www.PacktPub.com, you can use this to access PacktLib today and view nine entirely free books. Simply use your login credentials for immediate access.

Table of Contents

Preface

Spring Web-Services (Spring-WS), introduced by the SpringSource community (`http://www.springsource.org/`), aims to create contract-first SOAP Web-Services in which either a WSDL or an XSD is required primarily for the creation of a Web-Service. Since Spring-WS is a Spring-based product, it takes advantage of Spring's concepts such as Inversion of Control (IOC) and dependency injection. Some of the key features of Spring-WS are:

- Powerful endpoint mappings: The incoming XML requests can be forwarded to any handler object, based on the payload, SOAP action, and an XPath expression

- Rich XML API support: The incoming XML messages can be read using a variety of Java's XML APIs such as DOM, JDOM, dom4j, and so on

- Built by Maven: Spring-WS can be easily integrated with your Maven project

- Support for Marshalling technologies: Several OXM technologies, such as JAXB, XMLBean, XStream, and JiBX, can be used alternatively for the conversion of XML messages to/from an object

- Security support: Security operations, such as encryption/decryption, signature, and authentication

Covering all of these key features of Spring-WS 2.x has been the main goal of this book.

However, in the last two chapters, a different approach toward Web-Service development using REST-style and contract-last development using Spring remoting feature are detailed.

What this book covers

Chapter 1, Building SOAP Web-Services: This chapter covers setting up SOAP Web-Services over HTTP, JMS, XMPP, and E-mail protocols. It also covers the different implementations of Web-Service's endpoint using technologies such as DOM, JDOM, XPath, and Marshaller.

Chapter 2, Building Clients for SOAP Web-Services: This chapters covers building SOAP Web-Services clients over HTTP, JMS, XMPP, and E-mail protocols, using Spring-WS template classes.

Chapter 3, Testing and Monitoring Web-Services: This chapter explains the testing of Web-Services using the latest features of Spring-WS and monitoring a Web-Service using tools such as soapUI and TCPMon.

Chapter 4, Exception/SOAP Fault Handling: This chapter explains exception handling in the case of application/system failure.

Chapter 5, Logging and Tracing of SOAP Messages: In this chapter, we will see how to log important events and trace Web-Services.

Chapter 6, Marshalling and Object-XML Mapping (OXM): We will discuss marshalling/un-marshalling technologies as well as creating a custom marshaller in this chapter.

Chapter 7, Securing SOAP Web-Services using XWSS Library: This chapter covers security topics, such as encryption, decryption, digital signature authentication, and authorization using the Spring-WS feature, based on XWSS, and has a recipe about creating key stores.

Chapter 8, Securing SOAP Web-Services using WSS4J Library: In this chapter, we will see security topics, such as encryption, decryption, digital signature authentication, and authorization using the Spring-WS feature, based on the WSS4J package.

Chapter 9, RESTful Web-Services: This chapter explains REST Web-Service development using RESTful support in Spring.

Chapter 10, Spring Remoting: We will discuss contract-last Web-Service development using Spring remoting features to expose local business services as a Web-Service using Hessian/Burlap, JAX-WS, JMS, and a recipe to set up a Web-Service by Apache CXF using JAX-WS API.

What you need for this book

Java knowledge as well as basic Maven knowledge is a prerequisite. Having experience with Web-Service makes it easier for you to use recipes in your development environment, professionally. Basic recipes in the book help beginners learn Web-Service topics quickly.

Who this book is for

This book is for those Java/J2EE developers that either have experience with Web-Service and for beginners. Since this book covers a variety of topics in Web-Service development, those who are already familiar with Web-Service can benefit from the book as a reference. Beginners can use this book to gain real-world experience of Web-Service development rapidly.

Conventions

In this book, you will find a number of styles of text that distinguish between different kinds of information. Here are some examples of these styles, and an explanation of their meaning.

Code words in text are shown as follows: "`MessageDispatcherServlet` is the core component of Spring-WS."

A block of code is set as follows:

```
<context-param>
  <param-name>contextConfigLocation</param-name>
  <param-value>/WEB-INF/classes/applicationContext.xml</param-value>
</context-param>
```

When we wish to draw your attention to a particular part of a code block, the relevant lines or items are set in bold:

```
<tns:placeOrderRequest ...>
  <tns:order>
......
  </tns:order>
</tns:placeOrderRequest>
```

Any command-line input or output is written as follows:

```
mvn clean package tomcat:run
```

New terms and **important words** are shown in bold. Words that you see on the screen, in menus or dialog boxes for example, appear in the text like this: "You can click on the **JUnit** tab, adjacent to the **Console** tab, to see whether the test case has succeeded or not".

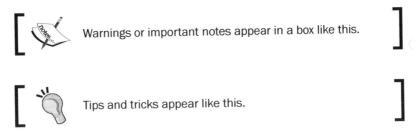

Warnings or important notes appear in a box like this.

Tips and tricks appear like this.

Reader feedback

Feedback from our readers is always welcome. Let us know what you think about this book—what you liked or may have disliked. Reader feedback is important for us to develop titles that you really get the most out of.

To send us general feedback, simply send an e-mail to `feedback@packtpub.com`, and mention the book title via the subject of your message.

If there is a book that you need and would like to see us publish, please send us a note in the **SUGGEST A TITLE** form on `www.packtpub.com` or e-mail `suggest@packtpub.com`.

If there is a topic that you have expertise in and you are interested in either writing or contributing to a book, see our author guide on www.packtpub.com/authors.

Customer support

Now that you are the proud owner of a Packt book, we have a number of things to help you to get the most from your purchase.

Downloading the example code

You can download the example code files for all Packt books you have purchased from your account at http://www.PacktPub.com. If you purchased this book elsewhere, you can visit http://www.PacktPub.com/support and register to have the files e-mailed directly to you.

Errata

Although we have taken every care to ensure the accuracy of our content, mistakes do happen. If you find a mistake in one of our books—maybe a mistake in the text or the code—we would be grateful if you would report this to us. By doing so, you can save other readers from frustration and help us improve subsequent versions of this book. If you find any errata, please report them by visiting http://www.packtpub.com/support, selecting your book, clicking on the **errata submission form** link, and entering the details of your errata. Once your errata are verified, your submission will be accepted and the errata will be uploaded on our website, or added to any list of existing errata, under the Errata section of that title. Any existing errata can be viewed by selecting your title from http://www.packtpub.com/support.

Piracy

Piracy of copyright material on the Internet is an ongoing problem across all media. At Packt, we take the protection of our copyright and licenses very seriously. If you come across any illegal copies of our works, in any form, on the Internet, please provide us with the location address or website name immediately so that we can pursue a remedy.

Please contact us at copyright@packtpub.com with a link to the suspected pirated material.

We appreciate your help in protecting our authors, and our ability to bring you valuable content.

Questions

You can contact us at questions@packtpub.com if you are having a problem with any aspect of the book, and we will do our best to address it.

1
Building SOAP Web-Services

In this chapter, we will cover:

- ▶ Using Maven for building and running a Spring-WS project
- ▶ Creating a data contract
- ▶ Setting up a Web-Service using `DispatcherServlet`
- ▶ Simplifying the creation of a Web-Service using `MessageDispatcherServlet`
- ▶ Setting up a Web-Service on JMS transport
- ▶ Setting up a Web-Service on E-mail transport
- ▶ Setting up a Web-Service on embedded HTTP server transport
- ▶ Setting up a Web-Service on XMPP transport
- ▶ Setting up a simple endpoint mapping for the Web-Service
- ▶ Setting up a contract-first Web-Service
- ▶ Setting up an endpoint by annotating the payload-root
- ▶ Setting up a transport-neutral WS-Addressing endpoint
- ▶ Setting up an endpoint using an XPath expression
- ▶ Handling the incoming XML messages using DOM
- ▶ Handling the incoming XML messages using JDOM
- ▶ Handling the incoming XML messages using JAXB2
- ▶ Validating the XML messages on the server side using an interceptor

Introduction

SOAP (Simple Object Access Protocol) was designed to be language-, transport-, and platform-independent, which is an alternative to the old fashioned middleware technologies such as CORBA and DCOM. SOAP was also designed to be extensible. The standards referred to as WS-*—WS-Addressing, WS-Policy, WS-Security, and so on—are built on the SOAP protocol.

The Web-Services that use SOAP, along with WSDL and XML schema, have become the standard for exchanging the XML-based messages. The Spring Web-Services facilitate SOAP service development, by providing a comprehensive set of APIs and configurations for the creation of flexible Web-Services. The following diagram shows how a Spring-WS works when it receives an incoming message (the diagram is in abstract form):

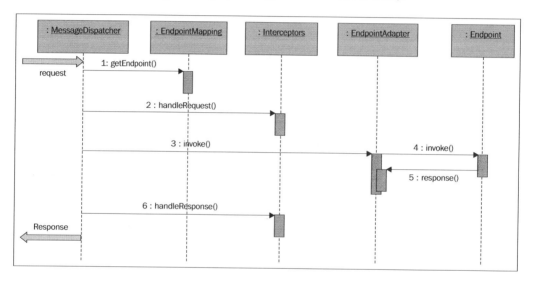

MessageDispatcher is the central point for a Spring Web-Service and dispatches Web-Service messages to the registered endpoint. In Spring-WS, request/response messages are wrapped inside the MessageContext object and the MessageContext will be passed to the MessageDispatcher (response will be set into MessageContext after invoking the endpoint). When a message arrives, MessageDispatcher uses the request object to get the endpoint. (Mapping a request to an endpoint is called **endpoint mapping** and it can be done by using data from beans registration within application context, scanning, and autodetection of annotations). Then the MessageDispatcher by using the endpoint, gets endpopint's interceptors (which range from zero to many) and calls handleRequest method on them.

An interceptor (`EndpointInterceptor` here), as the name suggests, intercepts the request/response to perform some operations prior to (for request)/after (for response) invoking the endpoint. This `EndpointInterceptor` gets called before/after calling the appropriate endpoint to perform several processing aspects such as logging, validating, security, and so on. Next, `MessageDispatcher` gets appropriate endpoint adapter for the endpoint method to be called. This adapter offers compatibility with various types of endpoint methods. Each adapter is specialized to call a method with specific method parameter and return type.

And Finally, `EndpointAdapter` invokes the endpoint's method and transforms the response to the desired form and set it into the `MessageContext` object. Now the initial message context that was passed to `MessageDispatcher`, contains the response object, that will be forwarded to the client (by the caller of `MessageDispatcher`).

Spring-WS only supports the contract-first development style in which creating the contract (XSD or WSDL) is the first step. The required steps to build a contract-first Web-Service using Spring-WS are as follows:

1. Contract definition (either XSD or WSDL)
2. Creating endpoint: the class that receives and processes an incoming message.
3. Configuration of Spring beans and the endpoint.

There are two types of endpoints, namely, payload endpoints and message endpoints. While message endpoints can access the entire XML SOAP envelop, the payload endpoint will only access the payload part of a SOAP envelop, that is, the body of a SOAP envelop. In this book, the focus is on creating payload endpoints.

In this chapter, after a recipe for the explanation of creating contract from a set of XML messages, the major focus will be on implementing endpoints and its related configuration.

For the purpose of illustrating the construction process of Web-Services, this book uses a simple business scenario of a fictitious restaurant, Live Restaurant, which needs to accept online orders from customers. Live Restaurant decides to publish its `OrderService` component as a Web-Service. For simplicity, just two operations are considered for the `OrderService` (Java interface).

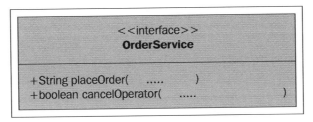

The project will follow the following domain model:

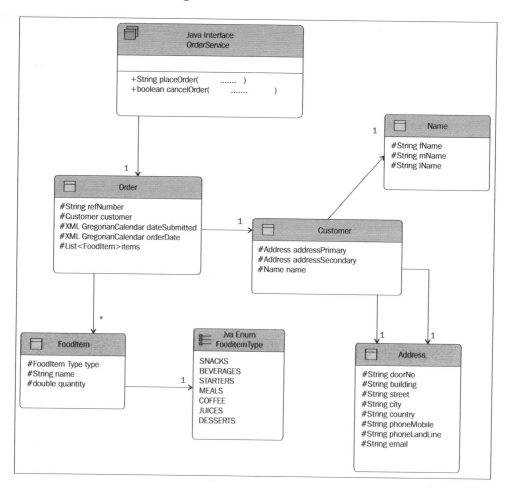

Each recipe in this book will incrementally build parts of the project to make it a complete Web-Service application. The Java project name is `LiveRestaurant`, and each recipe will use a slightly different version of the project, with the extension `_R-x.x`. For example, the first recipe in this chapter will use `LiveRestaurant_R-1.1` for the Web-Service server and `LiveRestaurant_R-1.1-Client for the client` as the project name.

>
> Setting up a Web-Service is the goal of this chapter, so more emphasis is on explanation of the server-side code and settings. Client-side code is used in this chapter for checking the functionality of the server. More about client side code, settings, and testing will be discussed in the following chapters.

Using Maven for building and running a Spring-WS project

Recent modern software development, based on enterprise-grade open source technologies, requires a new generation of build and project management tools. Such tools can make a standard way for building, managing, and deploying small scale to large scale applications.

Maven, hosted by the Apache Software Foundation, is a project management and automated build and deploy tool. Maven is built upon Ant's features and adds several features such as feature dependency and project management. Maven was initially used for Java programming, but it can also be used to build and manage projects written in other programming languages. In recent years, Maven has been used to automate the process of building, managing, and testing the deployments of major open source projects.

This recipe details the steps required to set up Maven for building, testing, and deploying the projects used in this book.

Getting ready

This recipe requires the installation of the following software or tools:

1. Java 6 or higher and Maven 3.0.2: For download and installation, refer to `http://maven.apache.org/` and `http://www.oracle.com/technetwork/java/javase/downloads/index.html`.

2. Add your custom repositories to `settings.xml` under `MAVEN_HOME/conf` or `.m2` folders (`MAVEN_HOME` is the folder in which Maven is installed and `.m2` is the folder in which Maven downloads its artifacts to).

   Later, you can add an extra repository to your custom repositories. You can disable this repository by setting `activeByDefault` to `false` (the file that contains repositories is in the `resources` folder):

```
<profile>
  <id>my-repository</id>
  <activation>
            <activeByDefault>true</activeByDefault>
  </activation>
  <!-- list of standard repository -->
   <repositories>
   ...
     ...
      <repository>
          <id>maven2-repository.java.net</id>
```

```
            <name>Java.net Repository for Maven</name>
            <url>http://download.java.net/maven/2</url>
        </repository>

    . . . .

        <repository>
            <id>maven1-repository.java.net</id>
            <name>Java.net Repository for Maven</name>
            <url>http://download.java.net/maven/1</url>
        </repository>
    </repositories>
    </profile>
```

An alternative way to include the Maven repositories to your Maven build is to include repository data in the POM file directly. Samples of both ways to include repositories are included under the `Using Maven` folder in the resource bundle of this chapter.

How to do it...

1. Build and deploy a project.

   ```
   mvn clean package   tomcat:run
   ```

2. Browse the following Web-Service WSDL file:

   ```
   http://localhost:8080/LiveRestaurant/OrderService.wsdl
   ```

   The following is the browser's output:

   ```
   <wsdl:definitions
     targetNamespace="http://www.packtpub.com/liverestaurant/
   OrderService/schema">
     <wsdl:types>
       <schema elementFormDefault="qualified"
   targetNamespace="http://www.packtpub.com/liverestaurant/
   OrderService/schema">
         <element name="placeOrderRequest">
           <complexType>
             <sequence>
               <element name="order" type="QOrder:Order" />
             </sequence>
           </complexType>
       ….. . . .
         </schema>
       </wsdl:types>
   ….. . . .
   ```

```xml
  <wsdl:binding name="OrderServiceSoap11" type="tns:OrderService">
    <soap:binding style="document"
      transport="http://schemas.xmlsoap.org/soap/http" />
    <wsdl:operation name="placeOrder">
      <soap:operation soapAction="" />
      <wsdl:input name="placeOrderRequest">
        <soap:body use="literal" />
      </wsdl:input>
      <wsdl:output name="placeOrderResponse">
        <soap:body use="literal" />
      </wsdl:output>
    </wsdl:operation>
    <wsdl:operation name="cancelOrder">
      <soap:operation soapAction="" />
      <wsdl:input name="cancelOrderRequest">
        <soap:body use="literal" />
      </wsdl:input>
      <wsdl:output name="cancelOrderResponse">
        <soap:body use="literal" />
      </wsdl:output>
    </wsdl:operation>
  </wsdl:binding>
  <wsdl:service name="OrderServiceService">
    <wsdl:port binding="tns:OrderServiceSoap11"
name="OrderServiceSoap11">
      <soap:address
        location="http://localhost:8080/LiveRestaurant/spring-ws/
OrderService" />
    </wsdl:port>
  </wsdl:service>
</wsdl:definitions>
```

The following is the output of the Maven command:

```
. . . . . . . . . . .
[INFO] Building war: C:\...\LiveRestaurant.war
. . . . . . .
[INFO] --- tomcat-maven-plugin:1.1:run ...@ LiveRestaurant ---
[INFO] Running war on http://localhost:8080/LiveRestaurant
[INFO] Creating Tomcat server configuration ...
Oct 15,...org.apache.catalina.startup.Embedded start
INFO: Starting tomcat server
Oct 15...org.apache.catalina.core.StandardEngine start
```

```
INFO: Starting Servlet Engine: Apache Tomcat/6.0.29
 org.apache.catalina.core.ApplicationContext log
...Set web app root ..: 'webapp.root' = [...src\main\webapp\]

INFO: Initializing log4j from..WEB-INF\log4j.properties]
...
INFO: Initializing Spring FrameworkServlet 'spring-ws'
......
INFO .. - FrameworkServlet 'spring-ws': initialization ..
Oct .. org.apache.coyote.http11.Http11Protocol init
INFO: Initializing Coyote HTTP/1.1 on http-8080
Oct .. org.apache.coyote.http11.Http11Protocol start
INFO: Starting Coyote HTTP/1.1 on http-8080
```

In order to import a Maven project into an Eclipse IDE:

Go to the root of the project (\chapterOne\LiveRestaurant_R-1.1) and execute:

mvn eclipse:eclipse -Declipse.projectNameTemplate="LiveRes taurant_R-1.1"

Then, you can import the Maven project as an Eclipse project.

In case Maven cannot find a JAR file, you can use your custom repository using the following command:

mvn -P my-repository clean package tomcat:run

How it works...

mvn clean package installs the required components into a local repository and creates a WAR/JAR file of the project:

[INFO] Building war: ...LiveRestaurant.war

mvn tomcat:run runs a WAR file of the project on the Tomcat plugin. mvn jetty:run runs the WAR file of the project on the Jetty plugin:

INFO] --- tomcat-maven-plugin:1.1:... LiveRestaurant ---

[INFO] Running war on http://localhost:8080/LiveRestaurant

[INFO] Creating Tomcat server configuration at

Creating a data contract

A WSDL document, known as a service contract, provides a standard way in which a Web-Service client and server exchange data. Using WSDL, the client and server could be on a different application or platform. XML Schema Definition(XSD), known as data contract, describes the structure of the datatypes that are being exchanged between the Web-Service server and client. XSD describes the types, fields, and any validation on those fields (such as max/min or pattern, and so on). While WSDL is specific to the Web-Service and describes a Web-Service's artifacts, such as methods and data passed through these methods (WSDL itself uses an XSD for that), URL, and so on; XSD only presents the structure of the data.

To be able to set up a Spring Web-Service, we need a contract. There are four different ways of defining such a contract for XML:

- DTDs
- XML Schema (XSD)
- RELAX NG
- Schematron

DTDs have limited namespace support, so they are not suitable for Web-Services. RELAX NG and Schematron certainly are easier than XML Schema. Unfortunately, they are not so widely supported across platforms. Spring-WS uses XML Schema.

A data contract is the center of Spring-WS and a service contract can be generated from a data contract. The easiest way to create an XSD is to infer it from the sample documents. Any good XML editor or Java IDE offers this functionality. Basically, these tools use some sample XML documents and generate a schema from it that validates them all. In this recipe, we will discuss sample XML data massages and how to convert them into a single schema file. The generated schema is used in this book as a data contract.

Getting ready

1. Install Java (as described in the first recipe).
2. Install xmlbeans-2.5.0 from `http://xmlbeans.apache.org/`.
3. The resources for this recipe are included in the folder Create Data Contract.

How to do it...

1. Copy your XML messages (`placeOrderRequest.xml`, `placeOrderResponse`, `cancelOrderRequest.xml`, and `cancelOrderResponse.xml`) to the `xmlbeans-2.5.0\bin` working folder.

2. Run the following command:

```
inst2xsd -design rd -enumerations never placeOrderRequest.xml
placeOrderResponse.xml cancelOrderRequest
```

3. The preceding command creates the `schema0.xsd` schema file. The generated schema result certainly needs to be modified, but it's a great starting point. Here is the final polished schema (`orderService.xsd`):

```
<?xml version="1.0" encoding="UTF-8"?>
…...
<schema...">
    <element name="placeOrderRequest">
        <complexType>
            <sequence>
                <element name="order" type="QOrder:Order"></
element>
            </sequence>
        </complexType>
    </element>
    <element name="placeOrderResponse">
        <complexType>
            <sequence>
                <element name="refNumber" type="string"></element>
            </sequence>
        </complexType>
    </element>
    .........
  <complexType name="Order">
     <sequence>
         <element name="refNumber" type="string"></element>
         <element name="customer" type="QOrder:Customer"></
element>
         <element name="dateSubmitted" type="dateTime"></element>
         <element name="orderDate" type="dateTime"></element>
         <element name="items" type="QOrder:FoodItem"
              maxOccurs="unbounded" minOccurs="1">
         </element>
     </sequence>
```

```
        </complexType>
        <complexType name="Customer">
            <sequence>
                <element name="addressPrimary" type="QOrder:Address"></
    element>
                <element name="addressSecondary"
    type="QOrder:Address"></element>
                <element name="name" type="QOrder:Name"></element>
            </sequence>
        </complexType>


        ....
    </schema>
```

How it works...

Initially, the input and output sample messages are required. In this book, there are four XML messages (`placeOrderRequest.xml`, `placeOrderResponse`, `cancelOrderRequest.xml`, and `cancelOrderResponse.xml`) and all the recipes use these message data formats for communication. `Inst2xsd` generates a schema file from the existing XML sample messages. Resources of this recipe are included under the `Create Data Contract` folder in the resource bundle of this chapter.

Setting up a Web-Service using DispatcherServlet

Spring-WS provides one of the easiest mechanisms to develop Web-Services in the Java platform. This recipe focuses on building a very simple Web-Service using the Spring-MVC `DispatcherServlet` and the components provided by Spring-WS.

Getting ready

In this recipe, the project's name is `LiveRestaurant_R-1.2` with the following Maven dependencies:

- `spring-ws-core-2.0.1.RELEASE.jar`
- `log4j-1.2.9.jar`

How to do it...

1. Copy the service contract from the `resources` folder (`orderService.wsdl`).

2. Create an endpoint (`OrderSeviceMessageReceiverEndpoint`).

3. Configure the endpoint, service contract,
   `WebServiceMessageReceiverHandlerAdapter`, `MessageDispatcher`,
   and `WsdlDefinitionHandlerAdapter`, in the server Spring configuration file
   (`Dispatcher-servlet.xml`).

4. Configure `DispatcherServlet` inside the `web.xml` file.

5. Run the server using the following command:

   ```
   mvn clean package tomcat:run
   ```

   The following is the output:

   ```
   …. . . . . . . . . . . . . . . . . . . . . . .

   [INFO] Running war on http://localhost:8080/LiveRestaurant

   …. . . . . . . . . . . . . . . . . . . . . . . . . . .

   18-Oct-2011 10:23:02.....ApplicationContext log

   INFO: Initializing Spring FrameworkServlet 'Dispatcher'

   18-Oct-2011 10:23:02 org.apache.coyote.http11.Http11Protocol init

   INFO: Initializing Coyote HTTP/1.1 on http-8080

   18-Oct-2011 10:23:02 org.apache.coyote.http11.Http11Protocol start

   INFO: Starting Coyote HTTP/1.1 on http-8080
   ```

6. To browse your service WSDL, open the following link inside your browser:

   ```
   http://localhost:8080/LiveRestaurant/Dispatcher/OrderService.
   wsdl
   ```

7. To test, open a new command window, go to the folder `LiveRestaurant_R-1.2-Client`, and run the following command:

   ```
   mvn clean package  exec:java
   ```

   The following is the server-side output:

   ```
   Inside method, OrderSeviceMethodEndpoint.receive - message content
   = <?xml version="1.0" encoding="UTF-8"?><tns:placeOrderRequest
   xmlns:tns="http://www.packtpub.com/liverestaurant/OrderService/
   schema">
     <tns:order>
       <tns:refNumber>9999</tns:refNumber>
       <tns:customer>
         …. . . . . .
   ```

```
        </tns:customer>
        <tns:dateSubmitted>2008-09-29T05:49:45</tns:dateSubmitted>
        <tns:orderDate>2014-09-19T03:18:33</tns:orderDate>
        <!--1 or more repetitions:-->
        <tns:items>
           <tns:type>Snacks</tns:type>
           <tns:name>Pitza</tns:name>
           <tns:quantity>2</tns:quantity>
        </tns:items>
      </tns:order>
   </tns:placeOrderRequest>
```

How it works...

`DispatcherServlet` receives all the incoming requests, and based on request context, it forwards the request to the endpoint (the general form of a request URL is `http://<host>:<port>/<appcontext>/<requestcontext>` (here `appcontext` is Liverestaurant and `requestcontext` should start with /Dispatcher/). The requests context that ends with /OrderService go to `OrderSeviceMessageReceiverEndpoint` and requests that end with *.wsdl go to `SimpleWsdl11Definition`).

`DispatcherServlet` configured in `web.xml` is responsible for receiving all requests with a URL mapping [/Dispatcher/*].

```
    <servlet>
        <servlet-name>Dispatcher</servlet-name>
        <servlet-class>org.springframework.web.servlet.
DispatcherServlet</servlet-class>
        <load-on-startup>1</load-on-startup>
    </servlet>
    <servlet-mapping>
        <servlet-name>Dispatcher</servlet-name>
        <url-pattern>/Dispatcher/*</url-pattern>
    </servlet-mapping>
```

 You can change the URL pattern to suit your requirement.

`DispatcherServlet` plays a major role in intercepting the HTTP requests and then loads the Spring bean configuration file. By default, it detects the bean configuration file by name `<servlet-name>-servlet.xml`. Since we have named the `DispatcherServlet` as `Dispatcher` in `web.xml` file, the server looks for `Dispatcher-servlet.xml` as application context filename. You may configure another file, using the following context param in the `web.xml`:

```
<context-param>
 <param-name>contextConfigLocation</param-name>
 <param-value>/WEB-INF/classes/applicationContext.xml</param-value>
</context-param>
```

`DispatcherServlet` needs separate instances of `WebServiceMessageReceiverHandlerAdapter`, `MessageDispatcher`, and `WsdlDefinitionHandlerAdapter` that in this recipe are configured inside `Dispatcher-servlet.xml`. The `DispatcherServlet`, by default, delegates to controllers for handling requests, but in the configuration file, it is configured to delegate to a `MessageDispatcher` (`WebServiceMessageReceiverHandlerAdapter`). `SaajSoapMessageFactory` is a specific message factory for message creation in Spring-WS.

```
<beans ...">
    <bean class="org.springframework.ws.transport.http.
WebServiceMessageReceiverHandlerAdapter">
        <property name="messageFactory">
          <bean class="org.springframework.ws.soap.saaj.
SaajSoapMessageFactory"></bean>
        </property>
    </bean>
    …..
```

To let `DispatcherServlet` handle the WSDL contract, `WsdlDefinitionHandlerAdapter`, which is registered in the configuration file; it reads the WSDL file source using the `WsdlDefinition` implementation (`SimpleWsdl11Definition`) and writes that as the result to the `HttpServletResponse`.

`SimpleUrlHandlerMapping` is to redirect the client requests to the appropriate endpoints using the URL patterns. Here the request URL that ends with `*.wsdl` will be redirected to `sampleServiceDefinition` (that is, `SimpleWsdl11Definition` that uses `OrderService.wsdl` to generate the response), and if the request URL contains `/OrderService`, it will be redirected to `OrderSeviceMessageReceiverEndpoint`. `SOAPMessageDispatcher` is to dispatch a SOAP message to the registered endpoint(s) (`OrderSeviceMessageReceiverEndpoint`).

```
…..
<bean class="org.springframework.web.servlet.handler.
SimpleUrlHandlerMapping">
        <property name="mappings">
            <props>
```

```
            <prop key="*.wsdl">sampleServiceDefinition</prop>
            <prop key="/OrderService">OrderServiceEndpoint</prop>
        </props>
      </property>
      <property name="defaultHandler" ref="messageDispatcher"/>
   </bean>
   <bean id="messageDispatcher" class="org.springframework.ws.soap.
server.SoapMessageDispatcher"/>
  <bean id="OrderServiceEndpoint" class="com.packtpub.liverestaurant.
service.endpoint.OrderSeviceMessageReceiverEndpoint"/>
    <bean class="org.springframework.ws.transport.http.
WsdlDefinitionHandlerAdapter"/>
      <bean id="sampleServiceDefinition" class="org.springframework.
ws.wsdl.wsdl11.SimpleWsdl11Definition">
        <property name="wsdl" value="/WEB-INF/OrderService.wsdl"/>
   </bean>
</beans>
```

OrderSeviceMessageReceiverEndpoint is a very basic endpoint
that get incoming message (messageContext.getRequest().
getPayloadSource()) and prin it out:

….....

```java
public class OrderSeviceMessageReceiverEndpoint implements
    WebServiceMessageReceiver {

  public OrderSeviceMessageReceiverEndpoint() {
  }

  public void receive(MessageContext messageContext) throws Exception
{

    System.out
        .println("Inside method, OrderSeviceMethodEndpoint.receive -
message content = "
            + xmlToString(messageContext.getRequest().
getPayloadSource()));
  }
```

You can change the URL pattern to suit your requirement.

```java
    private  String xmlToString(Source source) {
      try {
        StringWriter stringWriter = new StringWriter();
        Result result = new StreamResult(stringWriter);
        TransformerFactory factory = TransformerFactory.newInstance();
```

```
        Transformer transformer = factory.newTransformer();
        transformer.transform(source, result);
        return stringWriter.getBuffer().toString();
    } catch (TransformerConfigurationException e) {
        e.printStackTrace();
    } catch (TransformerException e) {
        e.printStackTrace();
    }
    return null;
}

}
```

See also

The *Setting up a Web-Service using MessageDispatcherServlet* recipe in this chapter.

Simplifying the creation of a Web-Service using MessageDispatcherServlet

`MessageDispatcherServlet` is the core component of Spring-WS. With simple configuration, a Web-Service can be set up in minutes. This servlet came as a simple way to configure an alternative to the Spring-MVC `DispatcherServlet`. As in the second recipe, *Setting up a Web-Service using DispatcherServlet*, `DispatcherServlet` needs separate instances of `WebServiceMessageReceiverHandlerAdapter`, `MessageDispatcher`, and `WsdlDefinitionHandlerAdapter`. However, `MessageDispatcherServlet` can dynamically detect `EndpointAdapters`, `EndpointMappings`, `EndpointExceptionResolvers`, and `WsdlDefinition` by setting inside the application context.

Since this is the default method for configuring Spring Web-Services, it will be used in later recipes. In this recipe, a very basic implementation of setting up a Spring-WS is detailed. More advance implementation will be explained later in the recipe *Setting up a contract-first Web-Service*.

Getting ready

In this recipe, the project's name is `LiveRestaurant_R-1.3` with the following Maven dependencies:

- `spring-ws-core-2.0.1.RELEASE.jar`
- `log4j-1.2.9.jar`

How to do it...

1. Copy the service contract from the `resources` folder (`orderService.wsdl`).

2. Create an endpoint (`OrderSeviceMethodEndpoint`).

3. Configure the endpoint. The service contract is in the server Spring configuration file (`spring-ws-servlet.xml`).

4. Configure `MessageDispatcherServlet` inside the `web.xml` file.

5. Run the server using the following command:

   ```
   mvn clean package tomcat:run
   ```

   The following is the output after the server is run successfully:

   ```
   ….......................
   [INFO] >>> tomcat-maven-plugin:1.1:run .. LiveRestaurant >>>
   [..............
   [INFO] Running war on http://localhost:8080/LiveRestaurant
   [I...........
   ..XmlBeanDefinitionReader.. Loading..spring-ws-servlet.xml]

   ...

   ..SimpleMethodEndpointMapping#0, OrderService,
   OrderServiceEndpoint]; root of factory hierarchy

   INFO [main] (SaajSoapMessageFactory.java:135) -..

   INFO [main] (FrameworkServlet.java:320) - FrameworkServlet '

   …......
   INFO: Starting Coyote HTTP/1.1 on http-8080
   ```

6. To browse your service WSDL, open the following link in your browser:

   `http://localhost:8080/LiveRestaurant/spring-ws/OrderService.wsdl`

7. To test, open a new command window, go to the folder `LiveRestaurant_R-1.3-Client`, and run the following command:

   ```
   mvn clean package  exec:java
   ```

   The following is the server-side output:

   ```
   Sent response

   ...

   <tns:placeOrderResponse....>
   <tns:refNumber>order-John_Smith_1234</tns:refNumber>
   </tns:placeOrderResponse>
   ```

```
.....
for request
<tns:placeOrderRequest.... >
  <tns:order>
    <tns:refNumber>9999</tns:refNumber>
    <tns:customer>
     ........
    </tns:customer>
    <tns:dateSubmitted>2008-09-29T05:49:45</tns:dateSubmitted>
    <tns:orderDate>2014-09-19T03:18:33</tns:orderDate>
    <!--1 or more repetitions:-->
    <tns:items>
      <tns:type>Snacks</tns:type>
      <tns:name>Pitza</tns:name>
      <tns:quantity>2</tns:quantity>
    </tns:items>
  </tns:order>
....
```

How it works...

The `MessageDispatcherServlet` is configured in the web configuration file `web.xml`:

```
<servlet>
  <servlet-name>spring-ws</servlet-name>
  <servlet-class>
    org.springframework.ws.transport.http.MessageDispatcherServlet</
servlet-class>
  <load-on-startup>1</load-on-startup>
</servlet>

<servlet-mapping>
  <servlet-name>spring-ws</servlet-name>
  <url-pattern>/*</url-pattern>
</servlet-mapping>
```

Downloading the example code

You can download the example code files for all Packt books you have purchased from your account at `http://www.PacktPub.com`. If you purchased this book elsewhere, you can visit `http://www.PacktPub.com/support` and register to have the files e-mailed directly to you.

`MessageDispatcherServlet` is the central element that handles the incoming SOAP requests, with the help of other components (`EndpointAdapters`, `EndpointMappings`, `EndpointExceptionResolvers`, and `WsdlDefinition`). It combines the attributes of both `DispatcherServlet` and `MessageDispatcher` that dispatch to the appropriate endpoint. This is the standard servlet recommended to build Web-Services with Spring-WS.

Since the `MessageDispatcherServlet` is inherited from `FrameworkServlet`, it looks for a configuration file named `<servlet-name>-servlet.xml` in the class path (you can change the configuration filename using the `context-param`, `contextConfigLocation` settings in the `web.xml`, as described in the recipe *Setting up a Web-Service using DispatcherServlet*). In the example, since the servlet name in the `web.xml` file is set to Spring-WS, the file `spring-ws-servlet.xml` is the Web-Services configuration file.

`MessageDispatcherServlet` then looks up for an endpoint mapping element in the configuration file, for the purpose of mapping the client requests to the endpoint. Here, `<sws:static-wsdl` sets the data contract in the WSDL format. This is the element to be configured in `spring-ws-servlet.xml` to set up a Web-Service:

```
<bean class="org.springframework.ws.server.endpoint.mapping.
SimpleMethodEndpointMapping">
    <property name="endpoints">
      <ref bean="OrderServiceEndpoint"/>
    </property>
    <property name="methodPrefix" value="handle"></property>
</bean>
  <sws:static-wsdl id="OrderService" location="/WEB-INF/orderService.
wsdl"/>

    <bean id="OrderServiceEndpoint" class="com.packtpub.liverestaurant.
service.endpoint.OrderSeviceMethodEndpoint">
    </bean>
```

The example uses `SimpleMethodEndpointMapping` that maps the client requests to `MethodEnpoints`. It maps the incoming request to a method that starts with the `handle+root` element of the message (`handle+placeOrderRequest`). In the endpoint class (`OrderSeviceMethodEndpoint`), a method with the name `handleplaceOrderRequest` should be defined.

In this method, the parameter source includes the incoming message and input parameters to call order service could be extracted from this parameter, then the method calls to the `orderService` method and wraps the outgoing message in the `StringSource` that is to be sent back to the client:

```
public class OrderSeviceMethodEndpoint {
  OrderService orderService;
  public void setOrderService(OrderService orderService) {
    this.orderService = orderService;
```

```
        }
    public @ResponsePayload
    Source handleplaceOrderRequest(@RequestPayload Source source) throws
Exception {
        //extract data from input parameter
        String fName="John";
        String lName="Smith";
        String refNumber="1234";
        return new StringSource(
            "<tns:placeOrderResponse xmlns:tns=\"http://www.packtpub.
com/liverestaurant/OrderService/schema\"><tns:refNumber>"+orde
rService.placeOrder(fName,lName,refNumber)+"</tns:refNumber></
tns:placeOrderResponse>");
    }
```

The endpoint mappings will be detailed in the later recipes.

See also

The recipes *Setting up a Web-Service using DispatcherServlet, Setting up a simple endpoint mapping for the Web-Service*, and *Setting up a contract-first Web-Service* discussed in this chapter.

Setting up a Web-Service on JMS transport

HTTP is the most common Web-Service protocol. However, Web-Services are currently built on multiple transports, each with different scenarios.

JMS was included in Java 2, J2EE by Sun Microsystems in 1999. Using JMS, systems are able to communicate synchronously or asynchronously and are based on point-to-point and publish-subscribe models. SOAP over JMS inherits the JSM features and meets the following requirements:

▸ Where asynchronous messaging is required

▸ Where the message consumers are slower than the producers

▸ To guarantee the delivery of messages

▸ To have a publisher/subscriber(multiple) model

▸ When sender/receiver might be disconnected

Spring Web-Services provide features to set up a Web-Service over JMS protocol that is built upon the JMS functionality in the Spring framework. In this recipe, how to set up a Spring-WS over JMS is presented.

Getting ready

In this recipe, the project's name is `LiveRestaurant_R-1.4` with the following Maven dependencies:

- `spring-ws-core-2.0.1.RELEASE.jar`
- `spring-ws-support-2.0.1.RELEASE.jar`
- `spring-test-3.0.5.RELEASE.jar`
- `spring-jms-3.0.5.RELEASE.jar`
- `junit-4.7.jar`
- `xmlunit-1.1.jar`
- `log4j-1.2.9.jar`
- `jms-1.1.jar`
- `activemq-core-4.1.1.jar`

In this recipe, Apache ActiveMQ is used to set up a JMS server and to create JMS server-related objects (queue and broker are used here). Spring-WS family JARs provide a functionality to set up a Spring-WS and `spring-jms` and `jms` JARs provide the JMS functionality that the Spring-WS, over JMS, is built upon it.

How to do it...

1. Create an endpoint (`OrderSeviceMethodEndpoint`).
2. Configure the `MessageListenerContainer`, `MessageListener`, and `connectionFactory` in the Spring configuration file (`applicationContext.xml`).
3. Configure `MessageDispatcher` that includes the endpoint mappings inside `applicationContext.xml`.
4. Run the recipe project using the following command:

   `mvn clean package`

5. The following is the output once the project runs successfully:

   ```
   INFO [main] (SaajSoapMessageFactory.java:135) -..
   INFO [main] (DefaultLifecycleProcessor.java:330) -..
   INFO [main] .. - ActiveMQ 4.1.1 JMS Message Broker (localhost)..
   ..
   INFO [JMX connector] ..
   INFO [main]..ActiveMQ JMS Message Broker ..started
   INFO [main] ..- Connector vm://localhost Started
   ```

```
.....
 Received response ....
<tns:placeOrderResponse ..><tns:refNumber>..</tns:refNumber>
</tns:placeOrderResponse>....
 for request ....
<tns:placeOrderRequest ....>
  <tns:order>
    <tns:refNumber>9999</tns:refNumber>
    <tns:customer>
      .....
    </tns:customer>
    <tns:dateSubmitted>2008-09-29T05:49:45</tns:dateSubmitted>
    <tns:orderDate>2014-09-19T03:18:33</tns:orderDate>
    <!--1 or more repetitions:-->
    <tns:items>
      <tns:type>Snacks</tns:type>
      <tns:name>Pitza</tns:name>
      <tns:quantity>2</tns:quantity>
    </tns:items>
  </tns:order>
</tns:placeOrderRequest>
….....
```

How it works...

DefaultMessageListenerContainer listens to destinationName (RequestQueue) for incoming messages. When a message arrives, this listener will use the message factory (messageFactory) to extract the message and use the dispatcher (messageDispatcher) to dispatch the message to the endpoint (SimplePayloadEndpoint).

In the application context, WebServiceMessageListener is a listener inside MessageListenerContainer. The message container uses connectionfactory to connect to the destination (RequestQueue):

```
    <bean id="connectionFactory" class="org.apache.activemq.
ActiveMQConnectionFactory">
        <property name="brokerURL" value="vm://localhost?broker.
persistent=false"/>
    </bean>
```

```xml
<bean id="messageFactory" class="org.springframework.ws.soap.saaj.
SaajSoapMessageFactory"/>

<bean class="org.springframework.jms.listener.
DefaultMessageListenerContainer">
    <property name="connectionFactory" ref="connectionFactory"/>
    <property name="destinationName" value="RequestQueue"/>
    <property name="messageListener">
        <bean class="org.springframework.ws.transport.jms.
WebServiceMessageListener">
            <property name="messageFactory" ref="messageFactory"/>
            <property name="messageReceiver"
ref="messageDispatcher"/>
        </bean>
    </property>
</bean>
```

This listener uses `message Dispatcher` and `messageFactory` to receive incoming messages and to send outgoing SOAP messages. Inside `messageDiapatcher`, endpoint's mapping is included, which sets the endpoint (`SimplePayloadEndpoint`) and type of endpoint mapping (`PayloadRootQNameEndpointMapping`):

```xml
<bean id="messageDispatcher" class="org.springframework.ws.soap.
server.SoapMessageDispatcher">
    <property name="endpointMappings">
        <bean class="org.springframework.ws.server.endpoint.
mapping.PayloadRootQNameEndpointMapping">
            <property name="defaultEndpoint">
                <bean class="com.packtpub.liverestaurant.service.
endpoint.SimplePayloadEndpoint">
                    <property name="orderService">
                     <bean class="com.packtpub.liverestaurant.service.
OrderServiceImpl"/>
                    </property>
                </bean>
            </property>
        </bean>
    </property>
</bean>
```

The `invoke` method from the endpoint (`SimplePayloadEndpoint`) will be called when a request comes to the server, and the response will be returned to be sent back to the client:

```
public class SimplePayloadEndpoint implements PayloadEndpoint {
  OrderService orderService;
  public void setOrderService(OrderService orderService) {
    this.orderService = orderService;
  }

    public Source invoke(Source request) throws Exception {
      //extract data from input parameter
    String fName="John";
    String lName="Smith";
    String refNumber="1234";

      return new StringSource(
      "<tns:placeOrderResponse xmlns:tns=\"http://www.packtpub.
com/liverestaurant/OrderService/schema\"><tns:refNumber>"+order
Service.placeOrder(fName, lName, refNumber)+"</tns:refNumber></
tns:placeOrderResponse>");
    }
```

`JmsTransportWebServiceIntegrationTest` is included in the project to load the application context, set up the JMS server, and test the Web-Service. However, these details are not discussed here. The client of JMS transport will be discussed in the next chapter.

See also

The *Creating a Web-Service client on JMS transport* recipe discussed in *Chapter 2, Building Clients for SOAP Web-Services* and the *Exposing Web-Services using JMS as the underlying communication protocol* recipe discussed in *Chapter 10, Spring Remoting*.

Setting up a Web-Service on E-mail transport

HTTP is easy to understand and therefore has been most often defined and implemented, but it's clearly not the most suitable transport for Web-Services in any scenario.

Web-Service on E-mail transport can take advantage of store-and-forward messaging to provide an asynchronous transport for SOAP. In addition, there is no firewall concern on e-mail and those applications that are able to communicate together don't need web servers to set up a Web-Service. This allows SOAP, over mail transport, to be used in a number of scenarios where HTTP is not suitable.

The reasons why setting up a Web-Service over HTTP is not suitable and e-mail might be a solution as a transport protocol are listed as follows:

▶ If a system is protected by a firewall, there is no control over the HTTP request/response, but e-mail is always is accessible.

▶ If a system expects no request/response conventional model. For example, publish/subscriber model is required.

▶ If a request takes too long to complete. For example, if the server has to run complex and time-consuming services, the client would get an HTTP timeout error. In such a scenario, Web-Service over e-mail is more appropriate.

In this recipe, setting up a Web-Service over E-mail transport is presented. To load the application context and test the Web-Service, a test class is used. This class also starts up and shuts down the server.

Getting ready

In this recipe, the project's name is `LiveRestaurant_R-1.5` with the following Maven dependencies:

▶ `spring-ws-core-2.0.1.RELEASE.jar`

▶ `spring-ws-support-2.0.1.RELEASE.jar`

▶ `spring-test-3.0.5.RELEASE.jar`

▶ `mail-1.4.1.jar`

▶ `mock-javamail-1.6.jar`

▶ `junit-4.7.jar`

▶ `xmlunit-1.1.jar`

Setting up a mail server outside a system that is using JavaMail for testing purpose is difficult. Mock JavaMail addresses this issue and provides a pluggable component to the system using JavaMail. The system can use this component to send/receive e-mails against the temporary in-memory *mailbox*.

How to do it...

1. Create an endpoint (`SimplePayloadEndpoint`).

2. Configure `MessageReceiver` and `MessageDispatcher` that include endpoint mappings inside `applicationContext.xml`.

3. Run the recipe project using the following command:

   `mvn clean package`

The following is the output:

```
. . . . . . . .
INFO [main] ...- Creating SAAJ 1.3 MessageFactory with SOAP 1.1
Protocol
..- Starting mail receiver  [imap://server@packtpubtest.com/INBOX]
. . . .
Received response...
<tns:placeOrderResponse xmlns:tns="....">
<tns:refNumber>...</tns:refNumber></tns:placeOrderResponse>
...for request ..
<tns:placeOrderRequest xmlns:tns="...">
  <tns:order>
    <tns:refNumber>9999</tns:refNumber>
    <tns:customer>
. . . .
    </tns:customer>
    <tns:dateSubmitted>2008-09-29T05:49:45</tns:dateSubmitted>
    <tns:orderDate>2014-09-19T03:18:33</tns:orderDate>
    <!--1 or more repetitions:-->
    <tns:items>
      <tns:type>Snacks</tns:type>
      <tns:name>Pitza</tns:name>
      <tns:quantity>2</tns:quantity>
    </tns:items>
  </tns:order>
</tns:placeOrderRequest>
. . . . . .
```

How it works...

Messages sent to an address will be saved in an inbox. The message receiver
(messageReceiver) monitors the inbox at continuous intervals and as soon as it detects
a new E-mail, it reads the E-mail, extracts the message, and forwards the message to a
message dispatcher (messageDispatcher). The message dispatcher will call the invoke
method inside its default endpoint (SamplePayloadEndpoint), and inside the handler
method (invoke), the response will be sent back to the client.

When the application context is being loaded, `MailMessageReceiver` starts up a mail receiver and its inbox folder (`imap://server@packtpubtest.com/INBOX`), that is, a temporary in-memory inbox. After loading the application context, the `messageReceiver` bean acts as a server monitor for the incoming messages based on a pluggable strategy (`monotoringStrategy`) that monitors the `INBOX` folder (`imap://server@packtpubtest.com/INBOX`) for new messages on `pollingInterval` of 1000 ms. `storeUri` is the location to be monitored for the incoming messages (`imap://server@packtpubtest.com/INBOX`) and `transportUri` is the mail server for sending the responses:

```
<bean id="messageFactory" class="org.springframework.ws.soap.saaj.
SaajSoapMessageFactory"/>
    <bean id="messagingReceiver" class="org.springframework.
ws.transport.mail.MailMessageReceiver">
        <property name="messageFactory" ref="messageFactory"/>
        <property name="from" value="server@packtpubtest.com"/>
        <property name="storeUri" value="imap://server@packtpubtest.
com/INBOX"/>
        <property name="transportUri" value="smtp://smtp.packtpubtest.
com"/>
        <property name="messageReceiver" ref="messageDispatcher"/>
        <property name="session" ref="session"/>
        <property name="monitoringStrategy">
            <bean class="org.springframework.ws.transport.mail.
monitor.Pop3PollingMonitoringStrategy">
                <property name="pollingInterval" value="1000"/>
            </bean>
        </property>
    </bean>
```

Inside `messageDiapatcher`, endpoint mapping is included that sets the endpoint (`SimplePayloadEndpoint`) and type of the endpoint mapping (`PayloadRootQNameEndpointMapping`):

```
<bean id="messageDispatcher" class="org.springframework.ws.soap.
server.SoapMessageDispatcher">
        <property name="endpointMappings">
            <bean class="org.springframework.ws.server.endpoint.
mapping.PayloadRootQNameEndpointMapping">
                <property name="defaultEndpoint">
                    <bean class="com.packtpub.liverestaurant.service.
endpoint.SimplePayloadEndpoint">
                        <property name="orderService">
                            <bean class="com.packtpub.liverestaurant.
service.OrderServiceImpl"/>
                        </property>
                    </bean>
```

```
            </property>
          </bean>
        </property>
      </bean>
```

`SimplePayloadEndpoint` receives a request and returns a fixed dummy response using `OrderService`. When a request comes to the server, the `invoke` method will be called and the response will be returned that is to be sent back to the client:

```
public class SimplePayloadEndpoint implements PayloadEndpoint {
  OrderService orderService;
  public void setOrderService(OrderService orderService) {
    this.orderService = orderService;
  }

    public Source invoke(Source request) throws Exception {
      //extract data from input parameter
    String fName="John";
    String lName="Smith";
    String refNumber="1234";

      return new StringSource(
      "<tns:placeOrderResponse xmlns:tns=\"http://www.packtpub.
com/liverestaurant/OrderService/schema\"><tns:refNumber>"+order
Service.placeOrder(fName, lName, refNumber)+"</tns:refNumber></
tns:placeOrderResponse>");
    }
```

To test this recipe, a `webServiceTemplate` is used. We will discuss it in the next chapter.

`MailTransportWebServiceIntegrationTest` is included in the project to load the application context, set up the mail server, and to test the Web-Service.

See also

The *Creating Web-Service client on E-mail transport* recipe, discussed in *Chapter 2, Building Clients for SOAP Web-Services*.

Setting up a Web-Service on embedded HTTP transport

External HTTP servers might be able to provide several features, but they are not light and they need a configuration to set up.

Spring-WS provides a feature to set up an HTTP-based Web-Service using embedded Sun's JRE 1.6 HTTP server. The embedded HTTP server is a light-weight standalone server that could be used as an alternative to external servers. While configuration of the web server is a must in a conventional external server (`web.xml`), the embedded HTTP server doesn't need any deployment descriptor to operate and its only requirement is to configure an instance of the server through the application context.

In this recipe, setting up a Spring Web-Service on the embedded HTTP server is presented. Since there is no external HTTP server, a Java class is used to load application context and start up the server.

Getting ready

In this recipe, the project's name is `LiveRestaurant_R-1.6` with the following Maven dependencies:

- `spring-ws-core-2.0.1.RELEASE.jar`
- `log4j-1.2.9.jar`

How to do it...

1. Copy the service contract (`OrderService.wsdl`) from the resource folder.

2. Create a service and an implementation of it and annotate its implementation with `@Service("serviceName")` (`OrderSevice`, `OrderServiceImpl`).

3. Configure the service in the application context (`applicationContext`) that is to be scanned and detected automatically.

4. Configure the embedded HTTP server inside the application context.

5. Add a Java class with the main method to load the application context to set up the embedded HTTP server.

6. Run the server using the following command:

   ```
   mvn clean package exec:java
   ```

7. From `LiveRestaurant_R-1.6-Client`, run the following command:

```
mvn clean package exec:java
```

The following is the output when the server runs successfully:

```
<tns:placeOrderRequest xmlns:tns="...">
  <tns:order>
    <tns:refNumber>order-John_Smith_1234</tns:refNumber>
    <tns:customer>
..… . . .
    </tns:customer>
    <tns:dateSubmitted>2008-09-29T05:49:45</tns:dateSubmitted>
    <tns:orderDate>2014-09-19T03:18:33</tns:orderDate>
    <!--1 or more repetitions:-->
    <tns:items>
      <tns:type>Snacks</tns:type>
      <tns:name>Pitza</tns:name>
      <tns:quantity>2</tns:quantity>
    </tns:items>
  </tns:order>
</tns:placeOrderRequest>
```

The following is the client-side output:

```
<tns:placeOrderResponse ...><refNumber>order-John_Smith_1234</
refNumber></tns:placeOrderResponse>>
..… . .
```

..… . .

How it works...

In the application context, `SimpleHttpFactoryBean` creates a simple HTTP server (from embedded Sun's JRE 1.6) and it starts the HTTP server on initialization and stops it on destruction.

The HTTP server that has a context property sets up a Web-Service with the service class (`orderServiceImpl`) set as the endpoint and specifies the URL defined by the properties inside the context (`localhost:3478/OrderService`). This service interface is registered within the context property.

However, the service implementation is autodetected using `component-scan`.
`HttpInvokerProxyFactoryBean` creates a client's proxy for a specific server URL.

```
<context:annotation-config />
<context:component-scan base-package="com.packtpub.liverestaurant.
service.endpoint" />
<bean id="httpServer" class="org.springframework.remoting.support.
SimpleHttpServerFactoryBean">
    <property name="contexts">
      <util:map>
        <entry key="/OrderService">
          <bean class="org.springframework.remoting.httpinvoker.
SimpleHttpInvokerServiceExporter">
            <property name="serviceInterface" value="com.packtpub.
liverestaurant.service.endpoint.IOrderServiceEndPoint" />
            <property name="service" ref="orderServiceImpl" />
          </bean>
        </entry>
      </util:map>
    </property>
    <property name="port" value="3478" />
    <property name="hostname" value="localhost" />
</bean>
```

`IOrderServiceEndPointImpl` and `IOrderServiceEndPoint` are simple service
interface and implementation classes. `IOrderServiceEndPointImpl` is annotated by
`@Service(orderServiceImpl)` and is to be detected as a service implementation.

```
package com.packtpub.liverestaurant.service.endpoint;
public interface OrderService {
    String invoke(String request) throws Exception;
}
```

```
package com.packtpub.liverestaurant.service.endpoint;
import org.apache.log4j.Logger;
import org.springframework.stereotype.Service;
@Service("orderServiceImpl")
public class OrderServiceImpl implements OrderService {
  static Logger logger = Logger.getLogger(OrderServiceImpl.class);
    private static final String responseContent =
"<tns:placeOrderResponse xmlns:tns=\"http://www.packtpub.com/
liverestaurant/OrderService/schema\"><refNumber>Order Accepted!</
refNumber></tns:placeOrderResponse>";

    public String invoke(String request) throws Exception {
      logger.info("invoke method request:"+request);
        return responseContent;

    }
}
```

`ServerStartUp.java` is used to load the application context and start up the server:

```
package com.packtpub.liverestaurant.server;
public class ServerStartUp {
  public static void main(String[] args) throws  IOException {
      ClassPathXmlApplicationContext appContext = new
ClassPathXmlApplicationContext("/applicationContext.xml");
      System.out.println(appContext);
    char c;
      // Create a BufferedReader using System.in
      BufferedReader br = new BufferedReader(new
                          InputStreamReader(System.in));
      System.out.println("Enter any character  to quit.");
      c = (char) br.read();
      appContext.close();
  }
}
```

Setting up Spring-WS on XMPP transport

HTTP is most often used as a Web-Service transport protocol. However, it is not able to meet the asynchronous communication requirements.

Web-Service on XMPP transport is capable of asynchronous communication in which a client doesn't need to wait for a response from a service; instead, the service sends the response to the client when the process is completed. Spring-WS 2.0 includes XMPP (Jabber) support in which a Web-Service can communicate over the XMPP protocol. In this recipe, setting up a Spring-WS on XMPP transport is presented. Since there is no external HTTP server, a test class is used to load the application context.

Getting ready

In this recipe, the project's name is `LiveRestaurant_R-1.7`, which has the following Maven dependencies:

- `spring-ws-core-2.0.1.RELEASE.jar`
- `spring-ws-support-2.0.1.RELEASE.jar`
- `spring-test-3.0.5.RELEASE.jar`
- `junit-4.7.jar`
- `xmlunit-1.1.jar`
- `smack-3.1.0.jar`

How to do it...

1. Create an endpoint (`SamplePlayLoadEndPoint`).

2. Configure connection to the XMPP server in the application context (`applicationContext.xml`).

3. Configure the message receiver in the application context.

4. Run the following command:

   ```
   mvn clean package
   ```

   The following is the response received:

   ```
   <placeOrderRequest xmlns="..."><id>9999</id></placeOrderRequest>
   ```

   `...`

   ```
   for request
   ...<placeOrderRequest xmlns="...."><id>9999</id></
   placeOrderRequet>...
   ```

How it works...

In the application context, the `messageFactory` bean is responsible for creating the incoming and outgoing SOAP messages. The `messageReceiver` bean acts as a server, using a connection (`to XMPP server:google talk`), and listens to the host on a specific service with a username and password.

```xml
<bean id="messageFactory" class="org.springframework.ws.soap.saaj.SaajSoapMessageFactory"/>
<bean id="connection" class="org.springframework.ws.transport.xmpp.support.XmppConnectionFactoryBean">
    <property name="host" value="talk.google.com"/>
    <property name="username" value="yourUserName@gmail.com"/>
    <property name="password" value="yourPassword"/>
    <property name="serviceName" value="gmail.com"/>
</bean>

<bean id="messagingReceiver" class="org.springframework.ws.transport.xmpp.XmppMessageReceiver">
    <property name="messageFactory" ref="messageFactory"/>
    <property name="connection" ref="connection"/>
    <property name="messageReceiver" ref="messageDispatcher"/>
</bean>
```

Once the message is sent by the client, it will be forwarded to the endpoint (SamplePlayLoadEndPoint that is configured within messageDispatcher) by the message dispatcher and the response will be returned to the client:

```
<bean id="messageDispatcher"
  class="org.springframework.ws.soap.server.SoapMessageDispatcher">
    <property name="endpointMappings">
    <bean class="org.springframework.ws.server.endpoint.mapping.
PayloadRootQNameEndpointMapping">
        <property name="defaultEndpoint"> <bean class="com.packtpub.
liverestaurant.service.endpoint.SamplePlayLoadEndPoint"/>
      </property> </bean>
    </property>
  </bean>
```

Webservicetemplate is used here as a client; it will be discussed in the next chapter.

SamplePlayLoadEndPoint just receives a request and returns a response:

```
public class SamplePlayLoadEndPoint implements PayloadEndpoint {
  static Logger logger = Logger.getLogger(SamplePlayLoadEndPoint.
class);
  public Source invoke(Source request) throws Exception {
    return  request;
  }
```

A test class is included in the project to load the application context, set up the XMPP Web-Service server, and test the Web-Service.

See also

The *Creating Web-Service client on XMPP transport* recipe discussed in *Chapter 2, Building Clients for SOAP Web-Services*.

Setting up a contract-first Web-Service

Generating WSDL and XSD contracts from Java code and setting up a Web-Service is called **contract-last development**. The major drawback to this approach is the contracts (WSDL or XSD) of the Web-Service could eventually change if there are any changes in Java classes. In this way, the client side has to update the client-side classes and that always is not favorable. The contract-first approach was introduced as an alternative to tackle the contract-last's bottleneck. In the contract-first approach, the contract (WSDL or schema) are primary artifacts to set up a Web-Service.

Some of the advantages of the contract-first approach over contract-last are as follows:

▶ Performance: In contract-last, some extra data, that is, serialization of Java code might be exchanged between client and server, which decreases the performance, while contract-last precisely exchanges the required data and maximizes the performance.

▶ Consistency: Different vendors may generate different WSDL in the contract-last approach, while the contract-first approach eliminates this problem by standing on the same contract.

▶ Versioning: Changing the version of a contract-last Web-Service means changing Java classes in both client and server side and that might eventually be expensive in case there are a lot of clients that call a Web-Service, while in contract-first, since the contract is decoupled from implementation, versioning could be simply done by adding a new method implementation in the same endpoint class or using a stylesheet to convert an old message format into new message format.

▶ Maintenance/enhancement cost: Changing only a contract is much cheaper than changing Java code in both client and server side. In this recipe, we will discuss how to set up a contract-first Web-Service using Spring-WS.

Getting ready

In this recipe, the project's name is `LiveRestaurant_R-1.8`, with the following Maven dependencies:

▶ `spring-ws-core-2.0.1.RELEASE.jar`

▶ `jdom-1.0.jar`

How to do it...

1. Copy the data contract (`orderService.xsd`) from the resources folder.

2. Create an endpoint (`OrderEndpoint`).

3. Configure the auto-detection of the endpoint using the component scan in the server Spring configuration file (`spring-ws-servlet.xml`).

4. Configure the dynamic generation of WSDL from the data contract (`orderService.xsd`).

5. Run the server using the following command:

   mvn clean package tomcat:run

6. Browse to the following link to see the WSDL:

   `http://localhost:8080/LiveRestaurant/OrderService.wsdl`

7. Run client from `LiveRestaurant_R-1.8-Client`:

   mvn clean package

   The following is the output when the server runs successfully:

   ```
    Sent response....
   <tns:placeOrderResponse xmlns:tns="....."><tns:refNumber>tns:refNum
   ber>order-John_S
   mith_9999</tns:refNumber></tns:refNumber></
   tns:placeOrderResponse>...
    for request ...
   <tns:placeOrderRequest xmlns:tns="....">
     <tns:order>
       <tns:refNumber>9999</tns:refNumber>
       <tns:customer>
         ....
       </tns:customer>
       <tns:dateSubmitted>2008-09-29T05:49:45</tns:dateSubmitted>
       <tns:orderDate>2014-09-19T03:18:33</tns:orderDate>
       <!--1 or more repetitions:-->
       <tns:items>
         <tns:type>Snacks</tns:type>
         <tns:name>Pitza</tns:name>
         <tns:quantity>2</tns:quantity>
       </tns:items>
     </tns:order>
   </tns:placeOrderRequest>
   ```

How it works...

The steps of this recipe are the same as that of the recipe *Simplifying the creation of a Web-Service using MessageDispatcherServlet*, except the implementation of endpoint handling methods.

This annotation serves as a specialization of `@Component`, allowing for the implementation classes to be autodetected through classpath scanning, which is configured in the server application context file (`spring-ws-servlet.xml`):

```
    <context:component-scan base-package="com.packtpub.liverestaurant.
service"/>
    <sws:annotation-driven/>
```

`OrderEndpoint` is the `endPoint` of this recipe and the `@Endpoint` annotation is also the same as `@service`, allowing for the implementation classes to be autodetected through classpath scanning. A request with the root element `placeOrderRequest` (`localPart = "placeOrderRequest"`) and the namespace `http://www.packtpub.com/liverestaurant/OrderService/schema` will be forwarded to call the corresponding method (`handlePlaceOrderRequest`).

```
@Endpoint
public class OrderEndpoint {
  private static final Log logger = LogFactory.getLog(OrderEndpoint.
class);
    private static final String NAMESPACE_URI = "http://www.packtpub.
com/liverestaurant/OrderService/schema";
  private OrderService orderService;
    @Autowired
  public OrderEndpoint(OrderService orderService) {
    this.orderService = orderService;
  }
    @PayloadRoot(namespace = NAMESPACE_URI, localPart =
"placeOrderRequest")
    @ResponsePayload
    public Source handlePancelOrderRequest(@RequestPayload Element
placeOrderRequest) throws Exception {
      String refNumber=placeOrderRequest.getElementsByTagNameNS(NAMESP
ACE_URI, "refNumber") .item(0).getTextContent();
      String fName=placeOrderRequest.getElementsByTagNameNS(NAMESPAC
E_URI, "fName") .item(0).getTextContent();
      String lName=placeOrderRequest.getElementsByTagNameNS(NAMESPAC
E_URI, "lName") .item(0).getTextContent();
        return new StringSource(
      "<tns:placeOrderResponse xmlns:tns=\"http://www.packtpub.
com/liverestaurant/OrderService/schema\"><tns:refNumber>"+orde
rService.placeOrder(fName,lName, refNumber)+"</tns:refNumber></
tns:placeOrderResponse>");
    }
  }
```

Other details about annotations and how the request will be mapped to an endpoint method are contained in this chapter.

The following setting in the `spring-ws-servlet.xml` file causes the application to automatically generate the WSDL file from the data contract (`orderService.xsd`).

```
        <sws:dynamic-wsdl id="OrderService"
portTypeName="OrderService" locationUri="http://localhost:8080/
LiveRestaurant/spring-ws/OrderService"
```

```
                        targetNamespace="http://www.packtpub.com/
    liverestaurant/OrderService/schema">
        <sws:xsd location="/WEB-INF/orderService.xsd"/>
    </sws:dynamic-wsdl>
```

Even though WSDL can be generated automatically from the data contract (XSD), Spring-WS recommends avoiding autogeneration of WSDL for these reasons:

- To keep consistency between releases (there might be slight differences among autogenerated WSDLs for different versions)
- Autogeneration of WSDL is slow, although once generated, WSDL will be cached and used later.

Therefore, Spring-WS recommends, while developing, autogenerate WSDL once via the browser and save it and use static WSDL to expose the service contract.

See also

The recipes *Setting up an endpoint by annotating the payload-root, Simplifying the creation of a Web-Service using MessageDispatcherServlet*, discussed in this chapter and the *Creating a Web-Service client on HTTP transport* recipe, discussed in *Chapter 2, Building Clients for SOAP Web-Services*.

Also see the recipes discussed in *Chapter 10, Spring Remoting*, to find out how to set up contract-last Web-Services.

Setting up a simple endpoint mapping for the Web-Service

This recipe demonstrates a very simple endpoint mapping that maps a Web-Service request to a Java class method.

Getting ready

In this recipe, the project's name is LiveRestaurant_R-1.9, with the following Maven dependencies:

- spring-ws-core-2.0.1.RELEASE.jar
- log4j-12.9.jar

How to do it...

The steps of this recipe are the same as that of the previous recipe, *Setting up a contract-first Web-Service*, except that the registration of the endpoint, that is, method endpoint mapping and is configured in `spring-ws-servlet.xml`.

1. Define an endpoint (`OrderSeviceMethodEndpoint`) based on the method mapping standard (`SimpleMethodEndpointMapping`).

2. Configure the method endpoint mapping in `spring-ws-servlet.xml`.

3. Run the `mvn clean package tomcat:run` command and browse to see the WSDL:

   `http://localhost:8080/LiveRestaurant/OrderService.wsdl`

4. To test, open a new command window, go to `Liverestaurant_R-1.9-Client`, and run the following command:

   ```
   mvn clean package exec:java
   ```

   Here is the server-side output:

   ```
   Sent response ..
   <tns:placeOrderResponse xmlns:tns="..."><tns:refNumber>order-John_
   Smith_1234</tns:refNumber>
   </tns:placeOrderResponse>...
     for request ...
   <tns:placeOrderRequest xmlns:tns="...">
     <tns:order>
       <tns:refNumber>order-9999</tns:refNumber>
       <tns:customer>
        ........
       </tns:customer>
       <tns:dateSubmitted>2008-09-29T05:49:45</tns:dateSubmitted>
       <tns:orderDate>2014-09-19T03:18:33</tns:orderDate>
       <!--1 or more repetitions:-->
       <tns:items>
         <tns:type>Snacks</tns:type>
         <tns:name>Pitza</tns:name>
         <tns:quantity>2</tns:quantity>
       </tns:items>
     </tns:order>
   </tns:placeOrderRequest>
   ```

How it works...

`SimpleMethodEndpointMapping` maps from the local name of the request payload
(`placeOrderRequest`) to the methods of the POJO classes. Here is a sample of the
request payload (note the local name of the request payload):

```
<tns:placeOrderRequest ...>
  <tns:order>
......
  </tns:order>
</tns:placeOrderRequest>
```

The endpoint bean is registered using the `endpoints` property. This property tells you that
there should be a method in the `endpoint` class (`OrderServiceEndpoint`) with a name
that starts with `methodPrefix(handle)` and ends with the request payload local name
(`placeOrderRequest`). This increases the flexibility of the endpoint naming by using the
configuration in `spring-ws-servlet.xml`:

```
    <bean class="org.springframework.ws.server.endpoint.mapping.
SimpleMethodEndpointMapping">
      <property name="endpoints">
        <ref bean="OrderServiceEndpoint"/>
      </property>
      <property name="methodPrefix" value="handle"></property>
      <property name="interceptors">
        <list>
          <bean
            class="org.springframework.ws.server.endpoint.interceptor.
PayloadLoggingInterceptor">
            <property name="logRequest" value="true" />
            <property name="logResponse" value="true" />
          </bean>
        </list>
      </property>
    </bean>
    <bean id="OrderServiceEndpoint" class="com.packtpub.liverestaurant.
service.endpoint.OrderSeviceMethodEndpoint">
    </bean>
```

The endpoint method name should match the `handle+request` message root name
(`handleplaceOrderRequest`). In the body of the method, we should process the request
and finally return the response in the form of `javax.xml.transform.Source`:

```
public class OrderSeviceMethodEndpoint {
  private OrderService orderService;
  @Autowired
```

```
   public void setOrderService(OrderService orderService) {
     this.orderService = orderService;
   }
   public @ResponsePayload Source handleplaceOrderRequest(@
RequestPayload Source source) throws Exception {
     //extract data from input parameter
     String fName="John";
     String lName="Smith";
     String refNumber="1234";
       return new StringSource(
     "<tns:placeOrderResponse xmlns:tns=\"http://www.packtpub.
com/liverestaurant/OrderService/schema\"><tns:refNumber>"+order
Service.placeOrder(fName, lName, refNumber)+"</tns:refNumber></
tns:placeOrderResponse>");
   }
}
```

See also

The recipes *Setting up a transport-neutral WS-Addressing endpoint* and *Setting up an endpoint by annotating the payload-root*, discussed in this chapter.

Setting up an endpoint by annotating the payload-root

Spring-WS simplifies the creation of complex Web-Services further by its annotation features and reduces the code and configuration in XML.

Getting ready

In this recipe, the project's name is `LiveRestaurant_R-1.10`, with the following Maven dependencies:

- `spring-ws-core-2.0.1.RELEASE.jar`
- `log4j-12.9.jar`

How to do it...

The steps of this recipe are the same as that of *Setting up a contract-first Web-Service* and here we want to describe the endpoint mapping using annotation in the `endpoint` class.

1. Run the following command:

   ```
   mvn clean package tomcat:run
   ```

2. Browse to the following link to see the WSDL:

   ```
   http://localhost:8080/LiveRestaurant/OrderService.wsdl
   ```

3. To test, open a new command window, go to `LiveRestaurant-1.10-Client`, and run the following command:

   ```
   mvn clean package exec:java
   ```

   Here is the server-side output:

   ```
   Sent response ..
   <tns:placeOrderResponse xmlns:tns="..."><tns:refNumber>order-John_
   Smith_1234</tns:refNumber>
   </tns:placeOrderResponse>...
    for request ...
   <tns:placeOrderRequest xmlns:tns="...">
     <tns:order>
       <tns:refNumber>order-9999</tns:refNumber>
       <tns:customer>
        ........
       </tns:customer>
       <tns:dateSubmitted>2008-09-29T05:49:45</tns:dateSubmitted>
       <tns:orderDate>2014-09-19T03:18:33</tns:orderDate>
       <!--1 or more repetitions:-->
       <tns:items>
         <tns:type>Snacks</tns:type>
         <tns:name>Pitza</tns:name>
         <tns:quantity>2</tns:quantity>
       </tns:items>
     </tns:order>
   </tns:placeOrderRequest>
   ```

How it works...

By including component scan and annotation-driven settings in the Spring-WS configuration file (`spring-ws-servlet.xml`), the Spring container will scan the entire package for endpoints, services, and dependencies to inject and autowire each other to build the Web-Service blocks. You cannot see the adapters and other handlers here, since the container smartly picks the right/default adapter, dynamically (`messageDispatcher` runs support method of an adapter from a list of existing adapters for the endponit, and if support method returns `true`, that adapter is the right adapter):

```
    <context:component-scan base-package="com.packtpub.liverestaurant.
service"/>

    <sws:annotation-driven/>

    <sws:dynamic-wsdl id="OrderService" portTypeName="OrderService"
locationUri="http://localhost:8080/LiveRestaurant/spring-ws/
OrderService"
                        targetNamespace="http://www.packtpub.com/
liverestaurant/OrderService/schema">
        <sws:xsd location="/WEB-INF/orderService.xsd"/>
    </sws:dynamic-wsdl>
```

The `@Endpoint` annotation of `OrderSeviceAnnotationEndpoint` makes it an endpoint, with `PayloadRootAnnotationMethodEndpointMapping`, with the exact pointers to the method-endpoint mapping with the method-level annotations:

```
@Endpoint
public class OrderSeviceAnnotationEndpoint {
  private final String SERVICE_NS = "http://www.packtpub.com/
liverestaurant/OrderService/schema";
  private OrderService orderService;
  @Autowired
  public OrderSeviceAnnotationEndpoint(OrderService orderService) {
    this.orderService = orderService;
  }
  @PayloadRoot(localPart = "placeOrderRequest", namespace = SERVICE_
NS)
  public @ResponsePayload
  Source handlePlaceOrderRequest(@RequestPayload Source source) throws
Exception {

    //extract data from input parameter
    String fName="John";
    String lName="Smith";
    String refNumber="1234";
```

```
       return new StringSource(
     "<tns:placeOrderResponse xmlns:tns=\"http://www.packtpub.
  com/liverestaurant/OrderService/schema\"><tns:refNumber>"+order
  Service.placeOrder(fName, lName, refNumber)+"</tns:refNumber></
  tns:placeOrderResponse>");
    }


  @PayloadRoot(localPart = "cancelOrderRequest", namespace = SERVICE_
  NS)
    public @ResponsePayload
    Source handleCancelOrderRequest(@RequestPayload Source source)
  throws Exception {
      //extract data from input parameter
      boolean cancelled =true ;
       return new StringSource(
          "<tns:cancelOrderResponse xmlns:tns=\"http://www.packtpub.
  com/liverestaurant/OrderService/schema\"><cancelled>"+(cancelled?"true
  ":"false")+"</cancelled></tns:cancelOrderResponse>");
    }
```

@PayloadRoot helps the MessageDispatcher to map the request to the method, with
the help of an argument annotation, @RequestPayload, which specifies the exact message
payload part of the entire SOAP message as an argument into the method (it finds the method
by root element of a request equal to localPart, for example, placeOrderRequest
or placeCancelRequest). @RequestPayload tells the container that the argument
RequestPayload is to be extracted from the SOAP message and injected to the method
as an argument at runtime.

The return type annotation, @ResponsePayload, instructs MessageDispatcher that the
instance of javax.xml.transform.Source is ResponsePayload. The smart Spring-
WS framework detects the type of these objects at runtime and delegates to the appropriate
PayloadMethodProcessor. In this case, it is SourcePayloadMethodProcessor, since
the input argument and the return value are of the type javax.xml.transform.Source.

See also

The recipes *Setting up a transport-neutral WS-Addressing endpoint* and *Setting up a simple
endpoint mapping for the Web-Service*, discussed in this chapter.

Setting up a transport-neutral WS-Addressing endpoint

Using HTTP transport information inside the XML messages for routing messages to endpoints mixes data and operation together, and these messages will be replied to for the requested client.

WS-Addressing standardizes routing mechanism by separating routing data and including it inside the SOAP headers. WS-Addressing may use its own metadata instead of using HTTP transport data for endpoint routing. In addition, a request from a client may return to a different client in WS-Addressing. For example, considering the following request from a client, the client side can set `ReplyTo` to its own address and `FaultTo` to admin the endpoint address. Then, the server will send successful messages to the client and fault messages to the admin address `[<SOAP-ENV:Envelope xmlns:SOAP-ENV="http://schemas. xmlsoap.org/soap/envelope/">`.

```
<SOAP-ENV:Header xmlns:wsa="http://www.w3.org/2005/08/addressing">
  <wsa:To>server_uri</wsa:To>
  <wsa:Action>action_uri</wsa:Action>
  <wsa:From>client_address </wsa:From>
  <wsa:ReplyTo>client_address</wsa:ReplyTo>
  <wsa:FaultTo>admen_uri </wsa:FaultTo>
<wsa:MessageID>..</wsa:MessageID>
</SOAP-ENV:Header>
<SOAP-ENV:Body>
<tns:placeOrderRequest>....</tns:placeOrderReques>
</SOAP-ENV:Body></SOAP-ENV:Envelope>]
```

In this recipe, we will set up a Spring-WS using WS-Addressing.

Getting ready

In this recipe, the project's name is `LiveRestaurant_R-1.11` with the following Maven dependencies:

- `spring-ws-core-2.0.1.RELEASE.jar`
- `log4j-12.9.jar`

How to do it...

The steps of this recipe are the same as that of *Setting up an endpoint by annotating the payload-root*, except for the endpoint class. So, follow the steps of the mentioned recipe and define a new endpoint with WS-Addressing standards.

1. Run the following command:

   ```
   mvn clean package tomcat:run
   ```

2. To test, open a new command window to `Liverestaurant_R-1.11-Client` and run the following command:

   ```
   mvn clean package exec:java
   ```

   The following is the server-side output:

   ```
   Sent response [<SOAP-ENV:Envelope ...><SOAP-ENV:Header...>

   <wsa:To ...>http://www.w3.org/2005/08/addressing/anonymous</
   wsa:To>

   <wsa:Action>http://www.packtpub.com/OrderService/OrdReqResponse</
   wsa:Action>

   <wsa:MessageID>...</wsa:MessageID>

   <wsa:RelatesTo>urn:uuid:2beaead4-c04f-487c-86fc-caab64ad8461</
   wsa:RelatesTo>

   </SOAP-ENV:Header>

   <SOAP-ENV:Body>

   <tns:placeOrderResponse ...><tns:refNumber>order-John_Smith_1234</
   tns:refNumber></tns:placeOrderResponse>

   </SOAP-ENV:Body></SOAP-ENV:Envelope>...

    for request <SOAP-ENV:Envelope ..><SOAP-ENV:Header ...>

   <wsa:To SOAP-..>http://www.packtpub.com/liverestaurant/
   OrderService/schema</wsa:To>

   <wsa:Action>http://www.packtpub.com/OrderService/OrdReq</
   wsa:Action>

   <wsa:MessageID>...</wsa:MessageID>

   </SOAP-ENV:Header><SOAP-ENV:Body>

   <tns:placeOrderRequest ...>

     <tns:order>

       <tns:refNumber>9999</tns:refNumber>

       <tns:customer>

           ...
   ```

```
        </tns:customer>
        <tns:dateSubmitted>2008-09-29T05:49:45</tns:dateSubmitted>
    <tns:orderDate>2014-09-19T03:18:33</tns:orderDate>
    <!--1 or more repetitions:-->
    <tns:items>
      <tns:type>Snacks</tns:type>
      <tns:name>Pitza</tns:name>
      <tns:quantity>2</tns:quantity>
    </tns:items>
  </tns:order>
</tns:placeOrderRequest>
</SOAP-ENV:Body></SOAP-ENV:Envelope>
```

How it works...

Same as the previous recipe, *Setting up an endpoint by annotating the payload-root*, the incoming WS-Addressing SOAP messages will be forwarded to the endpoint (OrderEndpoint, which is autodetected by @Endpoint). As you can see from the output, a header is added to the SOAP envelop that WS-Addressing uses for mapping and dispatching purposes of the endpoint method.

```
<SOAP-ENV:Header ...>
<wsa:To SOAP-..>http://www.packtpub.com/liverestaurant/OrderService/
schema</wsa:To>
<wsa:Action>http://www.packtpub.com/OrderService/OrdReq</wsa:Action>
<wsa:MessageID>...</wsa:MessageID>
</SOAP-ENV:Header>
```

In this recipe, the server applies AnnotationActionEndpointMapping, which uses @Action (http://www.packtpub.com/OrderService/OrdReq). @Action is similar to @PayloadRoot for recognizing the handling methods (handleOrderRequest) in the endpoint (OrderEndpoint).

```
    @Endpoint
    public class OrderEndpoint {
      private OrderService orderService;
      @Autowired
        public void setOrderService(OrderService orderService) {
        this.orderService = orderService;
      }
```

```
@Action("http://www.packtpub.com/OrderService/OrdReq")
public @ResponsePayload
Source handleOrderRequest(@RequestPayload Source source) throws
Exception {
    //extract data from input parameter
    String fName="John";
    String lName="Smith";
    String refNumber="1234";

    return new StringSource(
    "<tns:placeOrderResponse xmlns:tns=\"http://www.packtpub.
com/liverestaurant/OrderService/schema\"><tns:refNumber>"+order
Service.placeOrder(fName, lName, refNumber)+"</tns:refNumber></
tns:placeOrderResponse>");
    }
}
```

See also

The recipe *Creating Web-Service client for WS-Addressing endpoint*, discussed in *Chapter 2, Building Clients for SOAP Web-Services*, and the recipe *Setting up an endpoint by annotating the payload root*, discussed in this chapter.

Setting up an endpoint using an XPath expression

Spring-WS allows us to extract the passed parameters in the `endpoint` method's signature using annotations with the XPath expressions. For example, in the `endpoint` method's `handleOrderRequest(@RequestPayload Source source)`, if you want to find the value of any element in the source object, you have to use Java API to extract the value. You can eliminate using Java API in the handler method by using XPath in the method's signature to extract the data from the incoming XML data, as shown as follows: `handleOrderRequest(@ XPathParam("/OrderRequest/message") String message)`.

This recipe illustrates the usage of XPath expressions in endpoint mapping with the help of annotation.

Getting ready

In this recipe, the project's name is `LiveRestaurant_R-1.12` with the following Maven dependencies:

- `spring-ws-core-2.0.1.RELEASE.jar`
- `log4j-12.9.jar`

How to do it...

The steps of this recipe are the same as that of *Setting up an endpoint by annotating the payload-root*, except for the implementation of endpoint handling methods. So, follow the steps of the mentioned recipe and use XPath expressions to extract data from incoming message and create a response.

1. Run the following command from `LiveRestaurant_R-1.12`:

   ```
   mvn clean package tomcat:run
   ```

2. Browse to the following link to see the Web-Service service contract:

   ```
   http://localhost:8080/LiveRestaurant/OrderService.wsdl
   ```

3. To test, open a new command window, go to `LiveRestaurant_R-1.12-Client`, and run the following command:

   ```
   mvn clean package exec:java
   ```

   The following is the server-side output:

   ```
    Sent response ..
   <tns:placeOrderResponse xmlns:tns="">
   <tns:refNumber>order-John_Smith_9999</tns:refNumber>
   </tns:placeOrderResponse>
   ...
   for request ...
   <tns:placeOrderRequest xmlns:tns="...">
     <order>
       <refNumber>9999</refNumber>
       <customer>
        ......
       </customer>
       <dateSubmitted>2008-09-29T05:49:45</dateSubmitted>
       <orderDate>2014-09-19T03:18:33</orderDate>
       <items>
         <type>Snacks</type>
         <name>Pitza</name>
         <quantity>2</quantity>
       </items>
     </order>
   ```

```
  </tns:placeOrderRequest>

  ...

    Sent response...

  <tns:cancelOrderResponse xmlns:tns="...">

  <tns:cancelled>true</tns:cancelled>

  </tns:cancelOrderResponse>

  ...

  for request ...

  <tns:cancelOrderRequest xmlns:tns="...">

    <refNumber>9999</refNumber>

  </tns:cancelOrderRequest>
```

How it works...

Passing the method parameter is the same as the recipe *Setting up an endpoint by annotating the payload-root*, except that it uses @XPathParam, which specifies the path of the data in a message that is to be passed as an argument into the method. Here XpathParamMethodArgumentResolver is responsible for extracting the value from the message and passing it to the method.

The annotation XpathParam helps the MethodArgumentResolvers (XpathParamMethodArgumentResolver) to extract information out of the XML and binds a node value to a method argument (using // cause, the whole message is searched recursively, for example, //lName searches the whole placeRequestRequest message). The same implementation is used for the method cancelOrderRequest:

```
@Endpoint
public class OrderEndpoint {

  private final String SERVICE_NS = "http://www.packtpub.com/
liverestaurant/OrderService/schema";

  private OrderService orderService;

  @Autowired
  public OrderEndpoint(OrderService orderService) {
    this.orderService = orderService;
  }

  @PayloadRoot(localPart = "placeOrderRequest", namespace = SERVICE_
NS)
  public @ResponsePayload
```

```
Source handleOrderRequest(@XPathParam("//fName") String fName,@
XPathParam("//lName") String lName,@XPathParam("//refNumber") String
refNumber) throws Exception {
    return new StringSource(
    "<tns:placeOrderResponse xmlns:tns=\"http://www.packtpub.
com/liverestaurant/OrderService/schema\"><tns:refNumber>" +
orderService.placeOrder(fName, lName, refNumber)+"</tns:refNumber></
tns:placeOrderResponse>");
    }


    @PayloadRoot(localPart = "cancelOrderRequest", namespace = SERVICE_
NS)
    public @ResponsePayload
    Source handleCancelOrderRequest(@XPathParam("//refNumber") String
refNumber) throws Exception {
        boolean cancelled = orderService.cancelOrder(refNumber);
        return new StringSource(
            "<tns:cancelOrderResponse xmlns:tns=\"http://www.packtpub.
com/liverestaurant/OrderService/schema\"><cancelled>"+(cancelled?"true
":"false")+"</cancelled></tns:cancelOrderResponse>");
    }
```

The method argument can be any of the following:

- boolean or Boolean
- double or Double
- String
- Node
- NodeList

See also

The recipe *Setting up an endpoint by annotating the payload-root*, discussed in this chapter.

Handling the incoming XML messages using DOM

The implementation of the endpoint requires us to get the incoming XML messages and extract its data. In Java, there are various methods (W3C DOM, SAX, XPath, JAXB, Castor, XMLBeans, JiBX, or XStream) for extracting data from an input XML message, but most of them are not language-neutral.

DOM was created to be language-neutral and initially used for JavaScript manipulation of HTML pages. In Java, W3C DOM library is provided to interact with XML data. Classes, such as `org.w3c.dom.Document`, `org.w3c.dom.Element`, `org.w3c.dom.Node`, and `org.w3c.dom.Text` from W3C DOM library, are for extracting data from an input XML message.

In this recipe, W3C DOM is used to extract the data from incoming messages.

Getting ready

In this recipe, the project's name is `LiveRestaurant_R-1.13`, with the following Maven dependencies:

- `spring-ws-core-2.0.1.RELEASE.jar`
- `log4j-1.2.9.jar`

How to do it...

The steps of this recipe are the same as that of the recipe *Setting up an endpoint by annotating the payload-root*, except for the implementation of the endpoint-handling methods. So, follow the steps of the mentioned recipe and use DOM to extract data from the incoming message and create the response.

1. Run the command `mvn clean package tomcat:run` and browse to the following link:

   `http://localhost:8080/LiveRestaurant/OrderService.wsdl`

2. To test, open a new command window and run the following command:

   `mvn clean package exec:java`

   The following is the server-side output:

   ```
   Sent response ....
   <placeOrderResponse xmlns="...">
   <refNumber>order-John_Smith_1234</refNumber></placeOrderResponse>
   ...
   for request ...
   <tns:placeOrderRequest xmlns:tns="...">
     <tns:order>
       <tns:refNumber>9999</tns:refNumber>
       <tns:customer>
   ....     </tns:customer>
   ```

```
    <tns:dateSubmitted>2008-09-29T05:49:45</tns:dateSubmitted>

    <tns:orderDate>2014-09-19T03:18:33</tns:orderDate>

    <!--1 or more repetitions:-->

    <tns:items>

      <tns:type>Snacks</tns:type>

      <tns:name>Pitza</tns:name>

      <tns:quantity>2</tns:quantity>

    </tns:items>

  </tns:order>

</tns:placeOrderRequest>
```

How it works...

Passing the method parameter is the same as the recipe *Setting up an endpoint by annotating the payload-root*, except that we use @RequestPayload, which specifies the DOM element of data in a message to be passed as an argument into the method. Here, DomPayloadMethodProcessor is responsible for extracting the value from the message and passing it to the method. Since the return type which is specified by @ResponsePayload is also a DOM element type, DomPayloadMethodProcessor is being used as return handler.

The @PayloadRoot annotation informs Spring-WS that the handleCancelOrderRequest method is a handling method for XML messages. The sort of message that this method can handle is indicated by the annotation values (the @RequestPayload element tells it is of the DOM element type). In this case, it can handle XML elements that have the placeOrderRequest local part and the http://www.packtpub.com/liverestaurant/OrderService/schema namespace.

```
    @PayloadRoot(namespace = NAMESPACE_URI, localPart =
    "placeOrderRequest")
        @ResponsePayload
        public Element handlePlaceOrderRequest(@RequestPayload Element
    placeOrderRequest) throws Exception {

            String refNumber=placeOrderRequest.getElementsByTagNameNS(NAMESP
    ACE_URI, "refNumber") .item(0).getTextContent();
            String fName=placeOrderRequest.getElementsByTagNameNS(NAMESPAC
    E_URI, "fName") .item(0).getTextContent();
            String lName=placeOrderRequest.getElementsByTagNameNS(NAMESPAC
    E_URI, "lName") .item(0).getTextContent();
```

The preceding code extracts the elements `refNumber`, `fName`, and `lName` from the incoming XML message (`placeOrderRequest`) via the method `getElementsByTagNameNS`. Then, it finds and returns the text content of the first item in the `refNumber`, `fName`, and `lName` elements (by `item(0).getTextContent()`).

The following part of the code creates an outgoing XML message by creating the `placeOrderResponse` element (using `document.createElementNS`). Then, it creates the child element `refNumber` (using `document.createElementNS`) and creates the text of this element (using `createTextNode and appendChild`). Then, it appends the `refNumber` element to the response element `placeOrderResponse` (using the `appendChild` method):

```
Document document = documentBuilder.newDocument();
Element responseElement = document.createElementNS(NAMESPACE_
URI,
    "placeOrderResponse");

    Element canElem=document.createElementNS(NAMESPACE_
URI,"refNumber");
    Text responseText = document.createTextNode(orderService.
placeOrder(fName, lName, refNumber));

    canElem.appendChild(responseText);
    responseElement.appendChild(canElem);
    return responseElement;
```

See also

The recipe *Setting up an endpoint by annotating the payload-root*, discussed in this chapter and the recipe *Creating a Web-Service client on HTTP transport*, discussed in *Chapter 2, Building Clients for SOAP Web-Services*.

Handling the incoming XML messages using JDOM

Implementation of endpoints requires us to get the incoming XML messages and extract its data. DOM can fetch the data from an XML document, but it is slow and memory consuming and has very basic features.

JDOM document is not built into the memory; it is built on demand (lazy initialization design pattern). In addition, JDOM makes navigating through the document tree or manipulating the elements easier by providing a standard Java-based collection interface. In this recipe, JDOM is used to extract data from incoming messages.

Getting ready

In this recipe, the project's name is `LiveRestaurant_R-1.14`, with the following Maven dependencies:

- `spring-ws-core-2.0.1.RELEASE.jar`
- `jdom-1.0.jar`
- `log4j-1.2.9.jar`
- `jaxen-1.1.jar`
- `xalan-2.7.0.jar`

How to do it...

The steps of this recipe are the same as that of the *Setting up an endpoint by annotating the payload-root* recipe, except for the implementation of the endpoint-handling methods. So, follow the steps of the aforementioned recipe, use JDOM to extract the data from incoming message, and create the response.

1. Run the following command:

   ```
   mvn clean package tomcat:run
   ```

2. Browse to the following link:

   ```
   http://localhost:8080/LiveRestaurant/OrderService.wsdl
   ```

3. To test, open a new command window and run the following command:

   ```
   mvn exec:java exec:java
   ```

   The following is the server-side output:

   ```
   Sent response ...
   <tns:placeOrderResponse xmlns:tns="...">
   <tns:refNumber>order-John_Smith_1234</tns:refNumber>
   </tns:placeOrderResponse>....
     for request ....
   <tns:placeOrderRequest xmlns:tns="....">
     <tns:order>
       <tns:refNumber>9999</tns:refNumber>
       <tns:customer>
        ........
       </tns:customer>
       <tns:dateSubmitted>2008-09-29T05:49:45</tns:dateSubmitted>
       <tns:orderDate>2014-09-19T03:18:33</tns:orderDate>
   ```

```
<!--1 or more repetitions:-->
<tns:items>
  <tns:type>Snacks</tns:type>
  <tns:name>Pitza</tns:name>
  <tns:quantity>2</tns:quantity>
</tns:items>
</tns:order>
```

How it works...

It works in the same way as explained in the previous recipe, except that it uses JDOM in its method implementation.

The following part of the code extracts the values refNumber, fName, and lName from the incoming XML message (placeOrderRequest) by using namespace and XPath object:

```
Namespace namespace = Namespace.getNamespace("tns", NAMESPACE_
URI);
XPath refNumberExpression = XPath.newInstance("//tns:refNumber");
refNumberExpression.addNamespace(namespace);

XPath fNameExpression = XPath.newInstance("//tns:fName");
fNameExpression.addNamespace(namespace);

XPath lNameExpression = XPath.newInstance("//tns:lName");
lNameExpression.addNamespace(namespace);

String refNumber = refNumberExpression.valueOf(placeOrderRequest);
String fName = fNameExpression.valueOf(placeOrderRequest);
String lName = lNameExpression.valueOf(placeOrderRequest);
```

The following part of the code creates an outgoing message by creating the placeOrderResponse element (using new Element(...)). Then, it creates the child element refNumber (using new Element(...)) and creates the text of this element (using setText(...)). Then, it appends the message element to the response element placeOrderResponse (using the addContent method):

```
Namespace resNamespace = Namespace.getNamespace("tns",
NAMESPACE_URI);
Element root = new Element("placeOrderResponse", resNamespace);
Element message = new Element("refNumber", resNamespace);
message.setText(orderService.placeOrder(fName, lName, refNumber));
root.addContent(message);
Document doc = new Document(root);
return doc.getRootElement();
```

See also

The recipes *Setting up an endpoint by annotating the payload-root* and *Handling incoming XML Messages using DOM*, discussed in this chapter.

The recipe *Creating a Web-Service client on HTTP transport*, discussed in *Chapter 2, Building Clients for SOAP Web-Services.*

Handling the incoming XML messages using JAXB2

Java Architecture for XML Binding (JAXB) is a Java standard for Object-XML marshalling. JAXB defines a programmer API for reading and writing Java objects to / from XML documents. The object-XML mapping is generally annotated in classes. JAXB provides a set of useful annotations with the default values for most of them that make this marshalling an easy job.

This recipe demonstrates how to handle the incoming XML message in a Web-Service using JAXB in a very simple way. For simplicity and a continuation from the previous recipes, the same recipes are re-used with little improvements in converting the XML schema into domain classes to demonstrate the usage of JAXB.

Getting ready

In this recipe, the project's name is `LiveRestaurant_R-1.15` and has the following Maven dependencies:

- `spring-ws-core-2.0.1.RELEASE.jar`
- `log4j-1.2.9.jar`

How to do it...

The steps of this recipe are the same as that of the recipe *Setting up an endpoint by annotating the payload-root*, except for the implementation of the endpoint handling methods. So, follow the steps of the aforementioned recipe and use JAXB Marshaller/Un-Mashaller to convert payload into/from POJO.

1. First, we define a set of domain objects we need to marshal to/from XML from the data contract `OrderService.xsd` (refer to the recipe *Marshalling with JAXB2*, discussed in *Chapter 6, Marshalling and Object-XML Mapping (OXM)—Converting POJO to/from XML messages using Marshallers and Un-Marshallers*).

2. Change the implementation of the endpoint (`OrderEndpoint`) to use JAXB.

3. Run the following command:

```
mvn clean package tomcat:run
```

4. Browse to the following link:

```
http://localhost:8080/LiveRestaurant/OrderService.wsdl
```

5. To test, open a new command window to `Liverestaurant_R-1.15-Client` and run the following command:

```
mvn clean package exec:java
```

The following is the server-side output:

```
Sent response ....
<placeOrderResponse xmlns="...">
<refNumber>order-John_Smith_1234</refNumber>
</placeOrderResponse>....
....
<tns:placeOrderRequest xmlns:tns="...">
  <tns:order>
    <tns:refNumber>9999</tns:refNumber>
    <tns:customer>
........
    </tns:customer>
    <tns:dateSubmitted>2008-09-29T05:49:45</tns:dateSubmitted>
    <tns:orderDate>2014-09-19T03:18:33</tns:orderDate>
    <!--1 or more repetitions:-->
    <tns:items>
      <tns:type>Snacks</tns:type>
      <tns:name>Pitza</tns:name>
      <tns:quantity>2</tns:quantity>
    </tns:items>
  </tns:order>
</tns:placeOrderRequest>
```

How it works...

In the preceding code, the XML is bound with Java classes at runtime using JAXB. The incoming XML is converted into Java objects (unmarshalling) and after processing the objects, the resultant objects are marshalled back to XML before returning to the caller:

```
@PayloadRoot(localPart = "placeOrderRequest", namespace = SERVICE_
NS)
  public @ResponsePayload
  Source handlePlaceOrderRequest(@RequestPayload Source source) throws
Exception {

     PlaceOrderRequest request = (PlaceOrderRequest) unmarshal(source,
PlaceOrderRequest.class);
    PlaceOrderResponse response = new PlaceOrderResponse();
    String refNumber=request.getOrder().getRefNumber();
    String fName=request.getOrder().getCustomer().getName().
getFName();
    String lName=request.getOrder().getCustomer().getName().
getLName();
    response.setRefNumber(orderService.placeOrder(fName,lName,refNumb
er));

    return marshal(response);
  }
  private Object unmarshal(Source source, Class clazz) throws
JAXBException {
    JAXBContext context;
    try {
      context = JAXBContext.newInstance(clazz);
      Unmarshaller um = context.createUnmarshaller();
      return um.unmarshal(source);
    } catch (JAXBException e) {
      e.printStackTrace();
      throw e;
    }
  }

  private Source marshal(Object obj) throws JAXBException {
    JAXBContext context = JAXBContext.newInstance(obj.getClass());
    return new JAXBSource(context, obj);
  }
```

The JAXB context binds the Java classes passed via the constructor with the incoming XML, with the help of annotations in the classes at runtime, which instructs the unmarshaller to instantiate and load data from the XML tags into the objects. The objects are now passed to the service classes (OrderServiceImpl) for processing:

```
public class OrderServiceImpl implements OrderService {
    @Service
public class OrderServiceImpl implements OrderService {

    public String placeOrder( String fName,String lName,String
refNumber){
        return "order-"+fName+"_"+lName+"_"+refNumber;
    }

    public boolean cancelOrder( String refNumber ){
        return true;
    }
}
```

This approach allows the developer to work with Java objects instead of XML code with simple marshalling technology.

See also

The recipe *Setting up an endpoint by annotating the payload-root*, discussed in this chapter.

The recipe *Marshalling with JAXB2*, discussed in *Chapter 6, Marshalling and Object-XML Mapping (OXM)—Converting POJO to/from XML messages using Marshallers and Un-Marshallers.*

Validating the XML messages at the server side using an interceptor

Data contract is a basic concept used to set up a Spring-WS. However, validation is a basic requirement before a SOAP message sends/replies on the server side/client side.

Spring-WS supports validation of messages on the server side as well as the client side. In this recipe, server-side validation is applied and when the incorrect request comes to the server or the incorrect response replays from the server to the client, it throws an exception.

Getting ready

In this recipe, the project's name is LiveRestaurant_R-1.16 with the following Maven dependencies:

- ▶ spring-ws-core-2.0.1.RELEASE.jar
- ▶ log4j-1.2.9.jar

How to do it...

The steps of this recipe are the same as that of _Handling the incoming XML messages using DOM_, except for the validation of request/response message.

1. Modify `spring-ws-servlet.xml` to include `PayloadValidatingInterceptor`.

2. Run the following command:

    ```
    mvn clean package tomcat:run
    ```

3. Browse to the following link:

    ```
    http://localhost:8080/LiveRestaurant/OrderService.wsdl
    ```

4. To test, open a new command window to `Liverestaurant_R-1.16-Client` and run the following command:

    ```
    mvn clean package exec:java
    ```

    The following is the server-side output:

    ```
    Sent response [...
    <placeOrderResponse xmlns="...">
    <refNumber>order-John_Smith_1234</refNumber>
    </placeOrderResponse>...
      for request ...
    <tns:placeOrderRequest xmlns:tns="...">
      <tns:order>
        <tns:refNumber>9999</tns:refNumber>
        <tns:customer>
          <tns:addressPrimary>
             .....
          </tns:addressPrimary>
           .......
        </tns:customer>
       ........
      </tns:order>
    </tns:placeOrderRequest>


      WARN [http-8080-1] (AbstractFaultCreatingValidatingInterceptor.
    java:156) - XML validation error on request: cvc-complex-
    type.2.4.a: Invalid content was found s
    ```

tarting with element 'tns:address'. One of '{"http://www.packtpub.com/liverestaurant/OrderService/schema":addressPrimary}' is expected.

```
........ Sent response....
```

```
<faultcode>SOAP-ENV:Client</faultcode><faultstring
xml:lang="en">Validation error</faultstring><detail><spring-
ws:ValidationErr
```

```
or xmlns:spring-ws="http://springframework.org/spring-ws">cvc-
complex-type.2.4.a: Invalid content was found starting with
element 'tns:address'. One of '{"http:
```

```
//www.packtpub.com/liverestaurant/OrderService/
schema":addressPrimary}' is expected.</spring-
ws:ValidationError></detail></SOAP-ENV:Fault></SOAP-ENV:Body></
SOAP
```

```
-ENV:Envelope>]
```

How it works...

`spring-ws-servlet.xml` is almost the same, as described in the recipe *Handling the incoming XML messages using DOM*, except that it includes the interceptor that uses schema for validation, `validateRequest`, and `validateResponse`.

```
        <sws:interceptors>
            <bean class="org.springframework.ws.soap.server.endpoint.
    interceptor.PayloadValidatingInterceptor">
                <property name="schema" value="/WEB-INF/OrderService.
    xsd"/>
                <property name="validateRequest" value="true"/>
                <property name="validateResponse" value="true"/>
            </bean>
            <bean class="org.springframework.ws.server.endpoint.
    interceptor.PayloadLoggingInterceptor">
            </bean>
        </sws:interceptors>
```

When running the client, two requests will be sent to the server. The first one will be processed and the response will be sent back to the client, while the second one contains the wrong element (`address` instead of `addressPrimary`) that will send the faulty response back:

```
Sent response....
```

```
<faultcode>SOAP-ENV:Client</faultcode><faultstring
xml:lang="en">Validation error</faultstring><detail><spring-
ws:ValidationErr
```

```
or xmlns:spring-ws="http://springframework.org/spring-ws">cvc-
complex-type.2.4.a: Invalid content was found starting with element
'tns:address'. One of '{"http: //www.packtpub.com/liverestaurant/
OrderService/schema":addressPrimary}' is expected.</spring-
ws:ValidationError></detail></SOAP-ENV:Fault></SOAP-ENV:Body></SOAP
-ENV:Envelope>]
```

….

See also

The recipe *Setting up an endpoint by annotating the payload-root*, discussed in this chapter.

The recipe *Creating a Web-Service client on HTTP transport*, discussed in *Chapter 2, Building Clients for SOAP Web-Services*.

2

Building Clients for SOAP Web-Services

In this chapter, we will cover:

- ▶ Setting up a Web-Service client development environment within Eclipse
- ▶ Setting up a Web-Service client development environment using Maven
- ▶ Creating a Web-Service client on HTTP transport
- ▶ Creating a Web-Service client on JMS transport
- ▶ Creating a Web-Service client on E-mail transport
- ▶ Creating a Web-Service client on XMPP transport
- ▶ Creating a Web-Service client using XPath expression
- ▶ Creating a Web-Service client for WS-Addressing endpoint
- ▶ Transforming a Web-Service message using XSLT

Introduction

Using Java API, such as `SAAJ`, client-side SOAP messages can be generated and transmitted to/from a Web-Service. However, it requires an extra amount of coding and knowledge about SOAP messages.

The package `org.springframework.ws.client.core` contains the core functionality of the client-side API, which facilitates calling the server-side Web-Service.

APIs in this package provide template classes like `WebServiceTemplate` that simplifies the use of Web-Services. Using these templates, you will be able to create a Web-Service client over various transport protocols (HTTP, JMS, e-mail, XMPP, and so on) and send/receive XML messages as well as marshal objects to XML before sending them. Spring also provides classes, such as `StringSource` and `Result`, which simplify passing and retrieving XML messages while using `WebServiceTemplate`.

In this chapter, the first two recipes explain how to set up the environment for calling a Web-Service client using Eclipse and Maven.

Then we will discuss the usage of `WebServiceTemplate` to create a Web-Service client over various transport protocols (HTTP, JMS, e-mail, XMPP, and so on). In addition to this, the recipe *Setting up a Web-Service client using an XPath expression* explains how to retrieve data from an XML message. Finally, in the last recipe, *Transforming a Web-Service message using XSLT*, how to convert the XML messages into different formats between the client and server is presented. To set up a Web-Service server, some recipes from *Chapter 1, Building SOAP Web-Services*, are used and a separate client project is created that calls the server-side Web-Service.

Setting up a Web-Service client development environment within Eclipse

A Web-Service client in the simplest form is a Java class that calls a server-side Web-Service. In this recipe, setting up the environment to call a server-side Web-Service is presented. Here, a client-side Java class calls a Web-Service on the server in two forms. The first one is a Java class that calls a Web-Service in the main method of the class. The second one uses the JUnit test class to call the server-side Web-Service.

Getting ready

This recipe is similar to the recipe *Using Maven for building and running a Spring-WS*, discussed in *Chapter 1, Building SOAP Web-Services*.

1. Download and install the Eclipse IDE for Java EE developers—Helios.
2. In this recipe, the project's name is `LiveRestaurant_R-2.1` (for server-side Web-Service), with the following Maven dependencies:
   - `spring-ws-core-2.0.1.RELEASE.jar`
   - `jdom-1.0.jar`
   - `log4j-1.2.9.jar`
   - `jaxen-1.1.jarb`
   - `xalan-2.7.0.jar`

3. The `LiveRestaurant_R-2.1-Client` (for the client side) has the following Maven dependencies:

   ❑ `spring-ws-core-2.0.1.RELEASE.jar`

   ❑ `jdom-1.0.jar`

   ❑ `log4j-1.2.9.jar`

   ❑ `jaxen-1.1.jar`

   ❑ `xalan-2.7.0.jar`

   ❑ `junit-4.7.jar`

4. Run the following Maven command to be able to import the client projects into Eclipse (for the client side):

```
mvn eclipse:eclipse -Declipse.projectNameTemplate="LiveRestaurant
_R-2.1-Client"
```

How to do it...

This recipe uses the recipe *Handling the incoming XML messages using JDOM*, discussed in *Chapter 1, Building SOAP Web-Services*, as the server-side project.

1. Run a Java class that calls a Web-Service in the main method.

2. Import `LiveRestaurant_R-2.1-Client` into the Eclipse workspace by going to **File | Import | General | Existing projects into workspace | LiveRestaurant_R-2..1-Client**.

3. Go to the folder `LiveRestaurant_R-2.1` in the command prompt and run the server using the following command:

```
mvn clean package tomcat:run
```

4. Select the class `OrderServiceClient` in the folder `src/main/java` from the package `com.packtpub.liverestaurant.client` and select **Run As | Java Application**.

   The following is the console output on running the Java class on the client side:

```
Received response ....
<tns:placeOrderResponse xmlns:tns=".."> <tns:refNumber>order-John_
Smith_9999</tns:refNumber>
</tns:placeOrderResponse>
for request...
<tns:placeOrderRequest xmlns:tns="...">
  <tns:order>
    <tns:refNumber>9999</tns:refNumber>
    <tns:customer>
```

```
       .......
     </tns:customer>
     <tns:dateSubmitted>2008-09-29T05:49:45</tns:dateSubmitted>
     <tns:orderDate>2014-09-19T03:18:33</tns:orderDate>
     <tns:items>
       <tns:type>Snacks</tns:type>
       <tns:name>Pitza</tns:name>
       <tns:quantity>2</tns:quantity>
     </tns:items>
   </tns:order>
 </tns:placeOrderRequest>....
```

5. Run a JUnit test case using Eclipse.

6. Select the class `OrderServiceClientTest` in the folder `src/test/java` from the package `com.packtpub.liverestaurant.client` and select **Run As | Junit Test**.

   The following is the console output on running the JUnit test case (you can click on the **JUnit** tab, adjacent to the **Console** tab, to see whether the test case has succeeded or not):

```
Received response ..
 <tns:placeOrderResponse xmlns:tns="...">
 <tns:refNumber>order-John_Smith_9999</tns:refNumber>
 </tns:placeOrderResponse>..
 ......
<tns:placeOrderRequest xmlns:tns=".....">
  <tns:order>
    <tns:refNumber>9999</tns:refNumber>
    <tns:customer>
 ......
    </tns:customer>
    <tns:dateSubmitted>2008-09-29T05:49:45</tns:dateSubmitted>
    <tns:orderDate>2014-09-19T03:18:33</tns:orderDate>
    <tns:items>
      <tns:type>Snacks</tns:type>
      <tns:name>Pitza</tns:name>
      <tns:quantity>2</tns:quantity>
    </tns:items>
  </tns:order>
</tns:placeOrderRequest>
```

To pass parameters or customize the settings for a test, select the test unit class, **Run As | Run Configuration |**, and double-click on **JUnit** on the left pane.

Then you will be able to customize the passed parameters or the settings and run the client.

How it works...

When a Java class that calls a Web-Service in the main method is run, Eclipse runs the following command internally using the following Java class path:

```
java -classpath com.packtpub.liverestaurant.client.OrderServiceClient
```

When a JUnit test case is run, Eclipse runs a test case using the JUnit framework by internally calling the following command:

```
java -classpath com.packtpub.liverestaurant.client.OrderServiceClientTest
```

See also

The recipes *Using Maven for building and running a Spring-WS project* and *Handling the incoming XML messages using JDOM*, discussed in *Chapter 1, Building SOAP Web-Services*.

The recipe *Creating a Web-Service client on HTTP transport*, discussed in this chapter.

Setting up a Web-Service client development environment using Maven

Maven supports running the main method of a class using command prompt as well as a JUnit test case.

In this recipe, setting up a Maven environment to call a client-side Web-Service is explained. Here, a client-side Java code calls a Web-Service on the server in two forms. The first one is a Java class that calls a Web-Service in the main method of the class. The second one uses JUnit to call a server-side Web-Service.

Getting ready

In this recipe, the project's name is `LiveRestaurant_R-2.2` (for a server-side Web-Service) with the following Maven dependencies:

- `spring-ws-core-2.0.1.RELEASE.jar`
- `log4j-1.2.9.jar`

The following are the Maven dependencies for `LiveRestaurant_R-2.2-Client` (for the client-side Web-Service):

- `spring-ws-core-2.0.1.RELEASE.jar`
- `junit-4.7.jar`

How to do it...

This recipe uses the recipe *Handling the incoming XML messages using DOM*, discussed in *Chapter 1, Building SOAP Web-Services*, as the server-side project.

1. Run a Java class that calls a Web-Service in the main method.

2. Go to the folder `LiveRestaurant_R-2.2` in the command prompt and run the server using the following command:

   ```
   mvn clean package tomcat:run
   ```

3. Go to the folder `LiveRestaurant_R-2.2-Client` and run the following command:

   ```
   mvn clean package exec:java
   ```

   The following is the output when the Maven command is run on the client side:

   ```
   Received response ....
   <placeOrderResponse xmlns="...">
   <refNumber>order-John_Smith_9999</refNumber>
   </placeOrderResponse>....
   <tns:placeOrderRequest xmlns:tns="...">
     <tns:order>
       <tns:refNumber>9999</tns:refNumber>
       <tns:customer>
       .....
       </tns:customer>
       <tns:dateSubmitted>2008-09-29T05:49:45</tns:dateSubmitted>
       <tns:orderDate>2014-09-19T03:18:33</tns:orderDate>
       <tns:items>
         <tns:type>Snacks</tns:type>
         <tns:name>Pitza</tns:name>
         <tns:quantity>2</tns:quantity>
       </tns:items>
     </tns:order>
   </tns:placeOrderRequest>
   ```

4. Run a JUnit test case using Maven.

5. Go to the folder `LiveRestaurant_R-2.2` from the command prompt and run the server using the following command:

```
mvn clean package tomcat:run
```

6. Go to the folder `LiveRestaurant_R-2.2-Client` and run the following command:

```
mvn clean package
```

Here is the output after running the JUnit test case using Maven on the client side:

```
Received response ...
<placeOrderResponse xmlns="...">
<refNumber>order-John_Smith_9999</refNumber>
</placeOrderResponse>...
for request ...
<tns:placeOrderRequest xmlns:tns="...">
  <tns:order>
    <tns:refNumber>9999</tns:refNumber>
    <tns:customer>
    .....
    </tns:customer>
    <tns:dateSubmitted>2008-09-29T05:49:45</tns:dateSubmitted>
    <tns:orderDate>2014-09-19T03:18:33</tns:orderDate>
    <tns:items>
      <tns:type>Snacks</tns:type>
      <tns:name>Pitza</tns:name>
      <tns:quantity>2</tns:quantity>
    </tns:items>
  </tns:order>
</tns:placeOrderRequest></SOAP-ENV:Body></SOAP-ENV:Envelope>]
Tests run: 1, Failures: 0, Errors: 0, Skipped: 0, Time elapsed:
0.702 sec


Results :


Tests run: 1, Failures: 0, Errors: 0, Skipped: 0
```

How it works...

Run a Java class that calls a Web-Service in the main method, `exec-maven-plugin`, set in the `pom.xml` file. The Java class tells Maven to run `mainClass` of `OrderServiceClient`:

```xml
<build>
  <finalName>LiveRestaurant_Client</finalName>
  <plugins>
    …..…
  </plugin>

        <plugin>
            <groupId>org.codehaus.mojo</groupId>
            <artifactId>exec-maven-plugin</artifactId>
             <version>1.2.1</version>
            <executions>
                <execution>
                    <goals>
                        <goal>java</goal>
                    </goals>
                </execution>
            </executions>
            <configuration>
                <mainClass>com.packtpub.liverestaurant.client.
    OrderServiceClient</mainClass>
            </configuration>
        </plugin>
    </plugins>
  </build>
```

Maven runs the following command internally using the project class path:

```
java -classpath com.packtpub.liverestaurant.client.OrderServiceClient
```

To set up and run a JUnit test case in Maven, the test class `OrderServiceClientTest` should be included in the folder `src/test/java` and the test class name should end with `Test` (`OrderServiceClientTest`). The command `mvn clean package` runs all the test cases in the `src/test/java` folder (internal Maven calls):

```
java -classpath …;junit.jar.. junit.textui.TestRunner   com.packtpub.
liverestaurant.client.OrderServiceClientTest ) .
```

The recipes *Using Maven for building and running a Spring-WS project* and *Handling the incoming XML messages using JDOM*, discussed in *Chapter 1, Building SOAP Web-Services*.

The recipe *Creating a Web-Service client on HTTP transport*, discussed in this chapter.

Creating a Web-Service client on HTTP transport

In this recipe, `WebServiceTemplate` is used to send/receive simple XML messages from the client side over the HTTP transport.

Getting ready

In this recipe, the project's name is `LiveRestaurant_R-2.3` (for server-side Web-Service) with the following Maven dependencies:

- `spring-ws-core-2.0.1.RELEASE.jar`
- `log4j-1.2.9.jar`

The following are the Maven dependencies for `LiveRestaurant_R-2.3-Client` (for the client-side Web-Service):

- `spring-ws-core-2.0.1.RELEASE.jar`
- `junit-4.7.jar`

How to do it...

This recipe uses the recipe *Setting up an endpoint by annotating the payload-root*, discussed in *Chapter 1, Building SOAP Web-Services*, as the server-side project. Here is how you set up the client side:

1. Create a class that calls the Web-Service server using `WebServiceTemplate` in `src/test`.
2. Configure `WebServiceTemplate` in the `applicationContext.xml` file.
3. From the folder `Liverestaurant_R-2.3`, run the following command:

   `mvn clean package tomcat:run`

4. Open a new command window to `Liverestaurant_R-2.3-Client` and run the following command:

```
mvn clean package
```

The following is the client-side output:

```
Received response ....

<tns:placeOrderResponse xmlns:tns="...">

<tns:refNumber>order-John_Smith_1234</tns:refNumber>

</tns:placeOrderResponse>...

<tns:placeOrderRequest xmlns:tns="....">

   <tns:order>

      <tns:refNumber>9999</tns:refNumber>

      <tns:customer>

      ......

      </tns:customer>

      <tns:dateSubmitted>2008-09-29T05:49:45</tns:dateSubmitted>

      <tns:orderDate>2014-09-19T03:18:33</tns:orderDate>

      <tns:items>

         <tns:type>Snacks</tns:type>

         <tns:name>Pitza</tns:name>

         <tns:quantity>2</tns:quantity>

      </tns:items>

   </tns:order>

</tns:placeOrderRequest>

.....

Tests run: 2, Failures: 0, Errors: 0, Skipped: 0, Time elapsed:
0.749 sec


Results :


Tests run: 2, Failures: 0, Errors: 0, Skipped: 0
```

How it works...

`Liverestaurant_R-2.3` is a server-side project that reuses the recipe *Setting up an endpoint by annotating the payload-root*, discussed in *Chapter 1, Building SOAP Web-Services*.

The `applicationContext.xml` file of the configured client `WebServiceTemplate` (id="webServiceTemplate") is used for sending and receiving XML messages. The instance of this bean can be fetched from the client-side program to send and receive XML messages.

`messageFactory` is an instance of `SaajSoapMessageFactory`, which is referenced inside `WebServiceTemplate`. `messageFactory` is used to create a SOAP packet from the XML messages. The default service URI is the URI that `WebServiceTemplate` uses by default to send/receive all requests/responses:

```
<bean id="messageFactory" class="org.springframework.ws.soap.saaj.
SaajSoapMessageFactory" />
<bean id="webServiceTemplate" class="org.springframework.ws.client.
core.WebServiceTemplate">
    <constructor-arg ref="messageFactory" />
    <property name="defaultUri" value="http://localhost:8080/
LiveRestaurant/spring-ws/OrderService" />
</bean>
```

`OrderServiceClientTest.java` is a simple JUnit test case that is used to fetch and initialize `WebServiceTemplate` from `applicationContext.xml` in the method `setUpBeforeClass()` (marked by `@BeforeClass`). In the methods `testCancelOrderRequest` and `testPlaceOrderRequest` (marked by `@Test`), `WebServiceTemplate` sends a simple XML message (created by a `StringSource` object from an existing input XML file) and receives a response from the server wrapped inside the `Result` object:

```
private static WebServiceTemplate wsTemplate = null;
private static InputStream isPlace;
private static InputStream isCancel;
@BeforeClass
public static void setUpBeforeClass() throws Exception {
    ClassPathXmlApplicationContext appContext = new
ClassPathXmlApplicationContext("/applicationContext.xml");
    wsTemplate = (WebServiceTemplate) appContext.
getBean("webServiceTemplate");
    isPlace = new OrderServiceClientTest().getClass().getResourceAsStr
eam("placeOrderRequest.xml");
    isCancel = new OrderServiceClientTest().getClass().getResourceAsSt
ream("cancelOrderRequest.xml");
}
@Test
public  final void testPlaceOrderRequest() throws Exception {
    Result result = invokeWS(isPlace);
    Assert.assertTrue(result.toString().indexOf("placeOrderRespon
se")>0);
}
```

```
@Test
public  final void testCancelOrderRequest() throws Exception {
    Result result = invokeWS(isCancel);
    Assert.assertTrue(result.toString().indexOf("cancelOrderRespon
se")>0);
  }
  private  static  Result invokeWS(InputStream is) {
        StreamSource source = new StreamSource(is);
        StringResult result = new StringResult();
        wsTemplate.sendSourceAndReceiveToResult(source, result);
        return result;
  }
```

See also

The recipe *Setting up an endpoint by annotating the payload-root*, discussed in *Chapter 1, Building SOAP Web-Services* and the recipe *Setting up a Web-Service client development environment using Maven*, discussed in this chapter.

Creating a Web-Service client on JMS transport

JMS (Java message Service) was introduced in 1999 by Sun Microsystems as part of Java 2, J2EE. The systems that use JMS can communicate synchronously or asynchronously and are based on point-to-point and publish-subscribe models. Spring Web-Services provide features to set up a Web-Service over the JMS protocol that is built upon the JMS functionality in the Spring framework. Spring Web-Service over JMS protocol provides the following communication features:

- The client and server could be disconnected and can be connected only when sending/receiving messages

- The client doesn't need to wait until the server replies (in case the server needs a lot of time to process, for example, while doing complex mathematical calculations)

- JMS provides features that guarantee the delivery of messages between the client and server

In this recipe, WebServiceTemplate is used to send/receive simple XML messages on the client side over JMS transport. A JUnit test case class is used to set up as on server side and send and receive messages using WebServiceTemplate.

Getting ready

In this recipe, the project's name is `LiveRestaurant_R-2.4`, with the following Maven dependencies:

- `spring-ws-core-2.0.1.RELEASE.jar`
- `spring-ws-support-2.0.1.RELEASE.jar`
- `spring-test-3.0.5.RELEASE.jar`
- `spring-jms-3.0.5.RELEASE.jar`
- `junit-4.7.jar`
- `xmlunit-1.1.jar`
- `log4j-1.2.9.jar`
- `jms-1.1.jar`
- `activemq-core-4.1.1.jar`

How to do it...

This recipe uses the recipe *Setting up a Web-Service on JMS transport*, discussed in *Chapter 1, Building SOAP Web-Services*, as a server-side project.

1. Create a JUnit test class that calls the Web-Service server using `WebServiceTemplate`.

2. Configure `WebServiceTemplate` in `applicationContext` to send messages over the JMS protocol.

3. Run the command `mvn clean package`. You will see the following as output:

```
Received response ..
<tns:placeOrderResponse xmlns:tns="...">
<tns:refNumber>order-John_Smith_1234</tns:refNumber>
</tns:placeOrderResponse>....
<tns:placeOrderRequest xmlns:tns="...">
  <tns:order>
    <tns:refNumber>9999</tns:refNumber>
    <tns:customer>
  .....
  </tns:customer>
    <tns:dateSubmitted>2008-09-29T05:49:45</tns:dateSubmitted>
    <tns:orderDate>2014-09-19T03:18:33</tns:orderDate>
```

```
        <tns:items>
            <tns:type>Snacks</tns:type>
            <tns:name>Pitza</tns:name>
            <tns:quantity>2</tns:quantity>
        </tns:items>
    </tns:order>
</tns:placeOrderRequest>
```

How it works...

In this project, we set up a Web-Service server, over JMS transport, using a JUnit class. The server uses `PayloadEndpoint` to receive the XML request message and returns a simple XML message as the response (the server is already described in the recipe *Setting up a Web-Service on JMS transport*, discussed in *Chapter 1, Building SOAP Web-Services*).

The `applicationContext.xml` file of the configured client `WebServiceTemplate` (id="webServiceTemplate") is used for sending and receiving XML messages. The instance of this bean can be fetched from the client-side program to send and receive XML messages. `messageFactory` is an instance of `SaajSoapMessageFactory`, referenced inside `WebServiceTemplate`. `messageFactory` is used to create a SOAP packet from the XML messages. The default service URI is the JMS URI that `WebServiceTemplate` uses by default to send/receive all requests/responses. `JmsMessageSender`, configured inside `WebServiceTemplate`, is used to send JMS messages. To use the `JmsMessageSender`, the `defaultUri` or JMS URI should contain the `jms:` prefix and a destination name. Some examples of JMS URI are `jms:SomeQueue`, `jms:SomeTopic?priority=3&deliveryM ode=NON_PERSISTENT`, `jms:RequestQueue?replyToName=ResponseName`, and so on. By default, the `JmsMessageSender` sends JMS `BytesMessage`, but this can be overridden to use `TextMessages` by using the `messageType` parameter on the JMS URI. For example, `jms:Queue?messageType=TEXT_MESSAGE`.

```
        <bean id="webServiceTemplate" class="org.springframework.
    ws.client.core.WebServiceTemplate">
            <constructor-arg ref="messageFactory"/>
            <property name="messageSender">
                <bean class="org.springframework.ws.transport.jms.
    JmsMessageSender">
                    <property name="connectionFactory"
    ref="connectionFactory"/>
                </bean>
            </property>
            <property name="defaultUri" value="jms:RequestQueue?deliveryMo
    de=NON_PERSISTENT"/>
        </bean>
```

`JmsTransportWebServiceIntegrationTest.java` is a JUnit test case that fetches and injects `WebServiceTemplate` from the `applicationContext.xml` file (marked by `@Conte xtConfiguration("applicationContext.xml")`). In the method `testSendReceive()` (marked by `@Test`), `WebServiceTemplate` sends a simple XML message (created by a `StringSource` object from a simple input string) and receives a response from the server wrapped inside the `Result` object. In the method `testSendReceive()` (marked by `@Test`), sending and receiving of messages is similar to the HTTP client and uses `WebServiceTemplate.sendSourceAndReceiveToResult` to send/receive messages:

```
@Test
public void testSendReceive() throws Exception {
    InputStream is = new JmsTransportWebServiceIntegrationTest().
getClass().getResourceAsStream("placeOrderRequest.xml");
    StreamSource source = new StreamSource(is);
    StringResult result = new StringResult();
    webServiceTemplate.sendSourceAndReceiveToResult(source,
result);
    XMLAssert.assertXMLEqual("Invalid content received",
expectedResponseContent, result.toString());
}
```

See also

The recipe *Setting up a Web-Service on JMS transport*, discussed in *Chapter 1, Building SOAP Web-Services*.

Unit testing a Web-Service using Spring Junit

Creating a Web-Service client on E-mail transport

In this recipe, `WebServiceTemplate` is used to send/receive simple XML messages on the client side, over E-mail transport. The *Setting up a Web-Service on E-mail transport* recipe from *Chapter 1, Building SOAP Web-Services*, is used to set up a Web-Service. A JUnit test case class is used to set up a Web-Service on the server side and messages are sent/received using `WebServiceTemplate`.

Getting ready

In this recipe, the project's name is `LiveRestaurant_R-2.5`, with the following Maven dependencies:

- `spring-ws-core-2.0.1.RELEASE.jar`
- `spring-ws-support-2.0.1.RELEASE.jar`

- ▸ `spring-test-3.0.5.RELEASE.jar`
- ▸ `mail-1.4.1.jar`
- ▸ `mock-javamail-1.6.jar`
- ▸ `junit-4.7.jar`
- ▸ `xmlunit-1.1.jar`

How to do it...

This recipe uses the recipe *Setting up a Web-Service on E-mail transport*, discussed in *Chapter 1, Building SOAP Web-Services*, as the server-side project.

1. Create a test class that calls the Web-Service server using `WebServiceTemplate`.

2. Configure `WebServiceTemplate` in `applicationContext` to send messages over the e-mail protocol.

3. Run the command `mvn clean package`. The following is the output of this command:

```
Received response
<tns:placeOrderResponse xmlns:tns="...">
<tns:refNumber>order-John_Smith_1234</tns:refNumber>
</tns:placeOrderResponse>....
<tns:placeOrderRequest xmlns:tns="...">
  <tns:order>
    <tns:refNumber>9999</tns:refNumber>
    <tns:customer>
  .....
  </tns:customer>
    <tns:dateSubmitted>2008-09-29T05:49:45</tns:dateSubmitted>
    <tns:orderDate>2014-09-19T03:18:33</tns:orderDate>
    <tns:items>
      <tns:type>Snacks</tns:type>
      <tns:name>Pitza</tns:name>
      <tns:quantity>2</tns:quantity>
    </tns:items>
  </tns:order>
</tns:placeOrderRequest>
```

How it works...

This project sets up a Web-Service server over the E-mail transport, using a JUnit class. This class uses Spring JUnit that loads the application context, sets up the server first, and then runs the client unit test to verify that it functions as expected. The server is already explained in the recipe *Setting up a Web-Service on E-mail transport*, discussed in *Chapter 1, Building SOAP Web-Services*.

The `applicationContext.xml` file of the configured client `WebServiceTemplate` (`id="webServiceTemplate"`) is used for sending and receiving XML messages. The instance of this bean can be fetched from the client-side program to send and receive XML messages. `messageFactory` is an instance of `SaajSoapMessageFactory`, referenced inside `WebServiceTemplate`. `messageFactory` is used to create a SOAP packet from XML messages. `transportURI` is a URI used by `WebServiceTemplate` and indicates the server to use for sending requests. `storeURI` is a URI, configured inside `WebServiceTemplate`, and indicates the server to poll for responses (typically, a POP3 or IMAP server). The default URI is the e-mail address URI that `WebServiceTemplate` uses by default to send/receive all requests/responses:

```xml
    <bean id="webServiceTemplate" class="org.springframework.
ws.client.core.WebServiceTemplate">
        <constructor-arg ref="messageFactory"/>
        <property name="messageSender">
            <bean class="org.springframework.ws.transport.mail.
MailMessageSender">
                <property name="from" value="client@packtpubtest.
com"/>
                <property name="transportUri" value="smtp://smtp.
packtpubtest.com"/>
                <property name="storeUri" value="imap://client@
packtpubtest.com/INBOX"/>
                <property name="receiveSleepTime" value="1500"/>
                <property name="session" ref="session"/>
            </bean>
        </property>
        <property name="defaultUri" value="mailto:server@packtpubtest.
com"/>
    </bean>
    <bean id="session" class="javax.mail.Session" factory-
method="getInstance">
        <constructor-arg>
            <props/>
        </constructor-arg>
    </bean>
```

`MailTransportWebServiceIntegrationTest.java` is a JUnit test case that fetches and injects `WebServiceTemplate` from `applicationContext.xml` (marked by `@ContextConfiguration("applicationContext.xml")`). In the method `testWebServiceOnMailTransport()` (marked by `@Test`), `WebServiceTemplate` sends a simple XML message (created by a `StringSource` object from an input XML file) and receives a response from the server wrapped inside the `Result` object.

```
    @Test
     public void testWebServiceOnMailTransport() throws Exception {
        InputStream is = new MailTransportWebServiceIntegrationTest().
  getClass().getResourceAsStream("placeOrderRequest.xml");
        StreamSource source = new StreamSource(is);
        StringResult result = new StringResult();

         webServiceTemplate.sendSourceAndReceiveToResult(source,
  result);
        applicationContext.close();
        XMLAssert.assertXMLEqual("Invalid content received",
  expectedResponseContent, result.toString());
     }
```

See also..

The recipe *Setting up a Web-Service on E-mail transport*, discussed in *Chapter 1, Building SOAP Web-Services*.

Unit testing a Web-Service using Spring Junit

Setting up a Web-Service on XMPP transport

XMPP (The Extensible Messaging and Presence Protocol) is an open and decentralized XML routing technology on which systems can send XMPP messages to each other. The XMPP network consists of XMPP servers, clients, and services. Each system using XMPP is recognized by a unique ID known as the **Jabber ID** (**JID**). XMPP servers publish XMPP services to offer connected to a client remote service.

In this recipe, `WebServiceTemplate` is used to send/receive simple XML messages on the client side over XMPP transport. The recipe *Setting up a Web-Service on XMPP transport* from *Chapter 1, Building SOAP Web-Services*, is used to set up a Web-Service. A JUnit test case class is used to set up a Web-Service on the server side and send and receive messages using `WebServiceTemplate`.

In this recipe, the project's name is `LiveRestaurant_R-2.6`, with the following Maven dependencies:

- `spring-ws-core-2.0.1.RELEASE.jar`
- `spring-ws-support-2.0.1.RELEASE.jar`
- `spring-test-3.0.5.RELEASE.jar`
- `junit-4.7.jar`
- `xmlunit-1.1.jar`
- `smack-3.1.0.jar`

How to do it...

1. This recipe uses the recipe *Setting up a Web-Service on XMPP transport*, discussed in *Chapter 1, Building SOAP Web-Services*, as the server-side project.

2. Create a test class that calls the Web-Service server using `WebServiceTemplate`.

3. Configure `WebServiceTemplate` in `applicationContext` to send messages over the XMPP protocol.

4. Run the command `mvn clean package`. You will see the following output:

```
Received response ..
<tns:placeOrderResponse xmlns:tns="...">
<tns:refNumber>order-John_Smith_1234</tns:refNumber>
</tns:placeOrderResponse>....
<tns:placeOrderRequest xmlns:tns="...">
  <tns:order>
    <tns:refNumber>9999</tns:refNumber>
    <tns:customer>
  .....
  </tns:customer>
    <tns:dateSubmitted>2008-09-29T05:49:45</tns:dateSubmitted>
    <tns:orderDate>2014-09-19T03:18:33</tns:orderDate>
    <tns:items>
      <tns:type>Snacks</tns:type>
      <tns:name>Pitza</tns:name>
      <tns:quantity>2</tns:quantity>
    </tns:items>
  </tns:order>
</tns:placeOrderRequest>
```

How it works...

This project sets up a Web-Service server over the XMPP transport using a JUnit class. The server is already explained in the recipe *Setting up a Web-Service on e-mail transport*, discussed in *Chapter 1, Building SOAP Web-Services*.

The `applicationContext.xml` file of the configured client `WebServiceTemplate` (`id="webServiceTemplate"`) is used for sending and receiving XML messages. The instance of this bean can be fetched from the client-side program to send and receive XML messages. `messageFactory` is an instance of `SaajSoapMessageFactory`, referenced inside `WebServiceTemplate`. `messageFactory` is used to create a SOAP packet from XML messages. `WebServiceTemplate` uses `XmppMessageSender` to send messages to the server. The default URI is a XMPP address URI that `WebServiceTemplate` uses by default to send/receive all requests/responses:

```
<bean id="webServiceTemplate" class="org.springframework.
ws.client.core.WebServiceTemplate">
    <constructor-arg ref="messageFactory"/>
    <property name="messageSender">
        <bean class="org.springframework.ws.transport.xmpp.
XmppMessageSender">
            <property name="connection" ref="connection"/>
        </bean>
    </property>
    <property name="defaultUri" value="xmpp:yourUserName@gmail.
com"/>
</bean>
```

`XMPPTransportWebServiceIntegrationTest.java` is a JUnit test case that fetches and injects `WebServiceTemplate` from `applicationContext.xml` (marked by `@ContextConfiguration("applicationContext.xml")`). In the method `testWebServiceOnXMPPTransport()` (marked by `@Test`), `WebServiceTemplate` sends an XML message (created by a `StringSource` object from a simple input XML file) and receives a response from the server wrapped inside the `Result` object.

```
@Autowired
private GenericApplicationContext applicationContext;
@Test
public void testWebServiceOnXMPPTransport() throws Exception {
    StringResult result = new StringResult();
    StringSource sc=new StringSource(requestContent);
    webServiceTemplate.sendSourceAndReceiveToResult(sc, result);
    XMLAssert.assertXMLEqual("Invalid content received",
requestContent, result.toString());

    applicationContext.close();
}
```

The recipe *Setting up a Web-Service on XMPP transport*, discussed in *Chapter 1, Building SOAP Web-Services*.

Unit testing a Web-Service using Spring JUnit

Creating a Web-Service client using XPath expressions

Using XPath in Java programming is one of the standard ways of extracting data from XML messages. However, it mixes the XPath address of XML nodes/attributes (that might eventually turn out to be very long) with Java code.

Spring provides a feature to extract these addresses from Java and shift them into the Spring configuration file. In this recipe, the *Setting up an endpoint by annotating the payload-root* recipe from *Chapter 1, Building SOAP Web-Services*, is used to set up a Web-Service server.

Getting ready

In this recipe, the project's name is `LiveRestaurant_R-2.7` (for the server-side Web-Service), with the following Maven dependencies:

- `spring-ws-core-2.0.1.RELEASE.jar`
- `log4j-1.2.9.jar`

The following are the Maven dependencies for `LiveRestaurant_R-2.7-Client` (for the client-side Web-Service):

- `spring-ws-core-2.0.1.RELEASE.jar`
- `junit-4.7.jar`
- `log4j-1.2.9.jar`

How to do it...

This recipe uses the *Setting up an endpoint by annotating the payload-root* recipe discussed in *Chapter 1, Building SOAP Web-Services*, as the server-side project.

1. Configure the XPath expression inside `applicationContext.xml`.
2. Configure `WebServiceTemplate` in `applicationContext` to send messages over the HTTP protocol, as described in the recipe *Creating a Web-Service client on HTTP transport*.

3. Create a test class that calls the Web-Service server using `WebServiceTemplate` and uses the XPath expression in Java code to extract the desired values.

4. From the folder `Liverestaurant_R-2.7`, run the command `mvn clean package tomcat:run`.

5. Open a new command window to `Liverestaurant_R-2.7-Client` and run the following command:

```
mvn clean package.
```

The following is the output of the client-side code:

```
--Request
<tns:placeOrderRequest xmlns:tns="http://www.packtpub.com/
liverestaurant/OrderService/schema">
  <tns:order>
    <tns:refNumber>9999</tns:refNumber>
    <tns:customer>
      <tns:addressPrimary>
        <tns:doorNo>808</tns:doorNo>
        <tns:building>W8</tns:building>
        <tns:street>St two</tns:street>
        <tns:city>NY</tns:city>
        <tns:country>US</tns:country>
        <tns:phoneMobile>0018884488</tns:phoneMobile>
        <tns:phoneLandLine>0017773366</tns:phoneLandLine>
        <tns:email>d@b.c</tns:email>
      </tns:addressPrimary>
      <tns:addressSecondary>
        <tns:doorNo>409</tns:doorNo>
        <tns:building>W2</tns:building>
        <tns:street>St one</tns:street>
        <tns:city>NY</tns:city>
        <tns:country>US</tns:country>
        <tns:phoneMobile>0018882244</tns:phoneMobile>
        <tns:phoneLandLine>0019991122</tns:phoneLandLine>
        <tns:email>a@b.c</tns:email>
      </tns:addressSecondary>
      <tns:name>
        <tns:fName>John</tns:fName>
```

```
            <tns:mName>Paul</tns:mName>
            <tns:lName>Smith</tns:lName>
        </tns:name>
    </tns:customer>
    <tns:dateSubmitted>2008-09-29T05:49:45</tns:dateSubmitted>
    <tns:orderDate>2014-09-19T03:18:33</tns:orderDate>
    <tns:items>
        <tns:type>Snacks</tns:type>
        <tns:name>Pitza</tns:name>
        <tns:quantity>2</tns:quantity>
    </tns:items>
  </tns:order>
</tns:placeOrderRequest>
 <!--Received response-->
<tns:placeOrderResponse xmlns:tns="...">
<tns:refNumber>order-John_Smith_1234</tns:refNumber></
tns:placeOrderResponse>
 ...Request
 <tns:cancelOrderRequest xmlns:tns="http://www.packtpub.com/
liverestaurant/OrderService/schema">
   <tns:refNumber>9999</tns:refNumber>
</tns:cancelOrderRequest></SOAP-ENV:Body></SOAP-ENV:Envelope>]
 ...Received response..
<tns:cancelOrderResponse xmlns:tns="http://www.packtpub.com/
liverestaurant/OrderService/schema">
<tns:cancelled>true</tns:cancelled></tns:cancelOrderResponse>
```

How it works...

Setting up the client and server and using `WebserviceTemplate` are done in the same way
as we did in the recipe _Creating a Web-Service client on HTTP transport_. `xpathExpPlace`
and `xpathExpCancel` are configured in the client `applicationContext.xml` and
it creates an instance of `XPathExpressionFactoryBean` that gets a property of
`expression` as the XPath of the required data and `namespaces` of the XML messages:

```
    <bean id="xpathExpCancel"
        class="org.springframework.xml.xpath.XPathExpressionFactoryBean">
        <property name="expression" value="/tns:cancelOrderResponse/
  tns:cancelled" />
        <property name="namespaces">
          <props>
```

```
              <prop key="tns">http://www.packtpub.com/liverestaurant/
        OrderService/schema</prop>
            </props>
          </property>
        </bean>


          <bean id="xpathExpPlace"
          class="org.springframework.xml.xpath.XPathExpressionFactoryBean">
            <property name="expression" value="/tns:placeOrderResponse/
        tns:refNumber" />
            <property name="namespaces">
              <props>
                <prop key="tns">http://www.packtpub.com/liverestaurant/
        OrderService/schema</prop>
              </props>
            </property>
          </bean>
```

In the class `OrderServiceClientTest`, an instance of `XPathExpressionFactoryBean` can be extracted from `applicationContext`. `String message = xpathExp.` `evaluateAsString(result.getNode())` returns the required data using an XPath expression:

```
        @Test
        public  final void  testPlaceOrderRequest() {
          DOMResult result=invokeWS(isPlace);
           String message = xpathExpPlace.evaluateAsString(result.
        getNode());
           Assert.assertTrue(message.contains("Smith"));

        }
        @Test
        public  final void  testCancelOrderRequest() {
          DOMResult result= invokeWS(isCancel);
           Boolean cancelled = xpathExpCancel.evaluateAsBoolean(result.
        getNode());
           Assert.assertTrue(cancelled);

        }
```

See also

The recipe *Setting up an endpoint using an XPath expression*, discussed in *Chapter 1, Building SOAP Web-Services*.

The recipe *Creating a Web-Service client on HTTP transport*, discussed in this chapter.

Unit testing a Web-Service using Spring JUnit.

Creating a Web-Service client for a WS-Addressing endpoint

As described in the recipe _Setting up a transport-neutral WS-Addressing endpoint_, discussed in _Chapter 1, Building SOAP Web-Services_, WS-Addressing is an alternative way for routing. Instead of including the routing data within the body of the SOAP messages, WS-Addressing separates the routing data from the messages and includes it with the SOAP headers. Here is a sample of the WS-Addressing style of a SOAP message, sent from the client side:

```
<SOAP-ENV:Header xmlns:wsa="http://www.w3.org/2005/08/addressing">

   <wsa:To>server_uri</wsa:To>

   <wsa:Action>action_uri</wsa:Action>

   <wsa:From>client_address </wsa:From>

   <wsa:ReplyTo>client_address</wsa:ReplyTo>

   <wsa:FaultTo>admen_uri </wsa:FaultTo>
<wsa:MessageID>..</wsa:MessageID>

</SOAP-ENV:Header>

<SOAP-ENV:Body>

<tns:placeOrderRequest>....</tns:placeOrderReques>

</SOAP-ENV:Body></SOAP-ENV:Envelope>]
```

While using WS-Addressing, the client or server can access more features when compared to the other methods (including routing data within a message). For example, here the client side can set `ReplyTo` to its own and `FaultTo` to the admin endpoint address. Then the server sends successful messages to the client and fault messages to the admin address.

Spring-WS supports client-side WS-Addressing as well as on the server side. To create WS-Addressing headers for the client side, `org.springframework.ws.soap.addressing.client.ActionCallback` can be used. This callback keeps the `Action` header as a parameter. It also uses the WS-Addressing version and a `To` header.

In this recipe, the _Setting up a transport-neutral WS-Addressing endpoint_ recipe, discussed in _Chapter 1, Building SOAP Web-Services_, is used to set up a WS-Addressing Web-Service. A client application is used here to call the server and return the response object.

Getting ready

In this recipe, the project's name is `LiveRestaurant_R-2.8` (for server-side Web-Service), with the following Maven dependencies:

- `spring-ws-core-2.0.1.RELEASE.jar`
- `log4j-1.2.9.jar`

The following are the Maven dependencies for `LiveRestaurant_R-2.8-Client` (for the client-side Web-Service):

- `spring-ws-core-2.0.1.RELEASE.jar`
- `junit-4.7.jar`
- `log4j-1.2.9.jar`

How to do it...

This recipe uses the recipe *Setting up a transport-neutral WS-Addressing endpoint*, discussed in *Chapter 1, Building SOAP Web-Services*, as the server-side project. Creating a client for WS-Addressing is done in the same way as described in the recipe *Creating a Web-Service client on HTTP transport*, without using WebServiceTemplate. To add a WS-Addressing header on the client side, the method `sendSourceAndReceiveToResult` of `WebServiceTemplate` gets an `ActionCallBack` instance.

1. From the folder `LiveRestaurant_R-2.8`, run the following command:

   `mvn clean package tomcat:run`

2. Open a new command window to `LiveRestaurant_R-2.8-Client` and run the following command:

   `mvn clean package`

   The following is the client-side output:

   ```
   Received response [<SOAP-ENV:Envelope xmlns:SOAP-ENV="..../">
   <SOAP-ENV:Header xmlns:wsa="...">
   <wsa:To SOAP-ENV:mustUnderstand="1">....</
   wsa:To><wsa:Action>http://www.packtpub.com/OrderService/
   CanOrdReqResponse</wsa:Action>
   <wsa:MessageID>....</wsa:MessageID>
   <wsa:RelatesTo>...</wsa:RelatesTo>
   </SOAP-ENV:Header>
   <SOAP-ENV:Body>
   <tns:cancelOrderResponse xmlns:tns="http://www.packtpub.com/
   liverestaurant/OrderService/schema">
   <tns:cancelled>true</tns:cancelled></tns:cancelOrderResponse>
   </SOAP-ENV:Body></SOAP-ENV:Envelope>]
    for request ...
    <SOAP-ENV:Envelope xmlns:SOAP
   -ENV=".."><SOAP-ENV:Header xmlns:wsa="..">
   ```

```
<wsa:To SOAP-ENV:mustUnderstand="1">http://www.packtpub.com/
liverestaurant/OrderService/schema</wsa:To>

<wsa:Action>http://www.packtpub.com/OrderService/CanOrdReq</
wsa:Action>

<wsa:MessageID>..</wsa:MessageID>

</SOAP-ENV:Header><SOAP-ENV:Body/>

</SOAP-ENV:Envelope>]

<?xml version="1.0" encoding="UTF-8"?>

<tns:cancelOrderResponse xmlns:tns="http://www.packtpub.com/
liverestaurant/OrderService/schema">

<tns:cancelled>true</tns:cancelled></tns:cancelOrderResponse>
```

How it works...

The `Liverestaurant_R-2.8` project is a server-side Web-Service that supports the WS-Addressing endpoint.

The `applicationContext.xml` file of the configured client `WebServiceTemplate` (`id="webServiceTemplate"`) is used for sending and receiving XML messages, as described in the recipe *Creating a Web-Service client on HTTP transport*, except for the implementation of the Java class that used `WebServiceTemplate`.

WS-Addressing client passes an instance of `ActionCallBack` to the method `sendSourceAndReceiveToResult` of `WebServiceTemplate`. Using `ActionCallBack`, the client adds a custom header that contains the `Action` URI, for example, `http://www.packtpub.com/OrderService/OrdReq` and the `To` URI, for example, `http://www.packtpub.com/liverestaurant/OrderService/schema`.

```
@Test
public  final void testPlaceOrderRequest() throws URISyntaxException
{
        invokeWS(isPlace,"http://www.packtpub.com/OrderService/
OrdReq");
    }
    @Test
    public  final void testCancelOrderRequest() throws
URISyntaxException {
      invokeWS(isCancel,"http://www.packtpub.com/OrderService/
CanOrdReq");
}

    private static Result invokeWS(InputStream is,String action)
throws URISyntaxException {
```

```
        StreamSource source = new StreamSource(is);
        StringResult result = new StringResult();
        wsTemplate.sendSourceAndReceiveToResult(source, new
    ActionCallback(new URI(action),new Addressing10(),new URI("http://www.
    packtpub.com/liverestaurant/OrderService/schema")),
                result);
        return result;
    }
```

Using this header, the server side will be able to find the method in the endpoint (using the `@Action` annotation).

See also

The recipe *Setting up a transport-neutral WS-Addressing endpoint*, discussed in *Chapter 1, Building SOAP Web-Services*.

The recipe *Creating a Web-Service client on HTTP transport*, discussed in this chapter.

Unit testing a Web-Service using Spring JUnit

Transforming a Web-Service message using XSLT

Eventually, clients of a Web-Service may use different versions of XML messages and the requirement is to use the same Web-Service on the server side.

Spring Web-Services provide `PayloadTransformingInterceptor`. This endpoint interceptor uses XSLT stylesheets and is useful when you need multiple versions of a Web-Service. Using this interceptor, you can transform the old format of the message to a newer one.

In this recipe, the *Setting up a simple endpoint mapping for the Web-Service* recipe from *Chapter 1, Building SOAP Web-Services*, is used to set up a Web-Service and the client application here calls the server and returns the response message.

Getting ready

In this recipe, the project's name is `LiveRestaurant_R-2.9` (for a server-side web service), with the following Maven dependencies:

▶ `spring-ws-core-2.0.1.RELEASE.jar`
▶ `log4j-1.2.9.jar`

The following are the Maven dependencies for `LiveRestaurant_R-2.9-Client` (for the client-side Web-Service):

- `spring-ws-core-2.0.1.RELEASE.jar`
- `junit-4.7.jar`
- `log4j-1.2.9.jar`

How to do it...

This recipe uses the *Setting up a simple endpoint mapping for the Web-Service* recipe, discussed in *Chapter 1, Building SOAP Web-Services*, as a server-side project. The client side is the same as discussed in the recipe *Creating a Web-Service client on HTTP transport*, except for the XSLT files and their configuration in the server-side application context file:

1. Create the XSLT files (`oldResponse.xslt`, `oldRequest.xslt`).
2. Modify the file `spring-ws-servlet.xml` in `LiveRestaurant_R-2.9` to include the XSLT files
3. From the folder `Liverestaurant_R-2.9`, run the following command:

   `mvn clean package tomcat:run`

4. Open a new command window to `Liverestaurant_R-2.9-Client` and run the following command:

   `mvn clean package`

   The following is the client-side output:

   ```
   Received response...
   <ns:OrderResponse xmlns:ns="http://www.packtpub.com/
   LiveRestaurant/OrderService/schema" message="Order Accepted!"/>...

    for request ....
   <OrderRequest xmlns="http://www.packtpub.com/LiveRestaurant/
   OrderService/schema" message="This is a sample Order Message"/>
   ```

   The following is the server-side output:

   ```
   actual request ..
   <ns:OrderRequest  xmlns:ns="...">
   <ns:message>This is a sample Order Message</ns:message></
   ns:OrderRequest>


   actual response = <ns:OrderResponse xmlns:ns="..">
   <ns:message>Order Accepted!</ns:message></ns:OrderResponse>
   ```

How it works...

The server side is the same as that described in the recipe *Setting up a simple endpoint mapping for the Web-Service* from *Chapter 1, Building SOAP Web-Services*. On the client side, `WebServiceTemplate` and `OrderServiceClientTest.java` are the same as those described in the recipe *Creating a Web-Service client on HTTP transport*.

The only difference is the server application context file. The `transformingInterceptor` bean in `spring-servlet.xml` uses `oldRequests.xslt` and `oldResponse.xslt` to convert the old request XML message to the server's newer version and vice versa, respectively:

```
.   <bean  class="org.springframework.ws.server.endpoint.mapping.
    SimpleMethodEndpointMapping">
        <property name="endpoints">
          <ref bean="OrderServiceEndpoint" />
        </property>
        <property name="methodPrefix" value="handle"></property>
        <property name="interceptors">
          <list>
            <bean
              class="org.springframework.ws.server.endpoint.interceptor.
    PayloadLoggingInterceptor">
                <property name="logRequest" value="true" />
                <property name="logResponse" value="true" />
            </bean>
            <bean id="transformingInterceptor"
              class="org.springframework.ws.server.endpoint.interceptor.
    PayloadTransformingInterceptor">
                <property name="requestXslt" value="/WEB-INF/oldRequests.
    xslt" />
                <property name="responseXslt" value="/WEB-INF/oldResponse.
    xslt" />
            </bean>
          </list>
        </property>
      </bean>
```

See also

The recipe *Setting up a simple endpoint mapping for the Web-Service*, discussed in *Chapter 1, Building SOAP Web-Services*.

Unit testing a Web-Service using Spring JUnit.

3
Testing and Monitoring Web-Services

In this chapter, we will cover:

- ▶ Integration testing using Spring-JUnit support
- ▶ Server-side integration testing using `MockWebServiceClient`
- ▶ Client-side integration testing using `MockWebServiceServer`
- ▶ Monitoring TCP messages of a Web-Service using TCPMon
- ▶ Monitoring and load/functional testing a Web-Service using soapUI

Introduction

New software development strategies require comprehensive testing in order to achieve the quality in the software development process. Test-driven design (TDD) is an evolutionary approach to the development process, which combines the test-first development process and re-factoring. In the test-first development process, you write a test before writing the complete production code to simplify the test. This testing includes unit testing as well as integration testing.

Spring provides support for integration testing features using the spring-test package. These features include dependency injection and loading the application context within the test environment.

Writing a unit test that uses mock frameworks (such as EasyMock and JMock to test a Web-Service) is quite easy. However, it is not testing the content of the XML messages, so it is not simulating the real production environment of testing.

Spring Web-Services 2.0 provides features to create server-side integration tests as well as the client-side one. Using these integration test features, it is very simple to test a SOAP service without deploying it on the server when you are testing the server side, and without the need to set up a server when you are testing the client side.

In the first recipe, we will discuss how to use the Spring framework for Integration testing. In the next two recipes, new features for integration testing of Spring-WS 2.0 are detailed. In the last two recipes, using tools, such as soapUI and TCPMon for monitoring and testing Web-Services, are presented.

Integration testing using Spring-JUnit support

Spring supports integration testing features using the classes in the `org.springframework.test` package. These features provide dependency injection in your test case using either the production's application context or any customized one for testing purposes. This recipe presents how to use JUnit test cases using features, `spring-test.jar`, JUnit 4.7, and XMLUnit 1.1.

 Please note that to run Integration test, we need to start the server. However, in the next two recipes, we will use new features for integration testing of Spring-WS 2.0 that do not require starting up the server.

Getting ready

In this recipe, the project's name is `LiveRestaurant_R-3.1` (for server-side Web-Service) and has the following Maven dependencies:

- `spring-ws-core-2.0.1.RELEASE.jar`
- `log4j-1.2.9.jar`

The following are the Maven dependencies for `LiveRestaurant_R-3.1-Client` (for the client-side Web-Service):

- `spring-ws-core-2.0.1.RELEASE.jar`
- `spring-test-3.0.5.RELEASE.jar`
- `log4j-1.2.9.jar`
- `junit-4.7.jar`
- `xmlunit-1.1.jar`

How to do it...

This recipe uses the project used in the recipe *Setting up an endpoint by annotating the payload-root* discussed in *Chapter 1, Building SOAP Web-Services,* as the server-side project. Here is the setup for the client side:

1. Create a test class that calls the Web-Service server using `WebServiceTemplate` in `src/test`.

2. Configure `WebServiceTemplate` in `applicationContext.xml`.

3. From the folder `Liverestaurant_R-3.1`, run the following command:

   mvn clean package tomcat:run

4. Open a new command window to `Liverestaurant_R-3.1-Client` and run the following command:

   mvn clean package.

   The following is the client-side output:

```
…..............
-------------------------------------------------------------
   T E S T S
-------------------------------------------------------------
Running com.packtpub.liverestaurant.client.OrderServiceClientTest
..........................
Tests run: 2, Failures: 0, Errors: 0, Skipped: 0, Time elapsed:
1.633 sec


Results :


Tests run: 2, Failures: 0, Errors: 0, Skipped: 0
```

How it works...

The server-side projects set up a Web-Service server and the client-side project runs an integration test and sends predefined request messages to the server and gets the response message from the server. Then compare the server response with the expected response. Setting up a Web-Service and a client of the Web-Service have already been detailed in the first two chapters. Here, only the testing framework is detailed.

In `OrderServiceClientTest.java`, the method `setUpBefore()` will be called first to initialize data (since it is annotated by `@before`) and test methods that are annotated by `@Test` (`testCancelOrderRequest` or `testPalceOrderRequest`) to follow, and finally, the method `setUpAfter()` will be called to free up the resources (since it is annotated by `@after`).

When you run `mvn clean package`, Maven builds and runs any test class inside the `src/test/java` folder. So in `OrderServiceClientTest.java`, first the test application context will be loaded. In the application context, only the configuration of `WebServiceTemplate` is required:

```
    <bean id="messageFactory" class="org.springframework.ws.soap.saaj.
SaajSoapMessageFactory" />

    <bean id="webServiceTemplate" class="org.springframework.ws.client.
core.WebServiceTemplate">
       <constructor-arg ref="messageFactory" />
       <property name="defaultUri" value="http://localhost:8080/
LiveRestaurant/spring-ws/OrderService" />

    </bean>
```

In `OrderServiceClientTest.java`, to include the Spring dependency injection, and to set up and run the test, code is annotated with some information. The JUnit `@RunWith` annotation tells JUnit to use the Spring `TestRunner`. The `@ContextConfiguration` annotation from Spring tells to load which application context and use this context to inject `applicationContext` and `webServiceTemplate`, which are annotated with `@Autowired`:

```
@RunWith(SpringJUnit4ClassRunner.class)
@ContextConfiguration("/applicationContext.xml")
public class OrderServiceClientTest {
   @Autowired
     private  WebServiceTemplate webServiceTemplate;
   …......
```

`@Before` from JUnit tells to run the marked method (`setUpBefore`) before running the test case. JUnit `@After` causes the marked method to be called after the test case is executed. `@Test` from JUnit converts the marked methods (`testCancelOrderRequest` and `testPlaceOrderRequest`) into JUnit test methods:

```
@After
   public  void setUpAfter()  {
     applicationContext.close();
   }
   @Test
   public  final void testPlaceOrderRequest() throws Exception {
```

```
   Result result = invokeWS(placeOrderRequest);
    XMLAssert.assertXMLEqual("Invalid content received", getStringFro
mInputStream(placeOrderResponse), result.toString());
  }
  @Test
  public  final void testCancelOrderRequest() throws Exception {
    Result result = invokeWS(cancelOrderRequest);
     XMLAssert.assertXMLEqual("Invalid content received", getStringFro
mInputStream(cancelOrderResponse), result.toString());
  }
  private    Result invokeWS(InputStream is) {
      StreamSource source = new StreamSource(is);
      StringResult result = new StringResult();
      webServiceTemplate.sendSourceAndReceiveToResult(source,
result);
      return result;
  }
  public  String getStringFromInputStream (InputStream is)
    throws IOException {
    BufferedInputStream bis = new BufferedInputStream(is);
     ByteArrayOutputStream buf = new ByteArrayOutputStream();
     int result = bis.read();
     while(result != -1) {
       byte b = (byte)result;
       buf.write(b);
       result = bis.read();
     }
     return buf.toString();
  }
```

Note that for each test method, the @After and @Before methods will be executed once.
XMLAssert.assertXMLEqual compares the real result and the expected XML messages.

> In a real situation, the data will change dynamically every day.
> We should be able to build data dynamically based on dates
> and from the database. This helps continuous integration and
> smoke testing over a period of time.

See also

The recipe *Setting up an endpoint by annotating the payload-root*, discussed in *Chapter 1, Building SOAP Web-Service.*

The recipe *Creating a Web-Service client on HTTP transport*, discussed in *Chapter 2, Building Clients for SOAP Web-Services.*

Server-side integration testing using MockWebServiceClient

Writing a unit test that uses mock frameworks, such as EasyMock and JMock, to test a Web-Service is quite easy. However, it does not test the content of the XML messages, so it is not simulating the real production environment of testing (since these mock objects mimic a part of the software, which is not running, this is neither unit testing nor integration testing).

Spring Web-Services 2.0 provides features to create server-side integration tests. Using this feature, it is very simple to test a SOAP service without deploying on the server and without the need to configure a test client in the Spring configuration file.

The main class of server-side integration tests is `MockWebServiceClient` from the `org.springframework.ws.test.server` package. This class creates a request message, sends the request to the service, and gets the response message. The client compares the response with the expected message.

Getting ready

In this recipe, the project's name is `LiveRestaurant_R-3.2` (as the server-side Web-Service that includes a test case that uses `MockWebServiceClient`) and has the following Maven dependencies:

- `spring-ws-core-2.0.1.RELEASE.jar`
- `spring-ws-test-2.0.1.RELEASE.jar`
- `spring-test-3.0.5.RELEASE.jar`
- `log4j-1.2.9.jar`
- `junit-4.7.jar`

How to do it...

This recipe uses the project from *Setting up an endpoint by annotating the payload-root*, discussed in *Chapter 1, Building SOAP Web-Services*, as the server-side project. Here is the setup for the test case:

1. Include the following data in `pom.xml`:

```
<testResources>
 <testResource>
   <directory>src/main/webapp</directory>
 </testResource>
</testResources>
</build>
```

Add the test case class in the folder `src/test/java`.

2. Run the following command for `Liverestaurant_R-3.2`:

```
mvn clean package
```

The following is the server-side output:

```
…...............
----------------------------------------------------
 T E S T S
----------------------------------------------------
Running com.packtpub.liverestaurant.service.test.
OrderServiceServerSideIntegrationTest
l.........
Tests run: 2, Failures: 0, Errors: 0, Skipped: 0, Time elapsed:
1.047 sec


Results :


Tests run: 2, Failures: 0, Errors: 0, Skipped: 0
```

How it works...

In the class `OrderServiceServerSideIntegrationTest.java`, annotation and unit testing materials are the same as those used in the recipe *Integration testing using Spring-JUnit support*. The only difference here is that we are not setting up the server. Instead, we load the server application context in the test case class:

```
@RunWith(SpringJUnit4ClassRunner.class)
@ContextConfiguration("/WEB-INF/spring-ws-servlet.xml")
public class OrderServiceServerSideIntegrationTest {
…...................
```

The test case class, in the `@Before` method, initializes an instance of the client mock object and XML messages:

```
@Before
   public void createClient() {
       wsMockClient = MockWebServiceClient.createClient(applicationCon
text);
       placeOrderRequest = new OrderServiceServerSideIntegrationTest().
getClass().getResourceAsStream("placeOrderRequest.xml");
```

```
       cancelOrderRequest = new
OrderServiceServerSideIntegrationTest().getClass().getResourceAsStream
("cancelOrderRequest.xml");
       placeOrderResponse = new
OrderServiceServerSideIntegrationTest().getClass().getResourceAsStream
("placeOrderResponse.xml");
       cancelOrderRsponse = new
OrderServiceServerSideIntegrationTest().getClass().getResourceAsStream
("cancelOrderResponse.xml");
   }
```

Then, it sends a message and receives the response. It then compares the expected response and the real response:

```
@After
public  void setUpAfterClass()  {

  applicationContext.close();
}


@Test
public  final void testPlaceOrderRequest() throws Exception {
  Source requestPayload = new StreamSource(placeOrderRequest);
  Source responsePayload = new StreamSource(placeOrderResponse);
    wsMockClient.sendRequest(withPayload(requestPayload)).
      andExpect(payload(responsePayload));
}
@Test
public  final void testCancelOrderRequest() throws Exception {
  Source requestPayload = new StreamSource(cancelOrderRequest);
    Source responsePayload = new StreamSource(cancelOrderRsponse);
    wsMockClient.sendRequest(withPayload(requestPayload)).
      andExpect(payload(responsePayload));
}
```

In the method `createClient()`, `MockWebServiceClient.createClient(applica tionContext)` creates an instance of the client mock object (`wsMockClient`). In the test case methods (`testCancelOrderRequest`, `testPlaceOrderRequest`), using the code `wsMockClient.sendRequest(withPayload(requestPayload)).andExpect(pay load(responsePayload))`, the mock client sends an XML message and compares the response (from server endpoint) with the expected response (The client mock is aware of server endpoint from application context file and when it sends request to server, invokes the endpoint method and gets the response back).

See also

The recipes *Integration testing using Spring-JUnit support* and *Client-side integration testing using MockWebServiceServer*, discussed in this chapter.

The recipe *Setting up an endpoint by annotating the payload-root*, discussed in *Chapter 1, Building SOAP Web-Services*.

Client-side integration testing using MockWebServiceServer

Writing a client-side unit test that uses mock frameworks to test a client of a Web-Service is quite easy. However, it does not test the content of the XML messages that are sent over the wire, especially when mocking out the entire client class.

Spring Web-Services 2.0 provides features to create client-side integration tests. Using this feature, it is very simple to test the client of a SOAP service without setting up a server.

The main class of client-side integration tests is `MockWebServiceServer` from the `org.springframework.ws.test.server` package. This class accepts a request message from a client, verifies it against the expected request messages, and then returns the response message back to the client.

Since this project is a client-side test integration using `MockWebServiceServer`, it doesn't need any external server-side Web-Service.

Getting ready

In this recipe, the project's name is `LiveRestaurant_R-3.3-Client` (as the client-side project that includes a test case that uses `MockServiceServer` as the server) and has the following Maven dependencies:

- `spring-ws-core-2.0.1.RELEASE.jar`
- `spring-ws-test-2.0.1.RELEASE.jar`
- `spring-test-3.0.5.RELEASE.jar`
- `log4j-1.2.9.jar`
- `junit-4.7.jar`

How to do it...

This recipe uses the client-side project from *Creating a Web-Service client on HTTP transport*, discussed in *Chapter 2, Building Clients for SOAP Web-Services*. Here is the setup for the test case:

1. Create a test case class under `src/test`.

2. Create a class that extends `WebServiceGatewaySupport` to send/receive messages.

3. Run the following command for `Liverestaurant_R-3.3-Client`:

   `mvn clean package`

   The following is the client-side output:

   ```
   *************************

   -------------------------------------------------------

     T E S T S

   -------------------------------------------------------

   Running com.packtpub.liverestaurant.client.test.
   ClientSideIntegrationTest

   . . . . . . . .

   Tests run: 3, Failures: 0, Errors: 0, Skipped: 0, Time elapsed:
   0.945 sec

   Results :

   Tests run: 3, Failures: 0, Errors: 0, Skipped: 0
   ```

How it works...

The flow in the test case class `ClientSideIntegrationTest.java` is as follows:

1. Create a `MockWebServiceServer` using `WebServiceGatewaySupport` (`OrderServiceClient` that extends `WebServiceGatewaySupport`). You can also create `MockWebServiceServer` using `WebServiceTemplate` or using `ApplicationContext`.

2. Set up request expectations using `RequestMatcher` and return the response using `ResponseCreator`.

3. Make a client call by using the `WebServiceTemplate`.

4. Call the `verify` method to make sure all the expectations are met. The application context file is just a configuration of `WebServiceTemplate` and `OrderServiceClient`:

```xml
<bean id="client" class=" com.packtpub.liverestaurant.client.
test.OrderServiceClient">
        <property name="webServiceTemplate"
ref="webServiceTemplate"/>
    </bean>

    <bean id="webServiceTemplate" class="org.springframework.
ws.client.core.WebServiceTemplate">
        <property name="defaultUri" value="http://www.packtpub.
com/liverestaurant/OrderService/schema"/>
    </bean>
    </beans>
```

Inside `ClientSideIntegrationTest.java`, the annotation and unit testing materials are the same as those used in the recipe _Integration testing using Spring-JUnit support_. The method `createServer()` creates `MockWebServiceServer` using `WebServiceGatewaySupport` (`OrderServiceClient` extends `WebServiceGatewaySupport`):

```java
public class OrderServiceClient extends WebServiceGatewaySupport  {

    public Result getStringResult(Source source) {
        StringResult result = new StringResult();
        getWebServiceTemplate().sendSourceAndReceiveToResult(source,
result);
        return result;
    }
}
```

In the test, the method `testExpectedRequestResponse`, `mockServer.expect` sets the expected request and response (`webServiceTemplate` is configured in 'testing mode' in `client-integration-test.xml`. When the `sendSourceAndReceiveToResult` method is being called, the template calls server virtually without any real HTTP connection). Then `client.getStringResult` calls `webserviceTemplate` to call the server (`MockWebServiceServer`). Then, `mockServer.verify` checks if the returned response matches the expected one:

```java
    @Test
    public void testExpectedRequestResponse() throws Exception {

        Source requestPayload = new StringSource(getStringFromInputSt
ream(placeOrderRequest));
        Source responsePayload = new StringSource(getStringFromInputS
tream(placeOrderResponse));
        mockServer.expect(payload(requestPayload)).andRespond(withPay
load(responsePayload));
```

```
Result result = client.getStringResult(requestPayload);
    XMLAssert.assertXMLEqual("Invalid content received",
xmlToString(responsePayload), result.toString());
    mockServer.verify();
}
```

In the test method `testSchema`, instead of using a hardcoded request/response, the schema of the expected request and response is used. This test can test if the format of the request/response is as expected. This is shown as follows:

```
.  @Test
    public void testSchema() throws Exception {
        Resource schema=new FileSystemResource("orderService.xsd");
        mockServer.expect(validPayload(schema));
        client.getStringResult(new StreamSource(placeOrderRequest));
        mockServer.verify();
    }
```

In the test method `testSchemaWithWrongRequest`, the schema of the expected request and response is used. However, the client is trying to send invalid request, that is to be failed:

```
@Test(expected = AssertionError.class)
public void testSchemaWithWrongRequest() throws Exception {
    Resource schema=new FileSystemResource("orderService.xsd");
    mockServer.expect(validPayload(schema));
    client.getStringResult(new StringSource(getStringFromInputStre
am(cancelOrderRequestWrong)));
    mockServer.verify();
}
```

See also

The recipe *Integration testing using Spring-JUnit support*, discussed in this chapter.

Monitoring TCP messages of a Web-Service using TCPMon

TCPMon is an Apache project with a Swing UI, which provides features to monitor TCP-based messages transmitted between the client and server. A SOAP message can also be sent to the server using TCPMon.

This recipe presents how to monitor messages passed between a Web-Service client and the server. In addition, it shows how to send a SOAP message using TCPMon. The recipe *Integration testing using Spring-JUnit support* is used for server-side and client-side projects.

Getting ready

Download and install TCPMon 1.0 from the website `http://ws.apache.org/commons/tcpmon/download.cgi`.

How to do it...

Monitor the messages between the client and server as follows:

1. Run it on Windows using `tcpmon.bat` (`tcpmon.sh` for Linux).

2. Enter the values **8081** and **8080** into the **Listen port #** and **Target port #** fields and click on the **Add** option.

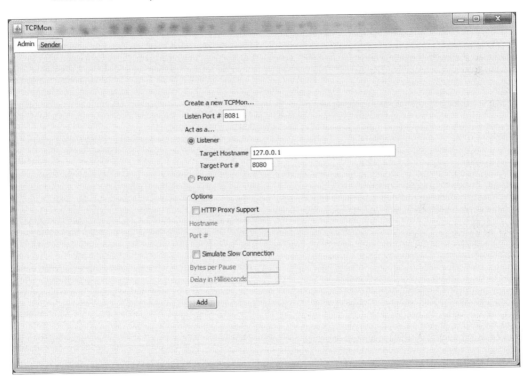

3. Change `applicationContext.xml` in `LiveRestaurant_R-3.1-Client` to use the **8081** port for `webserviceTemplate`:

```
<bean id="messageFactory" class="org.springframework.ws.soap.
saaj.SaajSoapMessageFactory" />

<bean id="webServiceTemplate" class="org.springframework.
ws.client.core.WebServiceTemplate">
```

```
        <constructor-arg ref="messageFactory" />
        <property name="defaultUri" value="http://localhost:8081/
    LiveRestaurant/spring-ws/OrderService" />

    </bean>
```

4. Run the server from the project `LiveRestaurant_R-3.1` using the following command:

   mvn clean package tomcat:run

5. Run the client from the project `LiveRestaurant_R-3.1-Client` using the following command:

   mvn clean package

6. Go to the **Port 8081** tab and see request and response messages, as shown in the following screenshot:

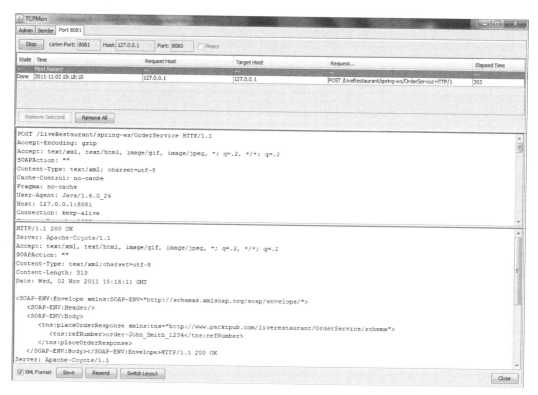

Send a SOAP request to the server as follows:

Go to the **Sender** tab. Enter the SOAP service address and a SOAP request message and click on the **Send** button to view the response:

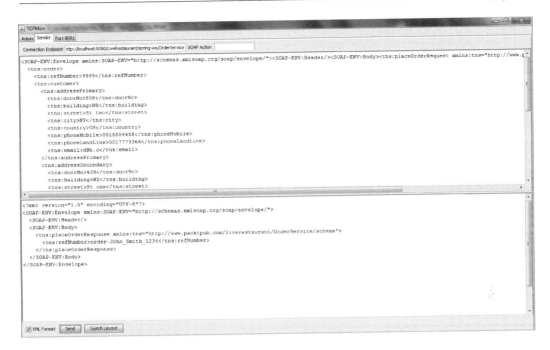

How it works...

Monitoring transmitted messages between a client and a Web-Service server is the most important usage of the TCPMon. In addition, TCPMon can be used as a client to send a message to a Web-Service server. This is an intermediary role that shows the transmitted messages between the client and server. The client has to point to the intermediary instead of the server service.

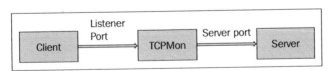

The second activity (sending a SOAP request to the server) shows the sending of a message using TCPMon to the server, the reception of the response, and shows all of this on TCPMon.

See also

The recipe *Integration testing using Spring-JUnit support* discussed in this chapter.

Monitoring and load/functional testing of a Web-Service using soapUI

soapUI is an open source testing solution for testing web services. Using a user-friendly GUI, this tool provides a feature to create and execute automated functional and load testing as well as monitor SOAP messages.

This recipe presents how to monitor SOAP messages of the Web-Service and functional and load testing using soapUI. To set up a Web-Service, `Recipe 3.1`, *Integration testing using Spring-JUnit support*, is used.

Getting ready

Get started by carrying out the following steps:

1. Install and run soapUI 4.0 (`http://www.soapui.org/`).
2. Run the following command from the folder `LiveRestaurant_R-3.1`:

   `mvn clean package tomcat:run`

How to do it...

To run the functional tests and monitor the SOAP messages, carry out the following steps:

1. Right-click on the **Projects** node. Select **New soapUI Project** and enter the WSDL URL and the **Project Name**.

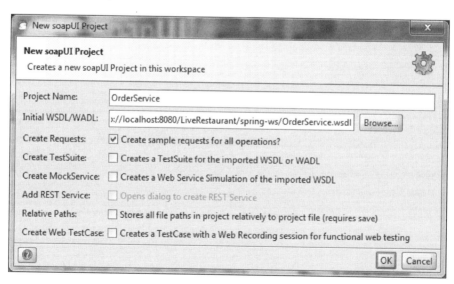

2. Right-click on the project's name, **OrderService**, in the navigator pane. Select **Launch HTTP Monitor** and enable the option **Set as Global Proxy**. Click on the **OK** button:

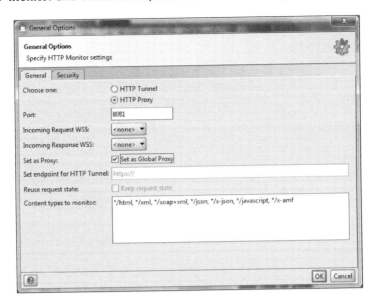

3. Expand the **OrderService** methods (**cancelOrder** and **placeOrder**). Double-click **cancelOrder**. Click on **Submit Request to Specific Endpoint URL** (The green icon on the top-left corner of the **Request1** screen). The following is the output of this action:

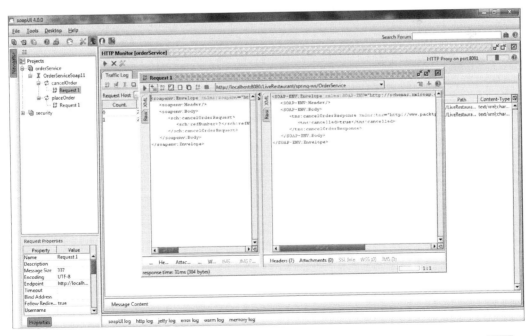

4. Right-click **OrderServiceSoap11** | **Generate Test Suite** | **OK**. Enter **OrderServiceSoap11 TestSuite**.

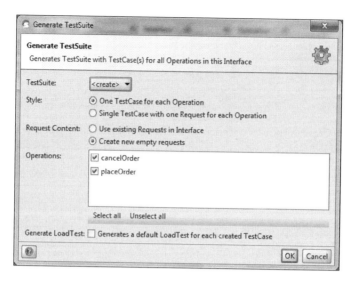

5. Double-click on **OrderServiceSoap11 TestSuite** on the navigator pane. Click Run the selected **TestCases**.

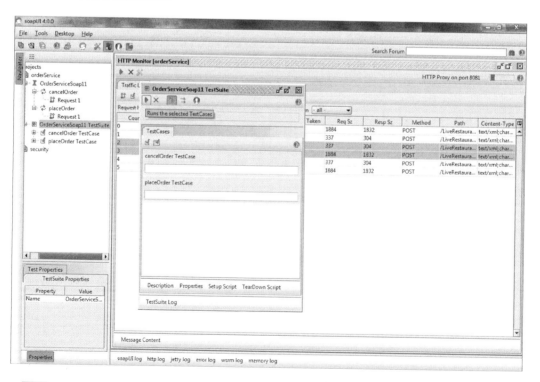

6. The following is the output when the test suite is run:

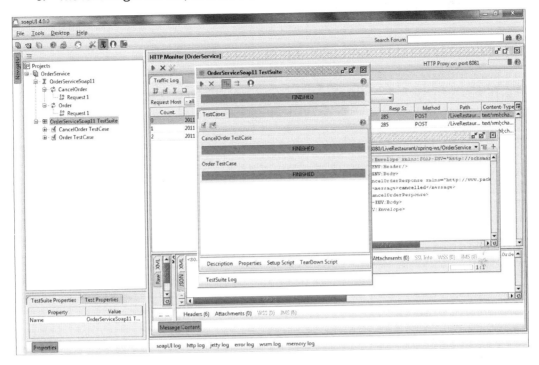

Run a load test as follows:

1. Right-click the **cancelOrder** test case. Select **New Local Test** and enter the **Load Test Name**.

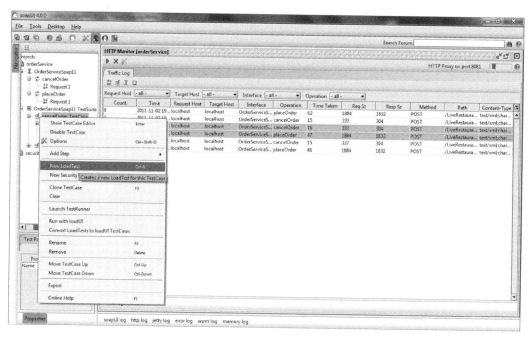

2. Double-click **Load test name**. Enter **Parameter** and click on **Run Load Test**.

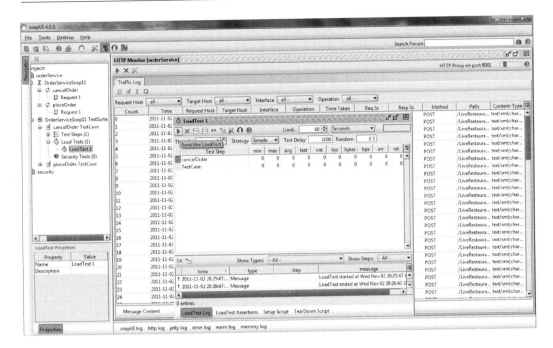

3. The following is the output of the test:

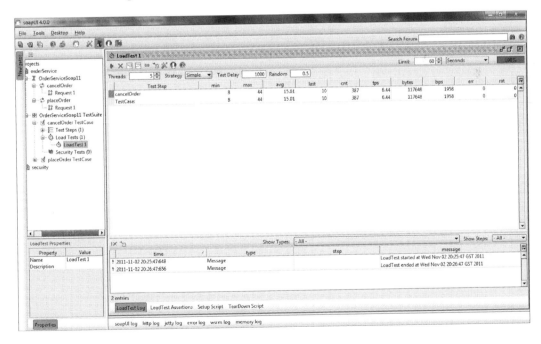

How it works...

Functional testing and monitoring SOAP messages: soapUI provides three levels of functional testing: test suites, test cases, and test steps.

Test cases are the unit tests that are generated from the WSDL file and test suites are a collection of these unit tests. Test steps control the flow of execution and validate the functionality of the service that is to be tested. For example, a test case in the test suite for the **cancelOrder** mentioned previously may test the database first. If there is such an order available, it cancels the order.

Load testing: soapUI provides a feature to run multiple threads (as many as your machine's hardware limits you to) on your test cases. When you run a load test, the underlying test case will be cloned internally for each thread. Delay settings let each thread wait before starting and let the Web-Service rest for each thread.

See also

The recipe *Integration testing using Spring-JUnit support*, discussed in this chapter.

4
Exception/SOAP Fault Handling

In this chapter, we will cover:

- ► Handling server-side exceptions by returning an exception's message as a SOAP fault string
- ► Mapping exception class names to SOAP faults
- ► Annotating exception classes with the `@SOAPFault`
- ► Writing your own exception resolvers in Spring-WS

Introduction

The server-side exceptions generated while processing a Web-Service are transmitted as SOAP faults. The `SOAP <Fault>` element is used to carry error and status information within a SOAP message.

The following code represents a general structure of the SOAP fault element in a SOAP message:

```
<SOAP-ENV:Fault>
    <faultcode xsi:type="xsd:string">SOAFP-ENV:Client</faultcode>
    <faultstring xsi:type="xsd:string">
        A human readable summary of the fault
        </faultstring>
    <detail xsi:type="xsd:string">
        Application specific error information related to the Body
element
        </detail>
</SOAP-ENV:Fault>
```

If a `Fault` element is present, it must appear as a child element of the `Body` element. A `Fault` element can only appear once in a SOAP message.

Spring Web-Services offer smart mechanisms to handle SOAP faults with its easy-to-use API. The exceptions that are thrown when handling the request get picked up by `MessageDispatcher` and get delegated to any of the endpoint exception resolvers that are declared in the application context (XML or annotation). This exception resolver-based handling mechanism allows the developer to define custom behaviors (such as returning a customized SOAP fault) when a particular exception gets thrown.

This chapter starts with recipes for easy exception-handling mechanisms and then moves on to slightly complex scenarios.

`org.springframework.ws.server.EndpointExceptionResolver` is the primary specification/contract for server-side exception handling in Spring-WS. `org.springframework.ws.soap.server.endpoint.SimpleSoapExceptionResolver` is the default implementation of `EndpointExceptionResolver`, available in the Spring-WS framework. If not explicitly handled by the developer, `MessageDispatcher` handles the server-side exceptions with `SimpleSoapExceptionResolver`.

The recipes in this chapter demonstrate different usages of `org.springframework.ws.server.EndpointExceptionResolver` and its implementations, including `SimpleSoapExceptionResolver`.

For demonstration purposes, the simplest recipe for building a Spring-WS is Simplifying the creation of a WebService using `MessageDispatcherServlet`.

Handling server-side exceptions by returning the exception's message as a SOAP fault string

Spring-WS framework automatically converts the description of application-level exception thrown in server-side into SOAP fault messages and includes it within response message and sends it back to the client. This recipe demonstrates catching the exception and setting a meaningful message to be sent back as a SOAP fault string in the response.

Getting ready

In this recipe, the project's name is `LiveRestaurant_R-4.1` (for server-side Web-Service) and has the following Maven dependencies:

▶ `spring-ws-core-2.0.1.RELEASE.jar`
▶ `log4j-1.2.9.jar`

The following are the Maven dependencies for `LiveRestaurant_R-4.1-Client` (for the client-side Web-Service):

- ▸ `spring-ws-core-2.0.1.RELEASE.jar`
- ▸ `spring-test-3.0.5.RELEASE.jar`
- ▸ `log4j-1.2.9.jar`

How to do it...

This recipe uses projects from *Setting up an endpoint by annotating the payload-root*, discussed in *Chapter 1, Building SOAP Web-Services*. The following steps describe how to modify the endpoint:

1. Modify the endpoint to throw an exception when an application/system error occurs.
2. Build and deploy the project in the Maven-embedded Tomcat server.
3. Run the following command from the root of the project, in a command-line window:

   `mvn clean package tomcat:run.`

4. To test, open a new command window, go to the folder `LiveRestaurant_R-4.1-Client`, and run the following command:

   `mvn clean package  exec:java`

   The following is the output from the server-side console (note the `SOAP-Env:Fault` element generated in the message):

   `DEBUG [http-8080-1] (MessageDispatcher.java:167) - Received request.....`

   `<SOAP-ENV:Fault><faultcode>SOAP-ENV:Server</faultcode>`

   `<faultstring xml:lang="en">Reference number is not provided!</faultstring>`

   `</SOAP-ENV:Fault>`

   `For request`

   `...`

   `<tns:placeOrderRequest xmlns:tns="....">`

   `....`

   `</tns:placeOrderRequest>`

   The following is the output from the client-side console:

   `Received response ....`

   `<SOAP-ENV:Fault>`

   `<faultcode>SOAP-ENV:Server</faultcode>`

```
<faultstring xml:lang="en">Reference number is not provided!</
faultstring>
</SOAP-ENV:Fault>
... for request....
<tns:placeOrderRequest xmlns:tns="...">
  ….......
</tns:placeOrderRequest>
....
[WARNING]
java.lang.reflect.InvocationTargetException
        at sun.reflect.NativeMethodAccessorImpl.invoke0(Native
Method)
        .........
        at org.codehaus.mojo.exec.ExecJavaMojo$1.run(ExecJavaMojo.
java:297)
        at java.lang.Thread.run(Thread.java:619)
Caused by: org.springframework.ws.soap.client.
SoapFaultClientException: Reference number is not provided!
        ..........
```

How it works...

In the endpoint (`OrderServiceEndpoint`) in the handler method
(`handlePlaceOrderRequest`), as the incoming message doesn't contain a reference
number, a simple `RuntimeException` is thrown. This symbolizes any unexpected runtime
exception. For clarification, a meaningful error description (**Reference number is not
provided!**) is passed to the exception:

```
@PayloadRoot(localPart = "placeOrderRequest", namespace = SERVICE_
NS)
public @ResponsePayload
Source handlePlaceOrderRequest(@RequestPayload Source source) throws
Exception {

    //extract data from input parameter
    String fName="John";
    String lName="Smith";
    String refNumber="";
    if(refNumber.length()>0)
       return new StringSource(
```

```
    "<tns:placeOrderResponse xmlns:tns=\"http://www.packtpub.
com/liverestaurant/OrderService/schema\"><tns:refNumber>"+order
Service.placeOrder(fName, lName, refNumber)+"</tns:refNumber></
tns:placeOrderResponse>");
    else
        throw new RuntimeException("Reference number is not provided!");
}
```

You can see that there are no explicit exception resolvers configured for this project. The smart `MessageDispatcher` of the Spring-WS framework allocates a default exception resolver to handle any exception when there is no exception resolver configured. It uses `SimpleSoapExceptionResolver` to handle the situation.

`SimpleSoapExceptionResolver` resolves the exception by performing the following operations:

- ▶ Logs the exception to the logger (console, log file)
- ▶ Generates the SOAP fault message with the exception message as the fault string and returns as part of the response message

When we check the response message at the client side, we can see the exact exception message (**Reference number is not provided!**) that is set inside the method, `OrderServiceEndpoint. handlePlaceOrderRequest` is returned as the SOAP fault string in the response message.

What is interesting here is that the developer doesn't need to do anything to handle and send the SOAP fault message, except for throwing an exception with a meaningful message.

See also

The recipe *Setting up an endpoint by annotating the payload-root*, discussed in *Chapter 1, Building SOAP Web-Services*.

The recipe *Creating a Web-Service client on HTTP transport*, discussed in *Chapter 2, Building Clients for SOAP Web-Services*.

Mapping exception class names to SOAP faults

Spring-WS framework allows the SOAP fault messages to be customized easily in the bean-configuration file, `spring-ws-servlet.xml`. It uses a special exception resolver, `SoapFaultMappingExceptionResolver`, to do that job. We can map exception classes to the corresponding SOAP fault to be generated and returned to the client.

Getting ready

In this recipe, the project's name is `LiveRestaurant_R-4.2` (for server-side Web-Service) and has the following Maven dependencies:

- `spring-ws-core-2.0.1.RELEASE.jar`
- `log4j-1.2.9.jar`

The following are the Maven dependencies for `LiveRestaurant_R-4.2-Client` (for the client-side Web-Service):

- `spring-ws-core-2.0.1.RELEASE.jar`
- `spring-test-3.0.5.RELEASE.jar`
- `log4j-1.2.9.jar`

How to do it...

This recipe uses the projects from *Setting up an endpoint by annotating the payload-root*, discussed in *Chapter 1, Building SOAP Web-Services*.

1. Create a custom exception class `DataOutOfRangeException.java`.
2. Modify `OrderServiceEndpoint` to throw `DataOutOfRangeException`.
3. Register `SoapFaultMappingExceptionResolver` in `spring-ws-servlet.xml`.
4. Build and deploy the project in the Maven-embedded Tomcat server.
5. Run the following command from the root of the project, in a command-line window:

   mvn clean package tomcat:run

6. To test, open a new command window, go to the folder `LiveRestaurant_R-4.2-Client`, and run the following command:

   mvn clean package exec:java

   The following is the output from the server-side console (note that the `SOAP-Env:Fault` element is generated in the message):

   DEBUG [http-8080-1] (MessageDispatcher.java:177) -

   Sent response

   ...

   <SOAP-ENV:Fault>

   <faultcode>SOAP-ENV:Server</faultcode>

   <faultstring xml:lang="en">such a data is out of range!</faultstring>

```
</SOAP-ENV:Fault>
</SOAP-ENV:Body>
... for request
<tns:placeOrderRequest xmlns:tns="....">

   …..
</tns:placeOrderRequest>
```

The following is the output from the client-side console:

```
 Received response...
<SOAP-ENV:Fault>
<faultcode>SOAP-ENV:Server</faultcode>
<faultstring xml:lang="en">such a data is out of range!</
faultstring>
</SOAP-ENV:Fault>
......
for request....
<tns:placeOrderRequest xmlns:tns="......">

   .......
</tns:placeOrderRequest>

.....
[WARNING]
java.lang.reflect.InvocationTargetException

        .........
Caused by: org.springframework.ws.soap.client.
SoapFaultClientException: such a data is out of range!

        .......
```

How it works...

In the preceding code, the `OrderServiceEndpoint.placeOrderRequest` method throws a custom exception, `DataOutOfRangeException`, which symbolizes a typical server-side exception:

```
    @PayloadRoot(localPart = "placeOrderRequest", namespace = SERVICE_
NS)
    public @ResponsePayload
    Source handlePlaceOrderRequest(@RequestPayload Source source) throws
Exception {
```

```
//extract data from input parameter
String fName="John";
String lName="Smith";
String refNumber="123456789";
if(refNumber.length()<7)
   return new StringSource(
   "<tns:placeOrderResponse xmlns:tns=\"http://www.packtpub.
com/liverestaurant/OrderService/schema\"><tns:refNumber>"+order
Service.placeOrder(fName, lName, refNumber)+"</tns:refNumber></
tns:placeOrderResponse>");
   else
      throw new DataOutOfRangeException("RefNumber is out of range");
}
```

This exception is caught by MessageDispatcher and delegated to the configured exception resolvers. In this project, SoapFaultMappingExceptionResolver is used, which is a special kind of resolver that allows the exception classes to be mapped with custom messages in the configuration file. In this example, a different message is used to map against DataOutOfRangeException. It acts as an interceptor that converts the SOAP fault message into whatever is given in the following mapping:

```
<bean id="exceptionResolver"
   class="org.springframework.ws.soap.server.endpoint.
SoapFaultMappingExceptionResolver">
      <property name="defaultFault" value="SERVER" />
      <property name="exceptionMappings">
         <value>
            com.packtpub.liverestaurant.service.exception.
DataOutOfRangeException=SERVER,
            such a data is out of range!
         </value>
      </property>
</bean>
```

The generated SOAP fault message is logged in at both the server-side as well as the client-side console screens. It displays the mapped SOAP fault message instead of what is originally thrown by the DataOutOfRangeException class.

There's more...

This powerful facility to map exceptions with SOAP fault strings is very useful for externalizing SOAP fault management from the code. It gives developers the flexibility to change the SOAP fault string, based on any business requirements at a later stage, without touching the code and rebuilding it. Moreover, if properly designed, this feature, with its configuration (SOAP fault mapping) in the spring-ws.xml file, can serve as a single point of reference for all possible SOAP fault messages of the services that can be maintained easily.

This is a good solution for B2B applications. Not good for B2C, when supporting multiple languages. In general, the best way to do this is by configuring messages in the database. This way, we can change them and fix them during runtime. The drawback in configuring in XML is that it needs to restart. In real time, one app runs on 30 servers. Deploying and restarting are painful processes.

See also

The recipe *Setting up an endpoint by annotating the payload-root*, discussed in *Chapter 1, Building SOAP Web-Services*.

The recipe *Creating a Web-Service client on HTTP transport*, discussed in *Chapter 2, Building Clients for SOAP Web-Services*.

The recipe *Handling server-side exceptions by returning exception's message as a SOAP fault string*, discussed in this chapter.

Annotating exception classes with @SOAPFault

Spring-WS framework allows application exceptions to be annotated to SOAP fault messages and customized easily in the exception class itself. It uses a special exception-resolver, `SoapFaultAnnotationExceptionResolver`, for that job. SOAP fault string and fault code can be customized by annotating in the class.

Getting ready

In this recipe, the project's name is `LiveRestaurant_R-4.3` (for the server-side Web-Service) and has the following Maven dependencies:

- `spring-ws-core-2.0.1.RELEASE.jar`
- `log4j-1.2.9.jar`

The following are the Maven dependencies for `LiveRestaurant_R-4.3-Client` (for the client-side Web-Service):

- `spring-ws-core-2.0.1.RELEASE.jar`
- `spring-test-3.0.5.RELEASE.jar`
- `log4j-1.2.9.jar`
- `junit-4.7.jar`
- `xmlunit-1.1.jar`

How to do it...

This recipe uses the project from *Setting up an endpoint by annotating the payload-root*, discussed in *Chapter 1, Building SOAP Web-Services*, as server-side and the recipe *How to integrate test using Spring-Junit support*, discussed in *Chapter 3, Testing and Monitoring Web-Services*, as client-side.

1. Create a custom exception class (`InvalidOrdeRequestException.java`), which is annotated with `@SoapFault`.

2. Create a custom exception class (`OrderProcessingFailedException.java`), which is annotated with `@SoapFault`.

3. Modify Endpoint (`OrderServiceEndpoint`) to throw both `InvalidOrderRequestException` and `OrderProcessingFailedException`.

4. Register `SoapFaultAnnotationExceptionResolver` in the server application context file (`spring-ws-servlet.xml`).

5. Build and deploy the project in the Maven-embedded Tomcat server.

6. Run the following command from the root of the project, in a command-line window:

   `mvn clean package tomcat:run.`

7. To test, open a new command window, go to the folder `LiveRestaurant_R-4.3-Client`, and run the following command:

   `mvn clean package`

   The following is the output from the client-side console (please note the `SOAP-Env:Fault` element generated in the message):

   ```
   DEBUG [main] (WebServiceTemplate.java:632) -
   Received response
   .....
   <SOAP-ENV:Fault><faultcode>SOAP-ENV:Client</faultcode>
   <faultstring xml:lang="en">Invalid Order Request: Request message
   incomplete</faultstring>
   </SOAP-ENV>
   for request....
   <tns:placeOrderRequest ....>
     ....
   </tns:placeOrderRequest>


   ...................
    Received response ...
   ```

```
<SOAP-ENV:Fault><faultcode>SOAP-ENV:Server</faultcode>

<faultstring xml:lang="en">Database server under maintenance,
please try after some time.</faultstring>

</SOAP-ENV:Fault>...

  for request ...

<tns:cancelOrderRequest ..>

  <tns:refNumber>9999</tns:refNumber>

</tns:cancelOrderRequest>

...

Tests run: 2, Failures: 0, Errors: 2, Skipped: 0, Time elapsed:
0.874 sec <<< FAILURE!
```

How it works...

In the endpoint's methods, `OrderServiceMethodEndoint.processOrder`
(`placeOrderRequest` and `cancelOrderRequest`), custom exceptions are thrown
(`ProcessingFailedException` and `InvalidOrderRequestException`) that
symbolize a typical server-side/client-side exception:

```
@PayloadRoot(localPart = "placeOrderRequest", namespace = SERVICE_
NS)
  public @ResponsePayload
  Source handlePlaceOrderRequest(@RequestPayload Source source) throws
Exception {

    //extract data from input parameter
    String fName="John";
    String lName="Smith";
    String refNumber="";
    if(refNumber.length()>0)
      return new StringSource(
    "<tns:placeOrderResponse xmlns:tns=\"http://www.packtpub.
com/liverestaurant/OrderService/schema\"><tns:refNumber>"+order
Service.placeOrder(fName, lName, refNumber)+"</tns:refNumber></
tns:placeOrderResponse>");
    else
      throw new InvalidOrderRequestException("Reference number is not
provided!");
  }
  @PayloadRoot(localPart = "cancelOrderRequest", namespace = SERVICE_
NS)
  public @ResponsePayload
  Source handleCancelOrderRequest(@RequestPayload Source source)
throws Exception {
```

```
     //extract data from input parameter
     boolean cancelled =true ;
     if ( isDataBaseServerRunning())
        return new StringSource(
            "<tns:cancelOrderResponse xmlns:tns=\"http://www.packtpub.
   com/liverestaurant/OrderService/schema\"><cancelled>"+(cancelled?"true
   ":"false")+"</cancelled></tns:cancelOrderResponse>");
        else
          throw new ProcessingFailedException("Database server is down!");
   }
   private boolean isDataBaseServerRunning(){
     return false;
   }
```

This exception is caught by the `MessageDispatcher` and delegates to the configured exception resolvers. In this project, `SoapFaultAnnotationExceptionResolver` is used, which is a special kind of resolver that allows the exception classes to be annotated with custom fault-code and fault-strings in the class. `SoapFaultAnnotationExceptionResolver` is configured to be used in `spring-ws-servlet.xml`, thus any exception handling is delegated to it by `MessageDispatcherServlet` at runtime:

```
   <bean id="exceptionResolver"
   class="org.springframework.ws.soap.server.endpoint.
   SoapFaultAnnotationExceptionResolver">
       <property name="defaultFault" value="SERVER" />
   </bean>
```

`ProcessingFailedException` represents a server-side system exception (`faultCode = FaultCode.SERVER`):

```
   @SoapFault(faultCode = FaultCode.SERVER,
       faultStringOrReason = "Database server under maintenance, please
   try after some time.")
   public class ProcessingFailedException extends Exception {
     public ProcessingFailedException(String message) {
       super(message);
     }
   }
```

`InvalidOrderRequestException` represents a client-side business logic exception (`faultCode = FaultCode.CLIENT`):

```
   @SoapFault(faultCode = FaultCode.CLIENT,
       faultStringOrReason = "Invalid Order Request: Request message
   incomplete")
   public class InvalidOrderRequestException extends Exception {
```

```
    public InvalidOrderRequestException(String message) {
      super(message);
    }
  }
```

You can see that the annotated `faultStringOrReason` is generated as a SOAP fault and is transmitted back to the client. The generated SOAP fault message, which is logged in both the server-side as well as client-side console screens, displays the annotated SOAP fault message instead of what is originally thrown in the `Endpoint` class.

There's more...

The attribute `faultCode` of the `@SoapFault` annotation has the following possible enumerated values:

- ► `CLIENT`
- ► `CUSTOM`
- ► `RECEIVER`
- ► `SENDER`

The selection of one from the enumerated list instructs the dispatcher which kind of SOAP fault is to be generated along with its specifics. Based on the preceding selection, dependent attributes become mandatory.

For example, if `FaultCode.CUSTOM` is selected for `faultCode`, the property `customFaultCode` string must be used instead of `faultStringOrReason`, as given in the code snippet of this recipe. The format used for `customFaultCode` is that of `QName.toString()`, that is, `"{" + Namespace URI + "}" + local part`, where the namespace is optional. Note that custom fault codes are only supported on SOAP 1.1.

The `@SoaPFault` annotation has one more attribute, namely, locale, which decides the language of the SOAP fault message. The default locale is English.

In general practice, we use error codes rather than error messages. Mapping will be done on the client side using mapping information. This avoids any load on the network and there will be no issue with multiple language support.

See also

The recipe *Setting up an endpoint by annotating the payload-root*, discussed in *Chapter 1, Building SOAP Web-Services*.

The recipe *How to integrate test using Spring-JUnit support*, discussed in *Chapter 3, Testing and Monitoring Web-Services*.

The recipe *Mapping exception class names to SOAP faults*, discussed in this chapter.

Writing your own exception resolvers in Spring-WS

While Spring-WS framework provides default mechanisms to handle exceptions using the standard exception resolvers, it allows developers to handle exceptions in their own way by building their own exception resolvers. SOAP faults can be customized to add custom details in their own formats and transmitted back to the client.

This recipe illustrates a custom exception resolver that adds the exception stack trace to the SOAP fault detail element of the SOAP response, so that the client will get the complete stack trace of the server-side exception, which is very useful for certain cases. This custom exception resolver already carries the power of annotations, as in the previous recipe.

Getting ready

In this recipe, the project's name is `LiveRestaurant_R-4.4` (for the server-side Web-Service) and has the following Maven dependencies:

- `spring-ws-core-2.0.1.RELEASE.jar`
- `log4j-1.2.9.jar`

`LiveRestaurant_R-4.4-Client` (for the client side) has the following Maven dependencies:

- `spring-ws-core-2.0.1.RELEASE.jar`
- `spring-test-3.0.5.RELEASE.jar`
- `log4j-1.2.9.jar`
- `junit-4.7.jar`
- `xmlunit-1.1.jar`

How to do it...

This recipe uses the project from *Setting up an endpoint by annotating the payload-root*, discussed in *Chapter 1, Building SOAP Web-Services*.

1. Create a custom exception resolver, `DetailedSoapFaultExceptionResolver`, extending `SoapFaultAnnotationExceptionResolver`.

2. Register `DetailedSoapFaultExceptionResolver` in `spring-ws-servlet.xml`.

3. Build and deploy the project in the Maven-embedded Tomcat server.

4. Run the following command from the root of the project, in a command-line window:

   mvn clean package tomcat:run.

5. To test, open a new command window, go to the folder `LiveRestaurant_R-4.4-Client`, and run the following command:

   mvn clean package `exec:java`

   The following is the output from the server-side console (note the `SOAP-Env:Fault` element generated in the message):

   DEBUG [http-8080-1] (MessageDispatcher.java:167) - Received request.....

   <tns:placeOrderRequest xmlns:tns="http://www.packtpub.com/ liverestaurant/OrderService/schema">

   ......

   </tns:placeOrderRequest></SOAP-ENV:Body>...

   DEBUG [http-8080-1] (MessageDispatcher.java:177) - Sent response

   ...

   <SOAP-ENV:Fault><faultcode>SOAP-ENV:Client</faultcode>

   <faultstring xml:lang="en">Invalid Order Request: Request message incomplete</faultstring>

   ><detail>

   <stack-trace xmlns=".....">

   ** at com.packtpub.liverestaurant.service.endpoint. OrderSeviceEndpoint.handlePlaceOrderRequest(OrderSeviceEndpoint. java:43)**

   **   at sun.reflect.NativeMethodAccessorImpl.invoke0(Native Method)**

   **   at sun.reflect.NativeMethodAccessorImpl. invoke(NativeMethodAccessorImpl.java:39)**

```
            at sun.reflect.DelegatingMethodAccessorImpl.invoke(Delegat
ingMethodAccessorImpl.java:25)&#13;

            at java.lang.reflect.Method.invoke(Method.java:597)&#13;

            at org.springframework.ws.server.endpoint.MethodEndpoint.
invoke(MethodEndpoint.java:132)&#13;

            at org.springframework.ws.server.endpoint.adapter.
DefaultMethodEndpointAdapter.invokeInternal(DefaultMethodEndpointA
dapter.java:229)&#13;

            at org.springframework.ws.server.endpoint.adapter.
AbstractMethodEndpointAdapter.invoke(AbstractMethodEndpointAdapt
er.java:53)&#13;

            at org.springframework.ws.server.MessageDispatcher.
dispatch(MessageDispatcher.java:230)&#13;


        . . . . . . .

</stack-trace></detail></SOAP-ENV:Fault>
```

How it works...

In the preceding code, our custom exception resolver,
DetailedSoapFaultExceptionResolver, which is a subclass of
SoapFaultAnnotationExceptionResolver, overrides the method custmizeFault()
to add an exception stack trace into the SOAP fault detail element. The method
stackTraceToString() returns the exception stack trace from a given exception, and it is
used to set the stack trace to the detail element of the SOAP fault of the response message.

There's more...

There are many different ways of creating custom exception resolvers. It is not just
SoapFaultAnnotationExceptionResolver that can be inherited for that purpose. Any
implementation of org.springframework.ws.server.EndpointExceptionResolver
can be configured appropriately to be used as an exception resolver. Developers can choose
from a set of very convenient implementations of EndpointExceptionResolver, available
in the Spring-WS API, leveraging the power of these implementations.

The place for customizing these classes is the method, customizeFault. The SOAP fault
can be customized by overriding the method customizeFault. Take a look at the package
org.springframework.ws.soap.server.endpoint for the readily available exception
resolvers that suit your requirement.

`AbstractSoapFaultDefinitionExceptionResolver` would be an ideal starting point to extend, if an exclusively custom exception resolver needs to be developed that doesn't fit with the currently available implementations, as it has already implemented some of the very common and basic functionality that are needed for any exception resolvers. The developer just needs to implement the abstract method, `resolveExceptionInternal()`, to suit your specific need.

What needs to be taken care of is that `MessageDispatcherServlet` should be instructed to consider the resolver in use, either by registering in `spring-ws-servlet.xml` or annotating in the exception class (in addition to registering in `spring-ws-servlet.xml`).

See also

The recipe *Setting up an endpoint by annotating the payload-root*, discussed in *Chapter 1, Building SOAP Web-Services*.

The recipe *Annotating Exception classes with @SOAP fault*, discussed in this chapter.

5
Logging and Tracing of SOAP Messages

In this chapter, we will cover:

- ► Logging the message payload manually
- ► Logging both request and response SOAP Envelopes using log4j
- ► Logging both request and response using Spring-WS's Interceptors
- ► Using Eclipse IDE to debug a Spring-WS

Introduction

Logging and tracing refers to capturing and recording events and data structures about a software program's execution to provide an audit trail. It helps the developers and support team to collect runtime information on the execution of the software program. For any serious software development team, it is very important to implement logging in their system.

For Web-Service development, it is quite useful to be able to see the SOAP messages being transported between client and server. Spring Web-Services offer logging and tracing of SOAP messages, when they arrive, or just before they are sent. Logging, in Spring-WS, is managed by the standard Commons Logging interface.

Generally, log4j is used as the concrete logging library in Spring Projects (as Spring logging feature are build upon log4j). This chapter illustrates a few simple ways of logging SOAP messages.

The recipes illustrated here can be applied to project sources of any recipe in this book. For demonstration purpose, an existing project source of the recipe *Setting up an endpoint by annotating the payload-root* is used, as this can be applied to any project used in this book.

Logging message payload manually

Message payload is the content of the SOAP message element, SOAP-ENV:Body. This is the exact message part of the whole SOAP Envelope for both request and response.

This recipe demonstrates logging the message payload manually from inside the code.

Getting ready

In this recipe, the project's name is LiveRestaurant_R-5.1 (for the server-side Web-Service) and has the following Maven dependencies:

- ▶ spring-ws-core-2.0.1.RELEASE.jar
- ▶ log4j-1.2.9.jar

And LiveRestaurant_R-5.1-Client (for the client side), with the following Maven dependencies:

- ▶ spring-ws-core-2.0.1.RELEASE.jar
- ▶ log4j-1.2.9.jar

How to do it...

This recipe uses projects used in the recipe *Setting up an endpoint by annotating the payload-root* in *Chapter 1, Building SOAP Web-Services*.

1. Modify log4j.properties to default the log level into INFO. Remove any type of debug setting for any package or API in log4j.properties.

2. Modify OrderServiceEndpoint to create two xmlToString methods and call these two methods to convert incoming messages into String and log it.

3. Build and deploy the project in the Maven-embedded Tomcat server. Run mvn clean package tomcat:run from the root of the project in a command line window.

4. To test this, open a new command line window and go to the folder LiveRestaurant_R-5.1-Client and run: mvn clean package exec:java.

5. Here is the output from the server-side console:

   ```
   INFO [http-8080-1] (OrderSeviceEndpoint.java:49) -

   Message Payload method handlePlaceOrderRequest   start ====

   <?xml version="1.0" encoding="UTF-8"?>
   <tns:placeOrderRequest xmlns:tns="....">
   ```

```
    <tns:order>
      <tns:refNumber>9999</tns:refNumber>
      ..........
      </tns:customer>
      <tns:dateSubmitted>2008-09-29T05:49:45</tns:dateSubmitted>
      <tns:orderDate>2014-09-19T03:18:33</tns:orderDate>
      <tns:items>
        <tns:type>Snacks</tns:type>
        <tns:name>Pitza</tns:name>
        <tns:quantity>2</tns:quantity>
      </tns:items>
    </tns:order>
  </tns:placeOrderRequest>


 ==== Message Payload End
 ......................

 INFO [http-8080-1] (OrderSeviceEndpoint.java:67) -

Message Payload method handleCancelOrderRequest  start ====

 <?xml version="1.0" encoding="UTF-8"?>
<tns:cancelOrderRequest xmlns:tns="...">
  <tns:refNumber>9999</tns:refNumber>
</tns:cancelOrderRequest>


 ==== Message Payload End
```

How it works...

The code simply logs the message payload manually, without any configuration change anywhere in the application. The changes in the log4j.properties makes sure that the log messages are printed to the console (as the appender is the ConsoleAppender) and no debug messages are printed:

```
log4j.rootLogger=INFO, stdout

log4j.appender.stdout=org.apache.log4j.ConsoleAppender
log4j.appender.stdout.layout=org.apache.log4j.PatternLayout

# Pattern to output the caller's file name and line number.
log4j.appender.stdout.layout.ConversionPattern=%5p [%t] (%F:%L) - %m%n
```

The method `xmlToString(...)` transforms the XML Source/Element Object into a `String` using a `StringWriter`:

```java
private String xmlToString(Node node) {
    try {
        Source source = new DOMSource(node);
        StringWriter stringWriter = new StringWriter();
        Result result = new StreamResult(stringWriter);
        TransformerFactory factory = TransformerFactory.
newInstance();
        Transformer transformer = factory.newTransformer();
        transformer.transform(source, result);
        return stringWriter.getBuffer().toString();
    } catch (TransformerConfigurationException e) {
        e.printStackTrace();
    } catch (TransformerException e) {
        e.printStackTrace();
    }
    return null;
}

private static String xmlToString(Source source) {
    try {
        StringWriter stringWriter = new StringWriter();
        Result result = new StreamResult(stringWriter);
        TransformerFactory factory = TransformerFactory.newInstance();
        Transformer transformer = factory.newTransformer();
        transformer.transform(source, result);
        return stringWriter.getBuffer().toString();
    } catch (TransformerConfigurationException e) {
        e.printStackTrace();
    } catch (TransformerException e) {
        e.printStackTrace();
    }
    return null;
}
```

In the `handleCancelOrderRequest()` and `handlePlaceOrderRequest()` methods, `xmlToString()` is invoked passing the Source/Element of the `RequestPayload` to return the message payload as a String instance, which is then logged into the configured logging appender (console in this case):

```java
@PayloadRoot(localPart = "placeOrderRequest", namespace = SERVICE_
NS)
public @ResponsePayload
```

```
  Source handlePlaceOrderRequest(@RequestPayload Source source) throws
Exception {
    String placeOrderRequestMessage = xmlToString(source);
  logger.info("\n\n Message Payload method handlePlaceOrderRequest
start ==== \n\n\n " + placeOrderRequestMessage + "\n\n\n ==== Message
Payload End\n\n");
    //extract data from input parameter
    String fName="John";
    String lName="Smith";
    String refNumber="1234";
      return new StringSource(
    "<tns:placeOrderResponse xmlns:tns=\"http://www.packtpub.
com/liverestaurant/OrderService/schema\"><tns:refNumber>"+order
Service.placeOrder(fName, lName, refNumber)+"</tns:refNumber></
tns:placeOrderResponse>");
  }
  @PayloadRoot(namespace = SERVICE_NS, localPart =
"cancelOrderRequest")
    @ResponsePayload
    public Source handleCancelOrderRequest(@RequestPayload Element
cancelOrderRequest) throws Exception {
      String refNumber=cancelOrderRequest.
getElementsByTagNameNS(SERVICE_NS, "refNumber") .item(0).
getTextContent();
        String cancelOrderRequestMessage = xmlToString(cancelOrderReq
uest);
      logger.info("\n\nMessage Payload method handleCancelOrderRequest
start ==== \n\n\n " + cancelOrderRequestMessage + "\n\n\n ==== Message
Payload End\n\n");
        return new StringSource(
    "<tns:cancelOrderResponse xmlns:tns=\"http://www.packtpub.com/
liverestaurant/OrderService/schema\"><tns:cancelled>"+orderService.
cancelOrder(refNumber)+"</tns:cancelled></tns:cancelOrderResponse>");
    }
```

As good practice, we log messages in debug mode. To get better performance, we do as follows:

```
If(logger.isDebugEnabled())
    logger.debug(message);
```

During runtime, we can enable and disable a log based on requirements.

There's more...

The example given in this recipe makes use of `SimpleMethodEndpointMapping`, which receives the message payload in the form of XML Source (`javax.xml.transform.Source`) or the Element (`org.w3c.dom.Element`) object as the method argument, with the help of the `RequestPayload` annotation, whereas in other cases, the incoming message will be in a different form. For example, marshalling endpoint—the input is already a marshalled object. You will need to adopt the appropriate mechanisms to transform the incoming argument in those cases. The recipes after that will give you insights on other approaches of logging and tracing.

See also

- ▸ *Setting up an endpoint by annotating the payload-root* in *Chapter 1, Building SOAP Web-Services.*

Logging both request and response SOAP Envelopes using log4j

Spring-WS framework allows the developer to log the entire SOAP message using simple logger configuration. This recipe illustrates configuring this internal logging of SOAP messages by the framework with log4j logger framework.

Getting ready

In this recipe, the project's name is `LiveRestaurant_R-5.2` (for the server-side Web Service) and has the following Maven dependencies:

- ▸ `spring-ws-core-2.0.1.RELEASE.jar`
- ▸ `log4j-1.2.9.jar`

It also has `LiveRestaurant_R-5.2-Client` (for the client side) with the following Maven dependencies:

- ▸ `spring-ws-core-2.0.1.RELEASE.jar`
- ▸ `log4j-1.2.9.jar`

How to do it...

This recipe uses projects used in the recipe *Setting up an endpoint by annotating the payload-root*:

1. Modify `log4j.properties` to set message tracing.

2. Build and deploy the project in the Maven-embedded Tomcat server. Run `mvn clean package tomcat:run` from the root of the project in a command-line window.

3. To test this, open a new command-line window, go to the folder `LiveRestaurant_R-5.1-Client`, and run `mvn clean package exec:java`.

The following is the output from the server-side console (please note the `SOAP-Env:Envelope` element of the Web-Service response generated in the message):

```
DEBUG [http-8080-1] (MessageDispatcher.java:167) - Received request
....
<SOAP-ENV:Envelope xmlns:SOAP-ENV="..."><SOAP-ENV:Body>
....
<tns:placeOrderRequest xmlns:tns="......">
  <tns:order>
    <tns:refNumber>9999</tns:refNumber>
    <tns:customer>
     ......
    </tns:customer>
    <tns:dateSubmitted>2008-09-29T05:49:45</tns:dateSubmitted>
    <tns:orderDate>2014-09-19T03:18:33</tns:orderDate>
    <tns:items>
      <tns:type>Snacks</tns:type>
      <tns:name>Pitza</tns:name>
      <tns:quantity>2</tns:quantity>
    </tns:items>
  </tns:order>
</tns:placeOrderRequest>
</SOAP-ENV:Body></SOAP-ENV:Envelope>
....
DEBUG [http-8080-1] (MessageDispatcher.java:177) - Sent response
....
<SOAP-ENV:Envelope xmlns:SOAP-ENV="..."><SOAP-ENV:Body>
....
<tns:placeOrderResponse xmlns:tns="...">
<tns:refNumber>order-John_Smith_1234</tns:refNumber></
tns:placeOrderResponse>
</SOAP-ENV:Body></SOAP-ENV:Envelope>
...
DEBUG [http-8080-1] (MessageDispatcher.java:167) - Received request ...
```

```
<SOAP-ENV:Envelope xmlns:SOAP-ENV="..."><SOAP-ENV:Body>

....

<tns:cancelOrderRequest xmlns:tns="....">

  <tns:refNumber>9999</tns:refNumber>

</tns:cancelOrderRequest>

</SOAP-ENV:Body></SOAP-ENV:Envelope>

...

DEBUG [http-8080-1] (MessageDispatcher.java:177) - Sent response

...

<SOAP-ENV:Envelope xmlns:SOAP-ENV="..."><SOAP-ENV:Body>

.....

<tns:cancelOrderResponse xmlns:tns="....">

<tns:cancelled>true</tns:cancelled></tns:cancelOrderResponse>

</SOAP-ENV:Body></SOAP-ENV:Envelope>

...
```

How it works...

The very core component of Spring-WS framework, namely, `MessageDispatcher`, logs every incoming SOAP message as soon as it receives it in the `receive()` method, after extracting the message content from the `MessageContext`, if logging is enabled for tracing or debugging.

In the `receive()` method, it checks for log settings for a named log instance, `org.springframework.ws.server.MessageTracing.received` checks for logging SOAP requests, and `org.springframework.ws.server.MessageTracing.sent` checks for SOAP responses. If those settings are given a value of either TRACE or DEBUG, it prints the entire SOAP Envelope of the corresponding request or response:

```
log4j.rootLogger=INFO, stdout, R

log4j.appender.stdout=org.apache.log4j.ConsoleAppender
log4j.appender.stdout.layout=org.apache.log4j.PatternLayout

# Pattern to output the caller's file name and line number.
log4j.appender.stdout.layout.ConversionPattern=%5p [%t] (%F:%L) - %m%n

  #RollingFileAppender
log4j.appender.R=org.apache.log4j.RollingFileAppender
log4j.appender.R.File=LiveRestaurant.log
```

```
log4j.appender.R.MaxFileSize=100KB
# Keep one backup file
log4j.appender.R.MaxBackupIndex=1

log4j.appender.R.layout=org.apache.log4j.PatternLayout
log4j.appender.R.layout.ConversionPattern=%p %t %c - %m%n
log4j.logger.org.springframework.ws.server.MessageTracing.
received=TRACE
log4j.logger.org.springframework.ws.server.MessageTracing.sent=TRACE
```

The easiest setting for the log tracing or debugging is in `log4j.properties`, as mentioned previously.

> Previously, for security purposes, messages were encrypted, so enabling logging was not useful all the time. It's better to log the message after completion of the decryption inside the entry method.

See also

▸   *Setting up an endpoint by annotating the payload-root* in *Chapter 1, , Building SOAP Web-Services.*

Logging both request and response using Spring-WS's Interceptors

Spring-WS provides features to log incoming/outgoing messages. These facilities are provided by using the `PayloadLoggingInterceptor` and `SoapEnvelopeLoggingInterceptor` classes that log using **Commons Logging Log.** While `PayloadLoggingInterceptor` logs only a message's payload, `SoapEnvelopeLoggingInterceptor` logs the whole SOAP Envelope including headers. To activate logging features using these two interceptors, log property within the `log4j` properties file should be set to debug for interceptors package.

In this recipe, logging Web-Service messages using `PayloadLoggingInterceptor` and `SoapEnvelopeLoggingInterceptor` are explained.

Getting ready

In this recipe, the project's name is `LiveRestaurant_R-5.3` (for the server-side Web-Service) and has the following Maven dependencies:

▸   `spring-ws-core-2.0.1.RELEASE.jar`
▸   `log4j-1.2.9.jar`

And `LiveRestaurant_R-5.3-Client` (for the client side) with the following Maven dependencies:

- `spring-ws-core-2.0.1.RELEASE.jar`
- `log4j-1.2.9.jar`

How to do it...

This recipe uses projects used in the recipe *Setting up an endpoint by annotating the payload-root*:

1. Open `log4j.properties` and set logging to debug the package `org.springframework.ws.server.endpoint.interceptor`.

2. Register `PayloadLoggingInterceptor` in the server-side application context.

3. Build and deploy the project in the Maven-embedded Tomcat server. Run `mvn clean package tomcat:run` from the root of the project in a command-line window.

4. To test this, open a new command-line window, go to the folder `LiveRestaurant_R-5.3-Client`, and run `mvn clean package exec:java`.

Here is the output from the server-side console:

```
DEBUG [http-8080-1] (AbstractLoggingInterceptor.java:160) - Request:
<tns:placeOrderRequest xmlns:tns=".....">
  <tns:order>
    <tns:refNumber>9999</tns:refNumber>
    <tns:customer>
    ......
    </tns:customer>
    <tns:dateSubmitted>2008-09-29T05:49:45</tns:dateSubmitted>
    <tns:orderDate>2014-09-19T03:18:33</tns:orderDate>
    <tns:items>
      <tns:type>Snacks</tns:type>
      <tns:name>Pitza</tns:name>
      <tns:quantity>2</tns:quantity>
    </tns:items>
  </tns:order>
</tns:placeOrderRequest>
DEBUG [http-8080-1] (AbstractLoggingInterceptor.java:160) - Response:
<tns:placeOrderResponse xmlns:tns="...">
```

```
<tns:refNumber>order-John_Smith_1234</tns:refNumber></
tns:placeOrderResponse>


DEBUG [http-8080-1] (AbstractLoggingInterceptor.java:160) - Request:

<tns:cancelOrderRequest xmlns:tns="...">

   <tns:refNumber>9999</tns:refNumber>

</tns:cancelOrderRequest>

DEBUG [http-8080-1] (AbstractLoggingInterceptor.java:160) - Response:

<tns:cancelOrderResponse xmlns:tns="...">

<tns:cancelled>true</tns:cancelled>

</tns:cancelOrderResponse>
```

To log Web-Service messages using `SoapEnvelopeLoggingInterceptor`, follow these steps:

1. Register `SoapEnvelopeLoggingInterceptor` in the server-side application context.

2. Open `log4j.properties` and set logging to debug the package `org.springframework.ws.soap.server.endpoint.interceptor`.

3. Build and deploy the project in the Maven-embedded Tomcat server. Run `mvn clean package tomcat:run` from the root of the project in a command-line window.

4. To test this, open a new command-line window, go to folder `LiveRestaurant_R-5.3-Client`, and run `mvn clean package exec:java`.

Here is the output from the server-side console:

```
DEBUG [http-8080-1] (AbstractLoggingInterceptor.java:160) - Request:

<SOAP-ENV:Envelope xmlns:SOAP-ENV=....">

<SOAP-ENV:Header/><SOAP-ENV:Body>

<tns:placeOrderRequest xmlns:tns="....">

   <tns:order>

     <tns:refNumber>9999</tns:refNumber>

     <tns:customer>

        .....

     </tns:customer>

     <tns:dateSubmitted>2008-09-29T05:49:45</tns:dateSubmitted>

     <tns:orderDate>2014-09-19T03:18:33</tns:orderDate>

     <tns:items>

        <tns:type>Snacks</tns:type>
```

```
        <tns:name>Pitza</tns:name>
        <tns:quantity>2</tns:quantity>
      </tns:items>
    </tns:order>
</tns:placeOrderRequest>
</SOAP-ENV:Body></SOAP-ENV:Envelope>
DEBUG [http-8080-1] (AbstractLoggingInterceptor.java:160) - Response:
 <SOAP-ENV:Envelope xmlns:SOAP-ENV=..."><SOAP-ENV:Header/><SOAP-ENV:Body>
<tns:placeOrderResponse xmlns:tns="...">
<tns:refNumber>order-John_Smith_1234</tns:refNumber>
</tns:placeOrderResponse>
</SOAP-ENV:Body></SOAP-ENV:Envelope>
DEBUG [http-8080-1] (AbstractLoggingInterceptor.java:160) - Request:
<SOAP-ENV:Envelope xmlns:SOAP-ENV="..."><SOAP-ENV:Header/><SOAP-ENV:Body>
<tns:cancelOrderRequest xmlns:tns="...">
   <tns:refNumber>9999</tns:refNumber>
</tns:cancelOrderRequest>
</SOAP-ENV:Body></SOAP-ENV:Envelope>
DEBUG [http-8080-1] (AbstractLoggingInterceptor.java:160) - Response:
 <SOAP-ENV:Envelope xmlns:SOAP-ENV="..."><SOAP-ENV:Header/><SOAP-
ENV:Body>
<tns:cancelOrderResponse xmlns:tns="...a">
<tns:cancelled>true</tns:cancelled></tns:cancelOrderResponse>
</SOAP-ENV:Body></SOAP-ENV:Envelope>
```

How it works...

`MessageDispatcherServlet` calls the Interceptor (if any) when the message is received as well as before calling the handler method in the endpoint and before sending back the response to the client.

Registering `PayloadLoggingInterceptor` inside `spring-ws-servlet.xml` only logs the message's payload:

```
    <sws:interceptors>
        <bean class="org.springframework.ws.server.endpoint.
interceptor.PayloadLoggingInterceptor"/>
    </sws:interceptors>
```

Similarly, registering `SoapEnvelopeLoggingInterceptor` inside `spring-ws-servlet.xml` logs the whole message's SOAP Envelope:

```
<sws:interceptors>
    <bean class="org.springframework.ws.soap.server.endpoint.
interceptor.SoapEnvelopeLoggingInterceptor"/>
    </sws:interceptors>
```

In both cases, the package name of these Interceptors should be set to debug for logging purpose:

```
….. . . . .
log4j.appender.R.layout=org.apache.log4j.PatternLayout
log4j.appender.R.layout.ConversionPattern=%p %t %c - %m%n

log4j.logger.org.springframework.ws.soap.server.endpoint.
interceptor=debug
log4j.logger.org.springframework.ws.server.endpoint.interceptor=debug
```

There's more...

Setting the `logRequest` and `logResponse` properties of `PayloadLoggingInterceptor` to true/false, enables/disables logging for request/response messages.

```
<bean class="org.springframework.ws.server.endpoint.interceptor.
PayloadLoggingInterceptor">
            <property name="logRequest" value="false" />
            <property name="logResponse" value="true" />

    </bean>
```

In addition to `logRequest` and `logResponse`, there is a `logFault` property for `SoapEnvelopeLoggingInterceptor` that setting these to true/false, enables/disables logging for request/response/fault messages:

```
….
        <bean class="org.springframework.ws.soap.server.endpoint.
interceptor.SoapEnvelopeLoggingInterceptor">
            <property name="logRequest" value="false" />
            <property name="logResponse" value="true" />
            <property name="logFault" value="true" ></property>
            </bean>
```

See also

▸ *Setting up an endpoint by annotating the payload-root in Chapter 1 , Building SOAP Web-Services.*

▸ *Logging both request and response SOAP Envelope using Log4j*

Using Eclipse IDE to debug a Spring-WS

The ability to debug an application during the development phase is one of the most important features of an IDE, as it helps the developers to find out the bugs easily and hence speeds up the development. For a server-side application, which is more complex, the debug ability is more important for defect-discovery. A remote debugger attached to an IDE like Eclipse can shorten the problem analysis time significantly and make the process more enjoyable.

Eclipse can be configured for debugging within a web/app server with both embedded and remote servers. This recipe explains how to debug a Spring-WS project as a web application from inside Eclipse, with an external remote Tomcat instance.

Getting ready

To get started:

1. Install Apache-Tomcat-6.0.14.
2. Download and install Eclipse IDE for Java EE Developers—Helios.

In this recipe, the project's name is `LiveRestaurant_R-5.4` (for the server-side WebService) and has the following Maven dependencies:

- `spring-ws-core-2.0.1.RELEASE.jar`
- `log4j-1.2.9.jar`

It also has `LiveRestaurant_R-5.4-Client` (for the client side) with the following Maven dependencies:

- `spring-ws-core-2.0.1.RELEASE.jar`
- `log4j-1.2.9.jar`

How to do it...

1. Modify the profile in user home (`/home/weblogic`) for Linux, or in the system variable in Windows for Tomcat.

   After installing Tomcat: On Linux > edit .profile>, add these lines for Tomcat:

   ```
   export TOMCAT_HOME=/opt2/apache-tomcat-6.0.14
   export PATH=$TOMCAT_HOME:$PATH
   ```

On Windows >edit system variable, set the system variable for Tomcat, as shown in the following screenshot:

2. In the `$TOMCAT_HOME/conf/tomcat-users.xml` file, set the role as `manager` and `username` and `password` as follows:

```xml
<?xml version='1.0' encoding='utf-8'?>
<tomcat-users>
  <role rolename="manager"/>
  <user username="tomcat" password="tomcat" roles="manager"/>
</tomcat-users>
```

3. In the `MAVEN_HOME/conf/settings.xml` file and if any `.m2/settings.xml` (`.m2` is maven repository folder), add a user login configuration named `tomcat` with the password `tomcat` as follows:

```xml
    <server>
  <id>myserver</id>

      <username>tomcat</username>
      <password>tomcat</password>
  </server>
```

4. Modify `debug.sh/debug.bat` `TOMCAT_HOME/bin/` at the end of the file:

   On Windows, modify `debug.bat`:

   ```
   set JPDA_TRANSPORT=dt_socket
   set JPDA_ADDRESS=8000
   call "%EXECUTABLE%" jpda start %CMD_LINE_ARGS%
   ```

   On Linux, modify `debug.sh`:

   ```
   export JPDA_ADDRESS=8000
   export JPDA_TRANSPORT=dt_socket
   exec "$PRGDIR"/"$EXECUTABLE" jpda start "$@"
   ```

5. Run Tomcat on Linux/Windows using `debug.sh/debug.bat` from `TOMCAT_HOME/bin/`.

6. Modify the `pom.xml` file of `LiveRestaurant_R-5.4`:

   ```
   <!--        <plugin>
           <groupId>org.codehaus.mojo</groupId>
           <artifactId>tomcat-maven-plugin</artifactId>
           <version>1.1</version>
       </plugin> -->

         <plugin>
           <groupId>org.codehaus.mojo</groupId>
               <artifactId>tomcat-maven-plugin</artifactId>
               <version>1.1</version>
       <configuration>
       <server>myserver</server>
       <path>/LiveRestaurant</path>
       </configuration>
       </plugin>
   ```

7. Import the project `LiveRestaurant_R-5.4` into Eclipse and set a break point in the class `com.packtpub.liverestaurant.service.endpoint.OrderEndpoint.java` in the method `handleCancelOrderRequest`.

8. Run `mvn clean package` from `LiveRestaurant_R-5.4` and then copy the WAR file into `tomcat/webapp` (the application will be deployed into Tomcat).

9. In Eclipse, set Maven installation: **Windows** | **Preferences** | **Maven** | **Installations**, click on the **Add** button, and set external Maven:

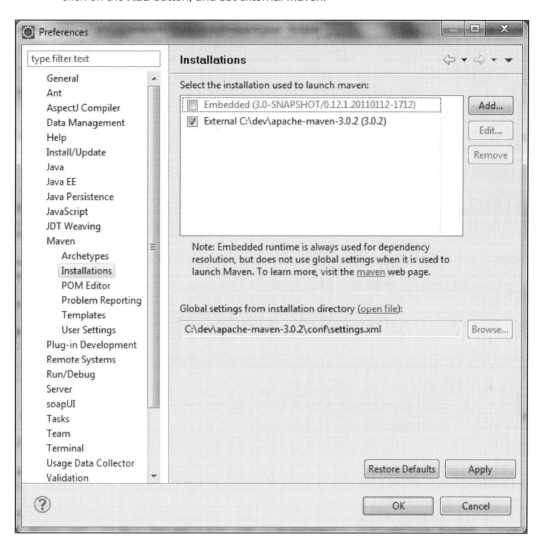

10. Open Eclipse. Right-click on **LiveRestaurant_R-5.4 | Debug as | Debug Configurations | Remote Java Application**, click on **New**, and then click on the **Debug** button:

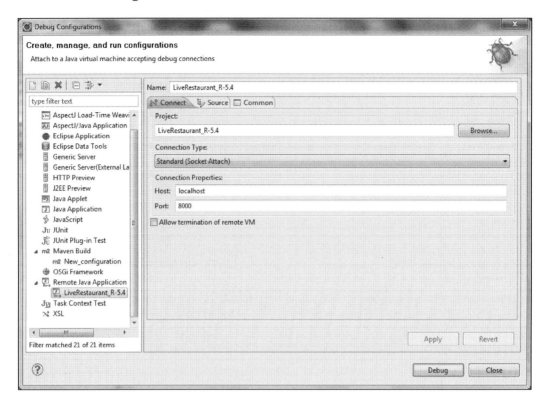

11. From the project `LiveRestaurant_R-5.4-Client`, run `mvn clean package`

The following is the output of this test:

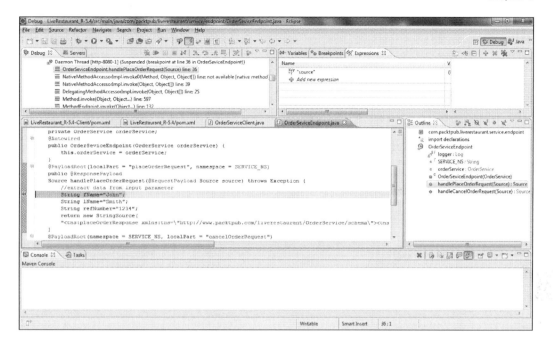

12. Now you can try different options for debugging the application, such as:

- ❑ Step Over (*F5*)
- ❑ Step Into (*F5*)
- ❑ Step Out (*F7*)
- ❑ Watch
- ❑ Inspect

How it works...

This recipe makes use of the **Java Debugger** (**JDB**) tool that helps find and fix bugs in the Java language programs both locally and on the server. JDB is part of the **Java Platform Debugging Architecture** (**JPDA**) that provides the infrastructure you need to build end-user debugger applications for the Java platform.

To use JDB in a Java EE application server or a servlet container, such as Tomcat, you must first launch it with debugging enabled and attach it to the server from the debugger through a JPDA port (the default port is 1044). At step 4, the JPDA port is set to 8000. Instead of the `run.bat/run.sh`, this recipe starts the server using the `debug.bat/debug.sh`, which means the server is started in debug mode.

The JDB parameters specify the way the debugger will operate. For instance, JPDA_TRANSPORT=dt_socket instructs the JVM that the debugger connections will be made through a socket, while the JPDA_ADDRESS=8000 parameter informs it that the port number will be 8000.

The Eclipse IDE is then attached to a JVM that accepts debugging connections. The project is set as a Remote Java Application inside Eclipse that listens to the same port, that is, 8000, for any debugging activity. In the next step, the break point will be set inside the service class that would be managed and redirected to the IDE by the JDB at runtime.

When the LiveRestaurant_R-5.4-Client project is executed as the client program of the service, the service class, OrderServiceEndpoint, is invoked and the break point is hit at the JVM, which is in the debug mode. It notifies the frontend as to where the JDI is implemented and which is the IDE in this case.

There's more...

Similar to the Tomcat server, you can attach any application server to any IDE such as Eclipse, Net Beans, or JDeveloper. The concepts are the same. However, the steps may vary for each application server and IDE.

 When debug mode is enabled, try to send the total time taken by a message in a given layer as one of the attributes in an XML message. This helps to troubleshoot in performance testing.

6
Marshalling and Object-XML Mapping (OXM)

In this chapter, we will cover the following topics:

- ▶ Marshalling with JAXB2
- ▶ Marshalling with XMLBeans
- ▶ Marshalling with JiBX
- ▶ Marshalling with XStream
- ▶ Marshalling with MooseXML
- ▶ Creating a custom marshaller using XPath for conditional XML parsing

Introduction

In Object/XML Mapping (OXM) terminology, marshalling (serializing) converts the object representation of data into the XML format and unmarshalling converts XML into the corresponding object.

Spring's OXM simplifies OXM operations by using rich aspects of the Spring framework. For example, the dependency injection feature can be used to instantiate different OXM technologies into objects to use them, and Spring can use annotations to map a class or a class's field to XML.

Spring-WS benefits from Spring's OXM for converting a Payload message into objects or vice versa. For example, set JAXB as the OXM framework using the following configuration in the application context:

```
<bean  class="org.springframework.ws.server.endpoint.adapter.
GenericMarshallingMethodEndpointAdapter">
   <constructor-arg ref="marshaller" />
</bean>

<bean id="marshaller" class="org.springframework.oxm.jaxb.
Jaxb2Marshaller">
    <property name="contextPath" value="com.packtpub.liverestaurant.
domain" />
</bean>
```

In addition, marshalling frameworks could be changed by changing the `marshaller` bean in the configuration file, while keeping the implementation of Web-Services unchanged.

There are many implementations of marshalling frameworks available. JAXB (Java Architecture for XML Binding), JiBX, XMLBeans, Castor, and so on are examples. For some of the OXM frameworks, tools are provided to convert schema into POJO classes and generate mapping data within these classes, or in a separate external configuration file.

This chapter provides recipes to illustrate the usage of different frameworks for Object/XML mapping.

For simplification, most of the recipes in this chapter use projects used in the *Integration testing using Spring-JUnit support* recipe, discussed in *Chapter 3, Testing and Monitoring Web-Services*, to set up a server and send and receive messages by client. However, in the recipe *Marshalling with XStream*, projects from the *Creating Web-Service client for WS-Addressing endpoint* recipe, discussed in *Chapter 2, Building Clients for SOAP Web-Services*, are used for the server and client sides.

Marshalling with JAXB2

Java Architecture for XML Binding (`http://jaxb.java.net/tutorial/`) is an API that allows developers to bind Java objects to XML representations. JAXB implementation is a part of the project Metro (`http://metro.java.net/`), which is a high-performance, extensible, and easy-to-use Web-Service stack. The main functionality of JAXB is to marshall Java objects into XML equivalents and unmarshall them back to the Java object (which can be called Object/XML binding or marshalling) as needed. JAXB is particularly useful when the specification is complex and changing.

JAXB provides many extensions and tools that make the Object/XML binding an easy job. Its annotation support allows developers to mark the O/X binding within the existing classes in order to generate the XML at runtime. Its Maven tool plugin (`maven-jaxb2-plugin`) enables the generation of Java classes from a given XML Schema file.

This recipe illustrates how to set up a marshalling end point and build a client program using JAXB2 as the marshalling library.

Getting ready

This recipe contains a server (`LiveRestaurant_R-6.1`) and a client (`LiveRestaurant_R-6.1-Client`) project.

`LiveRestaurant_R-6.1` has the following Maven dependencies:

- `spring-ws-core-2.0.1.RELEASE.jar`
- `log4j-1.2.9.jar`

`LiveRestaurant_R-6.1-Client` has the following Maven dependencies:

- `spring-ws-core-2.0.1.RELEASE.jar`
- `log4j-1.2.9.jar`
- `spring-test-3.0.5.RELEASE.jar`
- `junit-4.7.jar`

This recipe uses `maven-jaxb2-plugin` to generate classes from a schema.

How to do it...

1. Register the JAXB marshaller inside the server/client-side configuration file.
2. Configure `maven-jaxb2-plugin` inside server/client-side POM files.
3. Set up the server and run the client (it also generates classes from a schema):
   - Client project-root: `mvn clean package`
   - Server project-root: `mvn clean package tomcat:run`

The following is the client-side output:

```
- Received response ....
<ns2:cancelOrderResponse...>
<ns2:cancelled>true</ns2:cancelled>
</ns2:cancelOrderResponse>
...
```

```
for request ...
<ns2:cancelOrderRequest ...>
<ns2:refNumber>Ref-2010..</ns2:refNumber>
</ns2:cancelOrderRequest>
.....
....
- Received response ....
 <ns2:placeOrderResponse ...>
 <ns2:refNumber>Ref-2011-1..</ns2:refNumber>
 </ns2:placeOrderResponse>
 ...
 for request ...
 <ns2:placeOrderRequest ...>
 <ns2:order>.....
 </ns2:order></ns2:placeOrderRequest>
Tests run: 2, Failures: 0, Errors: 0, Skipped: 0, Time elapsed:
2.293 sec
```

How it works...

The main player in this marshalling business is
GenericMarshallingMethodEndpointAdapter, which utilizes a marshaller to perform
the Object/XML marshalling process. The marshaller used here is org.springframework.
oxm.jaxb.Jaxb2Marshaller, which performs O/X marshalling, utilizing the JAXB2
framework. If you examine the Java classes generated by the Maven plugin tool, you can see
the JAXB annotations such as @XmlType, @XmlRootElement, @XmlElement, and so on.
These annotations are the instructions to the JAXB engine that determines the structure of
the XML to be generated at runtime.

The following section in the POM files generates JAXB classes from the schema
(OrderService.xsd) in the folder src\main\webapp\WEB-INF (set by
schemaDirectory).

GeneratePackage set the package includes the generated classes and
generateDirectory set the folder host generatedPackage:

```
<plugins>
<plugin>
  <artifactId>maven-compiler-plugin</artifactId>
  <configuration>
    <source>1.6</source>
```

```
          <target>1.6</target>
        </configuration>
      </plugin>
      <plugin>
        <groupId>org.codehaus.mojo</groupId>
        <artifactId>tomcat-maven-plugin</artifactId>
        <version>1.1</version>
      </plugin>
      <plugin>
        <groupId>org.jvnet.jaxb2.maven2</groupId>
        <artifactId>maven-jaxb2-plugin</artifactId>
        <configuration>
          <schemaDirectory>src\main\webapp\WEB-INF</schemaDirectory>
          <schemaIncludes>
            <include>orderService.xsd</include>
          </schemaIncludes>
          <generatePackage>com.packtpub.liverestaurant.domain</
generatePackage>
        </configuration>
        <executions>
          <execution>
            <phase>generate-resources</phase>
            <goals>
              <goal>generate</goal>
            </goals>
          </execution>
        </executions>
      </plugin>

    </plugins>
```

The `OrderServiceEndPoint`, which is annotated as an `@Endpoint`, maps the Web-Service request, with a payload-root, `placeOrderRequest`, to the method `getOrder`, recognizing the annotation `@PayloadRoot`. While the marshaller marshalls the incoming XML into an instance of `PlaceOrderRequest`, the method `getOrder` returns `PlaceOrderResponse`. The same thing happens to the method `cancelOrder`:

```
    @PayloadRoot(localPart = "placeOrderRequest", namespace = SERVICE_
NS)
    public PlaceOrderResponse getOrder(
        PlaceOrderRequest placeOrderRequest) {

    PlaceOrderResponse response = JAXB_OBJECT_FACTORY
        .createPlaceOrderResponse();
    response.setRefNumber(orderService.placeOrder(placeOrderRequest
        .getOrder()));
```

```
      return response;
   }

   @PayloadRoot(localPart = "cancelOrderRequest", namespace = SERVICE_
NS)
   public CancelOrderResponse cancelOrder(
       CancelOrderRequest cancelOrderRequest) {

       CancelOrderResponse response = JAXB_OBJECT_FACTORY
           .createCancelOrderResponse();
       response.setCancelled(orderService.cancelOrder(cancelOrderRequest
           .getRefNumber()));
       return response;
   }
```

The following section in `spring-ws-servlet.xml` in the server sets the marshaller in the endpoint (`OrderServiceEndpoint`) to `Jaxb2Marshaller`. The setting `contextPath` in the `marshaller` bean registers all beans included in the package `com.packtpub.liverestaurant.domain` to be marshalled/unmarshalled by `Jaxb2Marshaller`:

```
    <bean   class="org.springframework.ws.server.endpoint.adapter.
GenericMarshallingMethodEndpointAdapter">
        <constructor-arg ref="marshaller" />
    </bean>

    <bean id="marshaller" class="org.springframework.oxm.jaxb.
Jaxb2Marshaller">
        <property name="contextPath" value="com.packtpub.liverestaurant.
domain" />
    </bean>
```

The same things happen in the client. The only difference is that the marshaller is set for `WebServiceTemplate`:

```
    <bean id="orderServiceTemplate" class="org.springframework.
ws.client.core.WebServiceTemplate">
        <constructor-arg ref="messageFactory" />
        <property name="marshaller" ref="orderServiceMarshaller"></
property>
        <property name="unmarshaller" ref="orderServiceMarshaller"></
property>
        …........</bean>

    <bean id="orderServiceMarshaller" class="org.springframework.oxm.
jaxb.Jaxb2Marshaller">
        <property name="contextPath" value="com.packtpub.
liverestaurant.domain" />
    </bean>
```

The `MessageDispatcherServlet`, with the help of the `Jaxb2Marshaller`, detects the O/X mapping annotations as well as the reflection and delegates the final marshalling process to the JAXB framework.

Marshalling with XMLBeans

XMLBeans (`http://xmlbeans.apache.org/`) is a technology for accessing XML by binding it to Java types. The library comes from the Apache Foundation and is a part of the Apache XML project. Known for its Java-friendliness, XMLBeans allows the developers to take advantage of the richness and features of XML and XML Schema and have these features mapped as naturally as possible to the equivalent Java language and typing constructs.

Two major features that make XMLBeans unique from other XML-Java binding options are:

- **Full XML Schema support**: XMLBeans fully supports (built-in) XML Schema and the corresponding Java classes provide constructs for all of the major functionality of XML Schema.

- **Full XML infoset fidelity**: While unmarshalling XML data, the full XML infoset is available to the developer. The XMLBeans provides many extensions and tools that make the Object/XML binding an easy job.

Getting ready

This recipe contains a server (`LiveRestaurant_R-6.2`) and a client (`LiveRestaurant_R-6.2-Client`) project.

`LiveRestaurant_R-6.2` has the following Maven dependencies:

- `spring-ws-core-2.0.1.RELEASE.jar`
- `log4j-1.2.9.jar`
- `xmlbeans-2.4.0.jar`

`LiveRestaurant_R-6.2-Client` has the following Maven dependencies:

- `spring-ws-core-2.0.1.RELEASE.jar`
- `log4j-1.2.9.jar`
- `xmlbeans-2.4.0.jar`
- `spring-test-3.0.5.RELEASE.jar`
- `junit-4.7.jar`

This recipe uses `xmlbeans-maven-plugin` to generate classes and bind files from a schema.

How to do it...

1. Register the XMLBean marshaller inside the server/client-side configuration file.

2. Configure `xmlbeans-maven-plugin` inside the server/client-side POM files.

3. Set up the server and run the client (it also generates classes from a schema):

4. Run the following commands:

   ❑ Server project-root: `mvn clean package tomcat:run`

   ❑ Client project-root: `mvn clean package`

The following is the client-side output:

```
[INFO]
[INFO]  --......
[INFO]
[INFO]  --- xmlbeans-maven-plugin:2.3.2:xmlbeans ....
[INFO]
[INFO]  .....
 Received response ...
 <sch:cancelOrderResponse ...>
 <sch:cancelled>true</sch:cancelled>
 </sch:cancelOr
derResponse>...
for request.....


......
- Received response ...
<sch:placeOrderResponse ...>
<sch:refNumber>Ref-2011-10-..</sch:refNumber>
</sch:placeOrderResponse>
...
for request ....
...
Tests run: 2, Failures: 0, Errors: 0, Skipped: 0, Time elapsed:
2.845 sec
```

How it works...

This recipe works exactly the same way as the first one, *Marshalling with JAXB2*, except that it is using a different marshaller, `XMLBeansMarshaller`. The scomp (Schema Compiler) tool used here generates the Java XMLBeans classes from the XML schema (`OrderService.xsd`). Besides the domain classes, it generates the classes representing the document root element, for example, `CancelOrderRequestDocument`. All the generated classes contain the `Factory` methods to instantiate them.

As can be noticed easily, the two main differences in the code are in `OrderServiceEndPoint` and `spring-ws-servlet.xml`. Unlike that of the previous recipe, the method `getOrder` returns an instance of `OrderResponseDocument` and it accepts `OrderRequestDocument` as an input argument. The same description is true about the method `cancelOrderDoc`:

```
  @PayloadRoot(localPart = "placeOrderRequest", namespace = SERVICE_
NS)
  public PlaceOrderResponseDocument getOrder(PlaceOrderRequestDocument
orderRequestDoc) {
    PlaceOrderResponseDocument orderResponseDocument
=PlaceOrderResponseDocument.Factory.newInstance();
    orderResponseDocument.addNewPlaceOrderResponse();
    orderResponseDocument.getPlaceOrderResponse().
setRefNumber(orderService.placeOrder(orderRequestDoc));
    return orderResponseDocument;
  }


  @PayloadRoot(localPart = "cancelOrderRequest", namespace = SERVICE_
NS)
  public CancelOrderResponseDocument placeCancelOrderDoc(
      CancelOrderRequestDocument cancelOrderRequestDoc) {

    CancelOrderResponseDocument cancelOrderResponseDocument=
CancelOrderResponseDocument.Factory.newInstance();
    cancelOrderResponseDocument.addNewCancelOrderResponse();
    cancelOrderResponseDocument.getCancelOrderResponse().
setCancelled(orderService.cancelOrder(cancelOrderRequestDoc.
getCancelOrderRequest().getRefNumber()));
    return cancelOrderResponseDocument;
  }
```

The marshaller used in `spring-ws-servlet.xml` is the `XMLBeansMarshaller`, which marshalls and unmarshalls between XML and Java using the XMLBeans library.

```
<bean      class="org.springframework.ws.server.endpoint.adapter.
GenericMarshallingMethodEndpointAdapter">
    <constructor-arg ref="marshaller" />
</bean>

<bean id="marshaller" class="org.springframework.oxm.xmlbeans.
XmlBeansMarshaller"/>
```

The contract between the `@Endpoint` class and `XMLBeansMarshaller` is that the `@PayloadRoot` methods should accept and return instances of `org.apache.xmlbeans.XmlObject`. Then it dynamically finds out the corresponding classes, and using their `Factory` methods, it creates instances and binds to the XML at runtime.

Same as the previous recipe, a plugin in the POM files generates `XMLBean` classes from the schema (`OrderService.xsd`) in the folder `src\main\webapp\WEB-INF` (set by `schemaDirectory`):

```
<plugin>
        <groupId>org.codehaus.mojo</groupId>
        <artifactId>xmlbeans-maven-plugin</artifactId>
        <version>2.3.2</version>
        <executions>
          <execution>
            <goals>
            <goal>xmlbeans</goal>
            </goals>
          </execution>
        </executions>
        <inherited>true</inherited>
        <configuration>
            <schemaDirectory>src/main/webapp/WEB-INF/</schemaDirectory>
        </configuration>
      </plugin>
```

The `MessageDispatcherServlet`, with the help of `XMLBeansMarshaller`, detects the O/X mapping annotations and the marshaller configuration, and delegates the final marshalling process to the XMLBeans framework.

There's more...

XMLBeans come with a set of built-in powerful tools to add much more functionality than merely marshalling between XML and Java. The recipe utilized just one such tool, `scomp`, the Schema Compiler that generates Java classes/compressed JAR files out of an XML Schema (`.xsd`) file. A few other tools that may be helpful are:

- `inst2xsd` (Instance to Schema Tool): Generates XML schema from XML instance files.

- `scopy` (Schema Copier): Copies the XML schema at the specified URL to the specified file

- `validate` (Instance Validator): Validates an instance against a schema

- `xpretty` (XML Pretty Printer): Pretty prints the specified XML to the console

- `xsd2inst` (Schema to Instance Tool): Prints an XML instance from the specified global element using the specified schema

- `xsdtree` (Schema Type Hierarchy Printer): Prints an inheritance hierarchy of the types defined in a schema

- `xmlbean Ant task`: Compiles a set of XSD and/or WSDL files into XMLBeans types

    The `xmlbean Ant task` is a nice way to automate the generation of Java classes in integration with your build scripts.

Marshalling with JiBX

JiBX (`http://jibx.sourceforge.net/`) is another tool and library for binding XML data to Java objects. JiBX is known to be the best for speed performance as well as flexibility. However, it has also been known for its complexity of binding, especially for a complex data model.

From version 1.2 onwards, JiBX has addressed these bottlenecks and now it has easy-to-use marshalling tools and framework. Using the JiBX tool, a user can generate a schema from existing Java code or generate Java code and binding files from an existing schema. JiBX library at runtime binds Java classes to XML data and vice versa.

In this recipe, the JiBX tool (`jibx-maven-plugin`) is used to generate POJO classes and bind a definition file from an existing schema, and then a Web-Service client and server will be built upon the JiBX libraries.

Getting ready

This recipe contains a server (`LiveRestaurant_R-6.3`) and a client (`LiveRestaurant_R-6.3-Client`) project.

`LiveRestaurant_R-6.3` has the following Maven dependencies:

- `spring-ws-core-2.0.1.RELEASE.jar`
- `log4j-1.2.9.jar`
- `spring-expression-3.0.5.RELEASE.jar`
- `jibx-run-1.2.3.jar`
- `jibx-extras-1.2.3.jar`
- `jibx-ws-0.9.1.jar`

`LiveRestaurant_R-6.3-Client` has the following Maven dependencies:

- `spring-ws-core-2.0.1.RELEASE.jar`
- `log4j-1.2.9.jar`
- `spring-expression-3.0.5.RELEASE.jar`
- `jibx-run-1.2.3.jar`
- `jibx-extras-1.2.3.jar`
- `jibx-ws-0.9.1.jar`
- `spring-test-3.0.5.RELEASE.jar`
- `junit-4.7.jar`

How to do it...

1. Register the JiBX marshaller inside the server/client-side configuration file.
2. Configure `xmlbeans-maven-plugin` inside the server/client-side POM files.
3. Set up the server and run the client (it also generates classes from a schema):
   - Server project root: `mvn clean package` (it also generates classes from schema). Copy the WAR file into the Tomcat `webapp` folder and run Tomcat (apache-tomcat-6.0.18)
   - Client project-root: `mvn clean package` (it also generate classes from schema)

The following is the client-side output:

```
. . . . . . .
. . . . . . . . .
[INFO] --- jibx-maven-plugin:1.2.3:bind (compile-binding) @
LiveRestaurant_Client ---
[INFO] Running JiBX binding compiler (single-module mode) on 1
binding file(s)
[INFO]
[INFO] ....
 Received response ...
 <tns:cancelOrderResponse ...>
 <tns:cancelled>true</tns:cancelled></tns:cancelOrderResponse>
 ...
 for request ...
 <tns:cancelOrderRequest ...><tns:refNumber>12345</tns:refNumber>
 </tns:cancelOrderRequest>
 . . . . .


Tests run: 2, Failures: 0, Errors: 0, Skipped: 0
```

How it works...

As explained in the previous recipe, the application context for the server/client uses a customized marshaller (`org.springframework.oxm.jibx.JibxMarshaller`) to perform the Object/XML marshalling process. This Spring marshaller uses JiBX libraries for binding and marshalling processes. The following POM plugin setting (goal: `schema-codegen`) generates POJO classes from a schema (`OrderService.xsd`) into a package (`com.packtpub.liverestaurant.domain`) and it also generates a binding file (goal: `bind`):

```xml
<plugin>
      <groupId>org.jibx</groupId>
      <artifactId>jibx-maven-plugin</artifactId>
      <version>1.2.3</version>
      <executions>
        <execution>
          <id>generate-java-code-from-schema</id>
          <goals>
            <goal>schema-codegen</goal>
          </goals>
        </execution>
        <execution>
```

```
            <id>compile-binding</id>
            <goals>
              <goal>bind</goal>
            </goals>
          </execution>
        </executions>
        <configuration>
          <schemaLocation>src/main/webapp/WEB-INF</schemaLocation>
          <includeSchemas>
            <includeSchema>orderService.xsd</includeSchema>
          </includeSchemas>
          <options>
            <package>com.packtpub.liverestaurant.domain</package>
          </options>
        </configuration>
      </plugin>
```

As described in the earlier recipes, this setting in the server and client Spring context file causes the client and server to use a customized marshaller (`JibxMarshaller`) for marshalling/unmarshalling POJO classes to/from XML data:

```
<bean id="marshaller"
    class="org.springframework.oxm.jibx.JibxMarshaller">
    <property name="targetClass"      value="com.packtpub.
liverestaurant.domain.CancelOrderRequest" />
  </bean>
```

`JibxMarshaller` uses mapping the `binding.xml` file for the marshalling task. As it is shown in the mapping file, JiBX supports for simple data binding (`<value style="element" name="fName"...`) as well as complex data binding known as structure (`<structure map-as="tns:Address"...`). This feature makes JiBX the most flexibility-binding framework among the others.

```
…..
<mapping abstract="true" type-name="tns:Customer" class="com.packtpub.
liverestaurant.domain.Customer">
    <structure map-as="tns:Address" get-method="getAddressPrimary"
set-method="setAddressPrimary" name="addressPrimary"/>
    <structure map-as="tns:Address" get-method="getAddressSecondary"
set-method="setAddressSecondary" name="addressSecondary"/>
    <structure map-as="tns:Name" get-method="getName" set-
method="setName" name="name"/>
  </mapping>
  <mapping abstract="true" type-name="tns:Name" class="com.packtpub.
liverestaurant.domain.Name">
```

```
        <value style="element" name="fName" get-method="getFName" set-
    method="setFName"/>
        <value style="element" name="mName" get-method="getMName" set-
    method="setMName"/>
        <value style="element" name="lName" get-method="getLName" set-
    method="setLName"/>
    </mapping>
    …..
```

The `OrderServiceEndPoint`, which is annotated as an `@Endpoint`, is almost the same as earlier recipes (*Marshalling with JAXB2*); only the implementation is slightly different.

```
    @PayloadRoot(localPart = "cancelOrderRequest", namespace = SERVICE_
    NS)
    public
    CancelOrderResponse handleCancelOrderRequest(CancelOrderRequest
    cancelOrderRequest) throws Exception {
        CancelOrderResponse cancelOrderResponse=new CancelOrderResponse();
        cancelOrderResponse.setCancelled(orderService.
    cancelOrder(cancelOrderRequest.getRefNumber()));
        return cancelOrderResponse;
    }

    @PayloadRoot(localPart = "placeOrderRequest", namespace = SERVICE_
    NS)
    public
    PlaceOrderResponse handleCancelOrderRequest(PlaceOrderRequest
    placeOrderRequest) throws Exception {
        PlaceOrderResponse orderResponse=new PlaceOrderResponse();
        orderResponse.setRefNumber(orderService.
    placeOrder(placeOrderRequest.getOrder()));
        return orderResponse;
    }
    …..
```

There's more...

JiBX provides more flexibility by letting users create their own customized marshaller. It means instead of using a generated binding file, a custom binding file and custom marshaller classes to marshal any kind of data structure inside an XML document.

Marshalling with XStream

XStream (`http://xstream.codehaus.org/`) is a simple library for marshalling/unmarshalling objects to/from XML data. The following major features make this library different from others:

- Doesn't need a mapping file

- Doesn't need to change POJO (no need for a setter/getter and default constructor)

- Alternative output format (JSON support and morphing)

- XStream does not have a tool to generate a schema from existing Java code or to generate Java code from an existing schema

- XStream does not support namespaces

In this recipe, a Web-Service client and server are created that use XStream libraries as a marshaller. Since XStream is not using any namespace in XML data (payload), a web address style of Web-Service is set up.

Getting ready

This recipe contains a server (`LiveRestaurant_R-6.4`) and a client (`LiveRestaurant_R-6.4-Client`) project.

`LiveRestaurant_R-6.4` has the following Maven dependencies:

- `spring-ws-core-2.0.1.RELEASE.jar`

- `log4j-1.2.9.jar`

- `spring-expression-3.0.5.RELEASE.jar`

- `jxstream-1.3.1.jar`

`LiveRestaurant_R-6.4-Client` has the following Maven dependencies:

- `spring-ws-core-2.0.1.RELEASE.jar`

- `log4j-1.2.9.jar`

- `jxstream-1.3.1.jar`

- `spring-test-3.0.5.RELEASE.jar`

- `junit-4.7.jar`

How to do it...

1. Register XStream marshaller inside the server/client-side configuration file.

2. Annotate domain classes with the `Xstream` annotation.

3. Set up the server and run the client:

   ❑ Server project-root: `mvn clean package tomcat:run`

   ❑ Client project-root: `mvn clean package`

   The following is the client-side output:

   ```
   Received response

    ..

    ...
   <wsa:Action>http://www.packtpub.com/OrderService/
   CancelOrdReqResponse</wsa:Action>

   <wsa:MessageID>urn:uuid:a4b681ff-00f5-429e-9ab9-f9054e796a89</
   wsa:MessageID>

    ....
   <cancelOrderResponse><cancelled>true</cancelled>

   </cancelOrderResponse></SOAP-ENV:Body>

    ....

    ...


   <wsa:Action>http://www.packtpub.com/OrderService/CancelOrdReq</
   wsa:Action>

   ...<cancelOrderRequest><refNumber>12345</refNumber></
   cancelOrderRequest>
   ```

How it works...

As explained in the previous recipe, the application context for server/client uses a customized marshaller (`org.springframework.oxm.xstream.XStreamMarshaller`) to perform the Object/XML marshalling process. This spring marshaller uses XStream libraries for the marshalling process. The beans that are input and output parameters of the method in the endpoint (`OrderServiceEndPoint.java`) have to be registered in XstreamMarshaller. `autodetectAnnotations` is set to detect annotating within POJO classes:

```
        <bean id="marshaller" class="org.springframework.oxm.
xstream.XStreamMarshaller">
        <property name="autodetectAnnotations" value="true"/>
```

```
            <property name="aliases">
                <map>
                    <entry key="placeOrderResponse" value="com.packtpub.
                      liverestaurant.domain.PlaceOrderResponse" />
                    <entry key="placeOrderRequest" value="com.packtpub.
                      liverestaurant.domain.PlaceOrderRequest" />
                    <entry key="cancelOrderRequest" value="com.packtpub.
                      liverestaurant.domain.CancelOrderRequest" />
                    <entry key="cancelOrderResponse" value="com.packtpub.
                      liverestaurant.domain.CancelOrderResponse" />
                </map>
            </property></bean>
```

`XStreamMarshaller` uses annotation in POJO classes (instead of the binding file) for the marshalling task. `@XstreamAlias` tells the marshaller that this class will be serialized/deserialized as 'name'. There is other annotation that is optional, but it tells marshaller how to serialize/deserialize the field of a class (`@XStreamAsAttribute`, `@XStreamImplicit`, and so on).

```
    import com.thoughtworks.xstream.annotations.XStreamAlias;
    @XStreamAlias("name")
    public class Name
    {
        private String FName;
        private String MName;
        private String LName;
```

The `OrderServiceEndPoint`, which is annotated as an `@Endpoint` is the same as JiBX recipes that " the endpoint method's input and and return parameters are POJO (`PlaceOrderResponse`, `PlaceOrderRequest`, and so on) that is mapped to the schema. The only difference is that the endpoint uses web addressing for method mapping:

```
    @Action("http://www.packtpub.com/OrderService/CancelOrdReq")
    public
    CancelOrderResponse handleCancelOrderRequest(CancelOrderRequest
    cancelOrderRequest) throws Exception {
        CancelOrderResponse cancelOrderResponse=new CancelOrderResponse();
        cancelOrderResponse.setCancelled(orderService.
    cancelOrder(cancelOrderRequest.getRefNumber()));
            return cancelOrderResponse;
    }
    @Action("http://www.packtpub.com/OrderService/OrdReq")
    public
    PlaceOrderResponse handlePancelOrderRequest(PlaceOrderRequest
    placeOrderRequest) throws Exception {
        PlaceOrderResponse orderResponse=new PlaceOrderResponse();
```

```
    orderResponse.setRefNumber(orderService.
placeOrder(placeOrderRequest.getOrder()));
    return orderResponse;
  }
```

Marshalling with MooseXML

Moose (`http://quigley.com/moose/`) is a lightweight framework for marshalling/unmarshalling objects to/from XML data. The schema generator of Moose is what makes this framework different from others. Moose is able to generate schema directly from annotated POJO classes. This is what is required to develop contract-last Web-Service development.

In this recipe, Moose is used to marshall/unmarshall objects to/from XML data in the Web-Service client and server communications.

Getting ready

This recipe contains a server (`LiveRestaurant_R-6.5`) and a client (`LiveRestaurant_R-6.5-Client`) project.

`LiveRestaurant_R-6.5` has the following Maven dependencies:

- `log4j-1.2.9.jar`
- `moose-0.4.6.jar`

`LiveRestaurant_R-6.5-Client` has the following Maven dependencies:

- `log4j-1.2.9.jar`
- `moose-0.4.6.jar`
- `spring-test-3.0.5.RELEASE.jar`
- `junit-4.7.jar`

How to do it...

1. Register Moose marshaller inside the server/client-side configuration file.
2. Annotate domain classes with the `@XML` annotation.
3. Set up the server and run the client:
   - Server project-root: `mvn clean package tomcat:run`
   - Client project-root: `mvn clean package`

The following is the client-side output:

```
 Received response ...
<ns:cancelOrderResponse...>
<ns:cancelled>true</ns:cancelled>
</ns:cancelOrderResponse>
...
for request ...
<ns:cancelOrderRequest...>
<ns:refNumber>12345</ns:refNumber>
</ns:cancelOrderRequest>
.......
```

How it works...

As explained in the previous recipe, the application context for the server/client uses a customized marshaller (`com.quigley.moose.spring.MooseMarshaller`) to perform the Object/XML marshalling process. A mapping provider is injected into this custom marshaller. The mapping provider is to set the namespace and `xmlPrefix` when the object is being marshalled into XML and when the XML data is being converted into an object. The mapping provider gets the list of registered POJO classes from `com.quigley.moose.mapping.provider.annotation.StaticClassesProvider`:

```
<bean class="org.springframework.ws.server.endpoint.adapter.
GenericMarshallingMethodEndpointAdapter">
        <constructor-arg ref="mooseMarshaller"/>
    </bean>
    <bean class="org.springframework.ws.server.endpoint.mapping.
PayloadRootAnnotationMethodEndpointMapping"/>

    <bean id="mooseMarshaller" class="com.quigley.moose.spring.
MooseMarshaller">
        <property name="mappingProvider"><ref
bean="mooseMappingProvider"/></property>
    </bean>

    <bean id="mooseMappingProvider"
        class="com.quigley.moose.mapping.provider.annotation.
AnnotationMappingProvider">
        <property name="xmlNamespace">
                <value>http://www.liverestaurant.com/OrderService/
schema</value></property>
```

```
        <property name="xmlPrefix"><value>ns</value></property>
        <property name="annotatedClassesProvider"><ref
          bean="mooseClassesProvider"/></property>
    </bean>

    <bean id="mooseClassesProvider"
        class="com.quigley.moose.mapping.provider.annotation.
          StaticClassesProvider">
        <property name="classes">
            <list>
                <value>com.packtpub.liverestaurant.domain.
                  CancelOrderRequest</value>
                <value>com.packtpub.liverestaurant.domain.
                  CancelOrderResponse</value>
                <value>com.packtpub.liverestaurant.domain.Order
                </value>
                 <value>com.packtpub.liverestaurant.domain.Address
                </value>
                 <value>com.packtpub.liverestaurant.domain.Customer
                </value>
                 <value>com.packtpub.liverestaurant.domain.FoodItem
                </value>
                 <value>com.packtpub.liverestaurant.domain.Name
                </value>
                <value>com.packtpub.liverestaurant.domain.
                  PlaceOrderResponse</value>
                <value>com.packtpub.liverestaurant.domain.
                  PlaceOrderRequest</value>

            </list>
        </property>
    </bean>
```

MooseMarshaller, just like XStreamMarshaller, uses annotation in POJO classes for marshalling tasks. @XML tells the marshaller that this class will be serialized/deserialized as 'name'. @XMLField is the tag that should be placed for each class field.

```
    @XML(name="cancelOrderRequest")
    public class CancelOrderRequest
    {
      @XMLField(name="refNumber")
        private String refNumber;

        /**        * Get the 'refNumber' element value.
```

```
     *
     * @return value
     */
    public String getRefNumber() {
        return refNumber;
    }

    /**
     * Set the 'refNumber' element value.
     *
     * @param refNumber
     */
    public void setRefNumber(String refNumber) {
        this.refNumber = refNumber;
    }
}
```

The `OrderServiceEndPoint`, which is annotated as an `@Endpoint`, is the same as the JiBX recipes that passing and return parameter is mapped POJO (`PlaceOrderResponse`, `PlaceOrderRequest`, and so on) that is mapped to the schema.

```
    @PayloadRoot(localPart = "cancelOrderRequest", namespace =
SERVICE_NS)
    public
    CancelOrderResponse handleCancelOrderRequest(CancelOrderRequest
cancelOrderRequest) throws Exception {
        CancelOrderResponse cancelOrderResponse=new CancelOrderResponse();
        cancelOrderResponse.setCancelled(orderService.
cancelOrder(cancelOrderRequest.getRefNumber()));
        return cancelOrderResponse;
    }


    @PayloadRoot(localPart = "placeOrderRequest", namespace = SERVICE_
NS)
    public
    PlaceOrderResponse handleCancelOrderRequest(PlaceOrderRequest
placeOrderRequest) throws Exception {
        PlaceOrderResponse orderResponse=new PlaceOrderResponse();
        orderResponse.setRefNumber(orderService.
placeOrder(placeOrderRequest.getOrder()));

        return orderResponse;
    }
```

Creating a custom marshaller using XPath for conditional XML parsing

Using the existing marshaller frameworks (JAXB, JiBX, and so on) is always the easiest way to handle a marshalling task. However, eventually you may need to write a customized marshaller. For example, you may get an XML input data, which is in a different format from the one that is generally is being used by the recognized marshaller.

Spring lets you define a customized marshaller and inject it into your endpoint marshaller as existing marshaller frameworks. In this recipe, the client sends/receives this data to/from the server in the following format:

```
<ns:placeOrderRequest xmlns:ns="http://www.packtpub.com/
LiveRestaurant/OrderService/schema">
  <ns:order refNumber="12345"  customerfName="fName"
customerlName="lName" customerTel="12345" dateSubmitted="2008-09-29
05:49:45" orderDate="2008-09-29 05:40:45">
    <ns:item type="SNACKS" name="Snacks" quantity="1.0"/>
     <ns:item type="DESSERTS" name="Desserts" quantity="1.0"/>
  </ns:order>
</ns:placeOrderRequest>
<ns:placeOrderResponse xmlns:ns="http://www.packtpub.com/
LiveRestaurant/OrderService/schema" refNumber="1234"/>
```

However, the XML input that can be mapped to/from the server's POJO is as follows:

```
<ns:placeOrderRequest xmlns:ns="http://www.packtpub.com/
LiveRestaurant/OrderService/schema">
<ns:order>
<ns:refNumber>12345</ns:refNumber>
<ns:customerfName>fName</ns:customerfName>
<ns:customerlName>lName</ns:customerlName>
<ns:customerTel>12345</ns:customerTel>
<ns:dateSubmitted>2008-09-29 05:49:45</ns:dateSubmitted>
<ns:orderDate>2008-09-29 05:40:45</ns:orderDate>
<ns:items>
<FoodItem>
<ns:type>SNACKS</ns:type>
<ns:name>Snack</ns:name>
<ns:quantity>1.0</ns:quantity>
</FoodItem>
<FoodItem>
<ns:type>COFEE</ns:type>
<ns:name>Cofee</ns:name>
```

```
<ns:quantity>1.0</ns:quantity>
</FoodItem>
</ns:items>
</ns:order>
</ns:placeOrderRequest>

<ns:placeOrderResponse xmlns:ns="http://www.packtpub.com/
LiveRestaurant/OrderService/schema" />
<ns:refNumber>1234</ns:refNumber>
</ns:placeOrderResponse>
```

In this recipe, a customized marshaller is used to map the incoming XML data to the server's POJO and the unmarshalling server response to the client format.

Getting ready

This recipe contains a server (`LiveRestaurant_R-6.6`) and a client (`LiveRestaurant_R-6.6-Client`) project.

`LiveRestaurant_R-6.6` has the following Maven dependencies:

- `spring-ws-core-2.0.1.RELEASE.jar`
- `log4j-1.2.9.jar`
- `dom4j-1.6.1.jar`

`LiveRestaurant_R-6.6-Client` has the following Maven dependencies:

- `spring-ws-core-2.0.1.RELEASE.jar`
- `log4j-1.2.9.jar`
- `spring-test-3.0.5.RELEASE.jar`
- `junit-4.7.jar`
- `dom4j-1.6.1.jar`

How to do it...

1. Create a customized marshaller class.
2. Register the new marshaller inside the server-side configuration file.
3. Set up the server and run the client:

    ❑ Server project-root: `mvn clean package tomcat:run`
    ❑ Client project-root: `mvn clean package`

The following is the server-side output:

Received request ..

...

<ns:placeOrderRequest ...>

  <ns:order customerTel="12345" customerfName="fName"
customerlName="lName" dateSubmitted="2008-09-29 05:49:45"
orderDate="2008-09-29 05:40:45" refNumber="12345">

    <ns:item name="Snacks" quantity="1.0" type="SNACKS"/>

     <ns:item name="Desserts" quantity="1.0" type="DESSERTS"/>

  </ns:order>

</ns:placeOrderRequest>

....

Sent response...

<ns:placeOrderResponse xmlns:ns="http://www.packtpub.com/
LiveRestaurant/OrderService/schema" refNumber="12345"/>

How it works...

To be able to work as an endpoint marshaller, a customized marshaller
(ServerCustomMarshaller) should implement Marshaller and Unmarshaller
interfaces. The method supports is for verifying if the POJO class is registered with this
marshaller. The value of the registered POJO comes from the Spring context file.

The method unmarshal will be called by the endpoint when the Web-Service calls the endpoint
method (handleOrderRequest) to build the passing parameter (PlaceOrderRequest). In
the unmarshal method, DOM4j and XPath are used to fetch a value from the incoming XML
data. These values will populate the POJO class and return it back to the endpoint. The method
marshal will be called by the endpoint when the endpoint method (handleOrderRequest)
returns the response (PlaceOrderResponse). Inside the marshal method,
XMLStreamWriter is used to return the desired format XML data to the client:

```
public boolean supports(Class<?> arg0) {
    return  registeredClassNames.contains(arg0.getSimpleName())  ;  }
@Override
  public Object unmarshal(Source source) throws IOException,
     XmlMappingException {
    PlaceOrderRequest placeOrderRequest=new PlaceOrderRequest();
    Order order=new Order();

          try {
            DOMSource in = (DOMSource)source;
```

```
                    org.dom4j.Document document = org.dom4j.
DocumentHelper.parseText( xmlToString(source) );
                    org.dom4j.Element orderRequestElem=document.
getRootElement();
                    org.dom4j.Node orderNode=orderRequestElem.
selectSingleNode("//ns:order");
                order.setRefNumber(orderNode.valueOf("@refNumber"));
                ….
                placeOrderRequest.setOrder(order);
                List orderItems=orderNode.selectNodes("//ns:order/
ns:item");

…..

                }


  @Override
  public void marshal(Object bean, Result result)    throws
IOException,
  XmlMappingException
        {
    XMLStreamWriter writer=null;
          PlaceOrderResponse placeOrderResponse=(PlaceOrderResponse)
bean;
      try {
        DOMResult out = (DOMResult)result;
         writer = XMLOutputFactory.newInstance().
createXMLStreamWriter(out);
        writer.writeStartElement("ns", "placeOrderResponse", "http://
www.packtpub.com/LiveRestaurant/OrderService/schema");
        writer.writeAttribute( "refNumber", placeOrderResponse.
getRefNumber());
        writer.writeEndElement();
        writer.flush();
          } catch (Exception e) {
        e.printStackTrace();
      } finally{
        try{writer.close();}catch (Exception e) {}
      }
   } …....
```

As explained in the previous recipe, the application context for the server/client uses this customized marshaller (`ServerCustomMarshaller`) to perform the Object/XML marshalling process. `RegisteredClassNames` is for registering the POJO classes eligible for marshalling/unmarshalling via the customized marshaller (`ServerCustomMarshaller`).

```
<bean id="customMarshaller"
class="com.packtpub.liverestaurant.marshaller.
ServerCustomMarshaller">

    <property name="registeredClassNames">
  <list>
     <value>PlaceOrderRequest</value>
     <value>PlaceOrderResponse</value>
  </list>
</property>

</bean>
```

The `OrderEndPoint`, which is annotated as an `@Endpoint`, is the same as the JiBX recipes that the endpoint method's input and and return parameters are POJO (`PlaceOrderResponse`, `PlaceOrderRequest`, and so on) that is mapped to the schema.

7
Securing SOAP Web-Services using XWSS Library

In this chapter, we will cover:

▶ Authenticating a Web-Service call using the username token with a plain/digested password

▶ Authenticating a Web-Service call using Spring security to authenticate a username token with a plain/digested password

▶ Authenticating a Web-Service call using the JAAS service to authenticate a username token

▶ Preparing pair and symmetric keystores

▶ Securing SOAP messages using a digital signature

▶ Authenticating a Web-Service call using X509 certificate

▶ Encrypting/decrypting SOAP messages

Introduction

WS-Security (WSS), published by OASIS, is an extension to SOAP to provide security-standard features to a Web-Service. XML and Web-Services Security (XWSS) is SUN's implementation of WSS, which is included in the Java Web-Services Developer Pack (WSDP).

XWSS is a form of message-level security in which security data is included within a SOAP message/attachment and allows security information to be transmitted with messages or attachments. For instance, while signing a message, a security token will be added to the message that is generated from the encryption of a part of the message for a specific receiver. When a sender sends this message, this token remains in the encrypted form and travels along with the message. When a receiver gets this message, the token can be decrypted only if he/she has the specific key for decryption. So if within transmission of this message, any non-authorized receiver (who doesn't have the specific key) gets this message, he/she cannot decrypt the token (this token will be used to check if the original message is altered). The originality of the message verification can be done by the regeneration of the token at the receiver's end (from the incoming message) and by comparing it with the incoming token that came along with the message.

An `EndpointInterceptor`, as the name suggests, intercepts the request and performs some action prior to invoking the endpoint. `EndpointInterceptors` are called before calling the appropriate endpoint to perform several processing aspects such as logging, validating, security, and so on. In earlier chapters, `SoapEnvelopeLoggingInterceptor`, `PayloadLoggingInterceptor`, and `PayloadValidatingInterceptor` were explained for logging and validation purposes.

In this chapter, and the next one, `SecurityInterceptors` will be explained.

Spring-WS `XwsSecurityInterceptor` is an `EndpointInterceptor` for performing security operations on a request message before calling the endpoint. This interceptor, which is based on XWSS, requires a policy configuration file to operate. Here is a sample of the policy configuration file that can include several security requirements:

```
<xwss:SecurityConfiguration ...>
    <xwss:RequireTimestamp .../>
    <xwss:RequireUsernameToken ...../>
    ........
</xwss:SecurityConfiguration>
```

The security interceptor uses this configuration to find what security information to expect from incoming SOAP messages (on the receiver side), and what information is to be added to outgoing messages (on the sender side).

In addition, this interceptor needs one or more `callBackHandlers` for security operations such as authentication, signing outgoing messages, verifying the signature of incoming messages, decryption, and encryption. These `callBackHandlers` need to be registered in the application context file:

```
<sws:interceptors>

  <bean
    class="...XwsSecurityInterceptor">
    <property name="policyConfiguration" value="/WEB-INF/
```

```
securityPolicy.xml" />
    <property name="callbackHandlers">
      <list>
        <ref bean="callbackHandler1" />
            <ref bean="callbackHandler2" />
              …...........
      </list>
    </property>
  </bean>
</sws:interceptors>
<bean id="callbackHandler1"
  class=".....SimplePasswordValidationCallbackHandler">
  <property name="users">
    <props>
      <prop key="admin">secret</prop>
      <prop key="clinetUser">pass</prop>
    </props>
  </property>
</bean>
….......
```

This chapter presents how to apply Spring-WS XWSS to different security operations. In every recipe's project, the client applies a security operation by adding or modifying data in the outgoing message and sends it to the server. The server receives the message, extracts security information, and proceeds with the message if the security information matches the expected requirement; otherwise it returns a *fault* message back to the client.

For simplification, most of the recipes in this chapter use the projects used in the *Integration testing using Spring-JUnit support* recipe, discussed in *Chapter 3*, *Testing and Monitoring Web Services*, to set up a server and send and receive messages by client. However, in the last recipe, projects from the *Creating Web-Service client for WS-Addressing endpoint* recipe, discussed in *Chapter 2*, *Building Clients for SOAP Web Services*, are used for the server and client side.

Authenticating a Web-Service call using plain/digested username token

Authentication simply means checking whether callers of a service are who they claim to be. One way of checking the authentication of a caller is to check the password.

XWSS provides APIs to get the usernames and passwords from incoming SOAP messages and compare them with what is defined in the configuration file. This goal will be accomplished by defining policy files for the sender and the receiver of the messages that on the sender side, client includes a username token in outgoing messages, and on the receiver side, the server expects to receive this username token along with the incoming messages for authentication.

Transmitting a plain password makes a SOAP message unsecured. XWSS provides the configuration setting in the policy file to include a digest of passwords (a hash generated from the password text by a specific algorithm) inside the sender message. On the server side, the server compares the digested password included in the incoming message with the digested password calculated from what is set in the configuration file (see the property users within the `callbackHandler` bean inside `spring-ws-servlet.xml`) using the same algorithms on the sender side. This recipe shows how to authenticate a Web-Service call using the username token with a plain/digest password. This recipe contains two cases. In the first case, the password will be transmitted in plain text format. However, in the second case, by changing the policy file configuration, the password will be transmitted in the digest format.

Getting ready

In this recipe, the project's name is `LiveRestaurant_R-7.1` (for the server-side Web-Service) and has the following Maven dependencies:

- `spring-ws-security-2.0.1.RELEASE.jar`
- `spring-expression-3.0.5.RELEASE.jar`
- `log4j-1.2.9.jar`

`LiveRestaurant_R-7.1-Client` (for the client-side Web-Service) has the following Maven dependencies:

- `spring-ws-security-2.0.1.RELEASE.jar`
- `spring-ws-test-2.0.0.RELEASE.jar`
- `spring-expression-3.0.5.RELEASE.jar`
- `log4j-1.2.9.jar`
- `junit-4.7.jar`

How to do it...

The following steps implement authentication using a username token with a plain password:

1. Register the security interceptor (`XwsSecurityInterceptor`) and callbackHandler (`SimplePasswordValidationCallbackHandler`) in the application context file (`applicationContext.xml`) of `LiveRestaurant_R-7.1-Client`.

2. Add the security policy file (`securityPolicy.xml`) for `LiveRestaurant_R-7.1-Client`.

3. Register the security interceptor (`XwsSecurityInterceptor`) and `callbackHandler` (`SimplePasswordValidationCallbackHandler`) in the application context file (`spring-ws-servlet.xml`) of `LiveRestaurant_R-7.1`.

4. Add the security policy file (`securityPolicy.xml`) for `LiveRestaurant_R-7.1`.

5. Run the following command from `Liverestaurant_R-7.1`:

```
mvn clean package tomcat:run
```

6. Run the following command from `Liverestaurant_R-7.1-Client`:

```
mvn clean package
```

The following is the client-side output (note the password's tag `wsse:Password` `...#PasswordText`) within the underlined section:

```
INFO: ==== Sending Message Start ====
<SOAP-ENV:Envelope ...">
<SOAP-ENV:Header>
<wsse:Security ..>
<wsu:Timestamp ...>
<wsu:Created>2011-11-06T07:19:16.225Z</wsu:Created>
<wsu:Expires>2011-11-06T07:24:16.225Z</wsu:Expires>
</wsu:Timestamp>
<wsse:UsernameToken .....>
<wsse:Username>clinetUser</wsse:Username>
<wsse:Password ...#PasswordText">****</wsse:Password>
<wsse:Nonce ..#Base64Binary">...</wsse:Nonce>
<wsu:Created>2011-11-06T07:19:16.272Z</wsu:Created>
</wsse:UsernameToken>
</wsse:Security>
</SOAP-ENV:Header>
<SOAP-ENV:Body>
<tns:placeOrderRequest xmlns:tns="...">
.....
.......
</tns:placeOrderRequest>
</SOAP-ENV:Body>
</SOAP-ENV:Envelope>
==== Sending Message End  ====
```

```
.....
INFO: ==== Received Message Start ====
......
<SOAP-ENV:Envelope....">
<SOAP-ENV:Header/>
<SOAP-ENV:Body>
<tns:placeOrderResponse .....>
<tns:refNumber>order-John_Smith_1234</tns:refNumber>
</tns:placeOrderResponse>
</SOAP-ENV:Body>
</SOAP-ENV:Envelope>
==== Received Message End  ====
```

The following steps implement authentication using the username token with the digest password:

1. Modify the security policy file (`securityPolicy.xml`) of `Liverestaurant_R-7.1` to get the digest password from the incoming message.

2. Modify the security policy file (`securityPolicy.xml`) of `Liverestaurant_R-7.1-Client` to send the digest password.

3. Run the following command from `Liverestaurant_R-7.1`:

   ```
   mvn clean package tomcat:run
   ```

4. Run the following command from `Liverestaurant_R-7.1-Client`:

   ```
   mvn clean package
   ```

   The following is the client-side output (note the password's tag `wsse:Password ...#PasswordDigest`) within the underlined section:

   ```
   Nov 6, 2011 12:19:25 PM com.sun.xml.wss.impl.filter.DumpFilter
   process
   INFO: ==== Sending Message Start ====
   ..
   <SOAP-ENV:Envelope .../">
   <SOAP-ENV:Header>
   <wsse:Security ...>
   <wsu:Timestamp ..>
   <wsu:Created>2011-11-06T08:19:25.515Z</wsu:Created>
   <wsu:Expires>2011-11-06T08:24:25.515Z</wsu:Expires>
   </wsu:Timestamp>
   ```

```
<wsse:UsernameToken...>
<wsse:Username>clinetUser</wsse:Username>
<wsse:Password ...#PasswordDigest">****</wsse:Password>
<wsse:Nonce ...#Base64Binary">...</wsse:Nonce>
<wsu:Created>2011-11-06T08:19:25.562Z</wsu:Created>
</wsse:UsernameToken>
</wsse:Security>
</SOAP-ENV:Header>
<SOAP-ENV:Body>
<tns:placeOrderRequest..">
......
</tns:placeOrderRequest>
</SOAP-ENV:Body>
</SOAP-ENV:Envelope>
==== Sending Message End  ====
........
INFO: ==== Received Message Start ====
<?xml version="1.0" ...>
<SOAP-ENV:Header/>
<SOAP-ENV:Body>
<tns:placeOrderResponse ...>
<tns:refNumber>order-John_Smith_1234</tns:refNumber>
</tns:placeOrderResponse>
</SOAP-ENV:Body>
</SOAP-ENV:Envelope>
==== Received Message End  ====
```

How it works...

The `Liverestaurant_R-7.1` project is a server-side Web-Service that requires its client to send a message along with the username token and password. The `Liverestaurant_R-7.1-Client` project is a client-side test project that sends a message to the server along with the username token and password.

On the server side, `XwsSecurityInterceptor` forces the server to apply
the policy inside `securityPolicy.xml` for all incoming messages and uses
`SimplePasswordValidationCallbackHandler` to compare incoming messages
username/password with includes username/password in the server configuration file
(see the property users within the `callbackHandler` bean):

```xml
<sws:interceptors>
...
    <bean     class="org.springframework.ws.soap.security.xwss.
XwsSecurityInterceptor">
        <property name="policyConfiguration" value="/WEB-INF/
securityPolicy.xml" />
        <property name="callbackHandlers">
          <list>
            <ref bean="callbackHandler" />
          </list>
        </property>
    </bean>
  </sws:interceptors>
  <bean id="callbackHandler"
    class="org.springframework.ws.soap.security.xwss.callback.
SimplePasswordValidationCallbackHandler">
      <property name="users">
        <props>
          <prop key="admin">secret</prop>
          <prop key="clinetUser">pass</prop>
        </props>
      </property>
  </bean>
```

In the `securityPolicy.xml` file, `<xwss:RequireUsernameToken
passwordDigestRequired="false" nonceRequired="true"/>` requires
that the incoming messages have username tokens with non-encrypted passwords.
`useNonce="true"` indicates that each incoming message will have a random number
that is not equal to the previous message:

```xml
<xwss:SecurityConfiguration dumpMessages="true" xmlns:xwss="http://
java.sun.com/xml/ns/xwss/config">
    <xwss:RequireTimestamp maxClockSkew="60"
timestampFreshnessLimit="300"/>
  <xwss:RequireUsernameToken passwordDigestRequired="false"
nonceRequired="true"/>
</xwss:SecurityConfiguration>
```

On the client side, `XwsSecurityInterceptor` forces the client to apply the policy inside `securityPolicy.xml` for all outgoing messages:

```xml
<bean id="webServiceTemplate" class="org.springframework.ws.client.
core.WebServiceTemplate">
         ....
    <property name="interceptors">

      <list>
        <ref local="xwsSecurityInterceptor" />
      </list>
    </property>
  </bean>
    <bean id="xwsSecurityInterceptor"
      class="org.springframework.ws.soap.security.xwss.
XwsSecurityInterceptor">
        <property name="policyConfiguration" value="/securityPolicy.
xml"/>
        <property name="callbackHandlers">
               <list>
                   <ref bean="callbackHandler"/>
                </list>
        </property>
  </bean>
    <bean id="callbackHandler" class="org.springframework.ws.soap.
security.xwss.callback.SimplePasswordValidationCallbackHandler"/>
```

In the `securityPolicy.xml` file, `<xwss:UsernameToken name="clinetUser" password="pass"    digestPassword="false" useNonce="true"/>` includes the username token with the password for all outgoing messages:

```xml
<xwss:SecurityConfiguration dumpMessages="true" xmlns:xwss="http://
java.sun.com/xml/ns/xwss/config">
    <xwss:Timestamp />

        <xwss:UsernameToken name="clinetUser" password="pass"
digestPassword="false" useNonce="true"/> ...
</xwss:SecurityConfiguration>
```

Here, `useNonce="true"` indicates that each request will be sent out with a new random number for each message (`Nonce` helps to protect against hijacking of the username token).

In the case of authentication using a username token with a plain password, since `digestPassword="false"` is in both the client- and server-side policy files, you see in the output result that the message sent by the client has a username and a plain text password included in the username token:

```
<wsse:UsernameToken ….>
<wsse:Username>clinetUser</wsse:Username>
<wsse:Password ..>****</wsse:Password>
...
</wsse:UsernameToken>
```

However, in the second case of authenticating using the digest username token with the digest password, since `digestPassword="true"` is in both the client- and server-side policy files, the digest of the password is included in the username token:

```
<wsse:UsernameToken ….>
<wsse:Username>clinetUser</wsse:Username>
<wsse:Password ...#PasswordDigest">****</wsse:Password>
...
</wsse:UsernameToken>
```

In this case, the server compares the incoming SOAP message digest password with the calculated digested password from inside `spring-ws-servlet.xml`. In this way, communication will be more secure by comparison with the first case in which the password was transmitted in plain text (the plain text password could be easily extracted from the SOAP messages. However, using an SSL connection can secure such a communication).

See also...

The recipes *Authenticating a Web-Service call using Spring security to authenticate a username token with plain/digested password, Authenticating a Web-Service call using JAAS service to authenticate a username token,* and *Authenticating a Web-Service call using X509 certificate,* discussed in this chapter.

Authenticating a Web-Service call using Spring security to authenticate a username token with a plain/digested password

Here we make use of the same authentication method used in the first recipe. The only difference here is that the Spring Security framework is used for authentication. Since the Spring Security framework is beyond the scope of this book, it is not described here. However, you can read more about it in the Spring Security reference documentation (`http://www.springsource.org/security`).

Same as the first recipe of this chapter, this recipe also contains two cases. In the first case, the password will be transmitted in plain text format. In the second case, by changing the policy file's configuration, the password will be transmitted in digest format.

Getting ready

In this recipe, the project's name is `LiveRestaurant_R-7.2` (for the server-side Web-Service) and has the following Maven dependencies:

- `spring-ws-security-2.0.1.RELEASE.jar`
- `spring-expression-3.0.5.RELEASE.jar`
- `log4j-1.2.9.jar`

`LiveRestaurant_R-7.2-Client` (for the client-side Web-Service) has the following Maven dependencies:

- `spring-ws-security-2.0.1.RELEASE.jar`
- `spring-ws-test-2.0.0.RELEASE.jar`
- `spring-expression-3.0.5.RELEASE.jar`
- `log4j-1.2.9.jar`
- `junit-4.7.jar`

How to do it...

In this recipe, all the steps are the same as in the previous recipe, *Authenticating a Web-Service call using username token with plain/digested password*, except the server-side application context file (`spring-ws.servlet.xml`) callback handler changes and uses the DAO layer to fetch data:

The following steps implement authentication of a Web-Service call using Spring Security to authenticate a username token with a plain password:

1. Register the security interceptor (`XwsSecurityInterceptor`) and callbackHandler(`SpringPlainTextPasswordValidationCallbackHandler`) in the application context file (`spring-ws-servlet.xml`) of `LiveRestaurant_R-7.2`.

2. Add the DAO layer classes to fetch data.

3. Run the following command from `Liverestaurant_R-7.2`:

   `mvn clean package tomcat:run`

4. Run the following command from `Liverestaurant_R-7.2-Client`:

   `mvn clean package`

The following is the client-side output:

```
Nov 6, 2011 1:42:37 PM com.sun.xml.wss.impl.filter.DumpFilter
process
INFO: ==== Sending Message Start ====
...
<SOAP-ENV:Envelope ....>
<SOAP-ENV:Header>
<wsse:Security ...>
<wsu:Timestamp....>
<wsu:Created>2011-11-06T09:42:37.391Z</wsu:Created>
<wsu:Expires>2011-11-06T09:47:37.391Z</wsu:Expires>
</wsu:Timestamp>
<wsse:UsernameToken ...>
<wsse:Username>clinetUser</wsse:Username>
<wsse:Password ...#PasswordText">****</wsse:Password>
<wsse:Nonce ...#Base64Binary">...</wsse:Nonce>
<wsu:Created>2011-11-06T09:42:37.442Z</wsu:Created>
</wsse:UsernameToken>
</wsse:Security>
</SOAP-ENV:Header>
<SOAP-ENV:Body>
<tns:placeOrderRequest ...>
......
</tns:placeOrderRequest>
</SOAP-ENV:Body>
</SOAP-ENV:Envelope>
==== Sending Message End  ====


INFO: ==== Received Message Start ====
<SOAP-ENV:Envelope ...">
<SOAP-ENV:Header/>
<SOAP-ENV:Body>
<tns:placeOrderResponse ....">
<tns:refNumber>order-John_Smith_1234</tns:refNumber>
</tns:placeOrderResponse>
</SOAP-ENV:Body>
</SOAP-ENV:Envelope>
==== Received Message End  ====
```

The following steps implement authentication of a Web-Service call using Spring Security to authenticate a digested username token:

1. Modify `springSecurityHandler` to `SpringDigestPasswordValidationCallbackHandler` in the server application context file (`spring-ws-servlet.xml`).

2. Modify the security policy file (`securityPolicy.xml`) in both the server side and client side to digest the password.

3. Run the following command from `Liverestaurant_R-7.2`:

   ```
   mvn clean package tomcat:run
   ```

4. Run the following command from `Liverestaurant_R-7.2-Client`:

   ```
   mvn clean package
   ```

   The following is the client-side output:

   ```
   Nov 6, 2011 2:04:37 PM com.sun.xml.wss.impl.filter.DumpFilter
   process
   INFO: ==== Sending Message Start ====
   ...
   <SOAP-ENV:Envelope ...>
   <SOAP-ENV:Header>
   <wsse:Security ...>
   <wsu:Timestamp ...>
   <wsu:Created>2011-11-06T10:04:36.622Z</wsu:Created>
   <wsu:Expires>2011-11-06T10:09:36.622Z</wsu:Expires>
   </wsu:Timestamp>
   <wsse:UsernameToken...>
   <wsse:Username>clinetUser</wsse:Username>
   <wsse:Password #PasswordDigest">****</wsse:Password>
   <wsse:Nonce #Base64Binary">...</wsse:Nonce>
   <wsu:Created>2011-11-06T10:04:36.683Z</wsu:Created>
   </wsse:UsernameToken>
   </wsse:Security>
   </SOAP-ENV:Header>
   <SOAP-ENV:Body>
   <tns:placeOrderRequest xmlns:tns="http://www.packtpub.com/
   liverestaurant/OrderService/schema">
   ......
   ```

```
        </tns:placeOrderRequest>
      </SOAP-ENV:Body>
    </SOAP-ENV:Envelope>
    ==== Sending Message End  ====


    Nov 6, 2011 2:04:37 PM com.sun.xml.wss.impl.filter.DumpFilter
    process
    INFO: ==== Received Message Start ====
    <?xml version="1.0" encoding="UTF-8"?><SOAP-ENV:Envelope
    xmlns:SOAP-ENV="http://schemas.xmlsoap.org/soap/envelope/">
    <SOAP-ENV:Header/>
    <SOAP-ENV:Body>
    <tns:placeOrderResponse...">
    <tns:refNumber>order-John_Smith_1234</tns:refNumber>
    </tns:placeOrderResponse>
    </SOAP-ENV:Body>
    </SOAP-ENV:Envelope>
    ==== Received Message End ====
```

How it works...

In the `Liverestaurant_R-7.2` project, every aspect of security for the client and server is almost the same as `Liverestaurant_R-7.1` that we made use of in the recipe *Authenticating a Web-Service call using username with plain/digested password token*, except for validating the user on the server side. A Spring Security class is responsible for validating the user and password by comparison with the incoming message's username/password with fetched data from a DAO layer (instead of hardcoding the username/password in `spring-ws-servlet.xml`). In addition, other data (such as `permissions`, `isAccountBlocked`, `isAccountExpired`, and so on) related to the successfully authenticated user (that matches the username and password) can be fetched from the DAO layer and returned for the authorization task or for any validation about the expiry date of the account and to check if the account is blocked or not.

In the first case, `CallbackHandler` `SpringPlainTextPasswordValidationCallbackHandler` compares the plain password included in the incoming SOAP message with the plain password that is fetched from the DAO layer.

```
    <sws:interceptors>
      <bean
        ....
```

```xml
<bean class="org.springframework.ws.soap.security.xwss.
XwsSecurityInterceptor">
        <property name="policyConfiguration" value="/WEB-INF/
securityPolicy.xml"/>
        <property name="callbackHandlers">
            <list>
                <ref bean="springSecurityHandler"/>
            </list>
        </property>
    </bean>
</sws:interceptors>



    <bean id="springSecurityHandler"
    class="org.springframework.ws.soap.security.xwss.callback.
SpringPlainTextPasswordValidationCallbackHandler">
    <property name="authenticationManager"
ref="authenticationManager"/>
  </bean>
    ....
```

In the second test, however, `CallbackHandler` is
`SpringDigestPasswordValidationCallbackHandler` that compares the digest
password included in the incoming SOAP message with the digest of the password that is
fetched from the DAO layer.

```xml
<bean id="springSecurityHandler"
    class="org.springframework.ws.soap.security.xwss.callback.
SpringDigestPasswordValidationCallbackHandler">
    <property name="userDetailsService" ref="userDetailsService"/>
</bean>
```

`springSecurityHandler` uses `MyUserDetailService.java`, which should implement
Spring's `UserDetailService` to get the username from the provider and internally fetch
all information for that user from a DAO layer (for example, password, roles, is expired, and
so on).

```java
public class MyUserDetailService implements UserDetailsService {

  @Override
  public UserDetails loadUserByUsername(String username)
      throws UsernameNotFoundException, DataAccessException {

    return getUserDataFromDao(username);
  }
```

```
    private MyUserDetail getUserDataFromDao(String username) {

      /**
       *Real scenario: find user data from a DAO layer  by userName,
       * if this user name found, populate  MyUserDetail with its
    data(username, password,Role, ....).
       */
      MyUserDetail mydetail=new MyUserDetail(username,"pass",true,true,
    true,true);
      mydetail.getAuthorities().add(new GrantedAuthorityImpl("ROLE_
    GENERAL_OPERATOR"));

      return mydetail;

    }
```

This service finally returns the populated data in `MyUserDetails.java`, which should implement Spring's `UserDetails`.

```
    public class MyUserDetail implements UserDetails {

      private String password;
      private String userName;
      private boolean isAccountNonExpired;
      private boolean isAccountNonLocked;
      private boolean isCredentialsNonExpired;
      private boolean isEnabled;

      public static  Collection<GrantedAuthority> authority =
           new ArrayList<GrantedAuthority>();

      public MyUserDetail( String userName, String password,boolean
    isAccountNonExpired, boolean isAccountNonlocked,boolean
    isCredentialsNonExpired, boolean isEnabled){
        this.userName=userName;
        this.password=password;
        this.isAccountNonExpired=isAccountNonExpired;
        this.isAccountNonLocked=isAccountNonlocked;
        this.isCredentialsNonExpired=isCredentialsNonExpired;
        this.isEnabled=isEnabled;
      }
      @Override
      public Collection<GrantedAuthority> getAuthorities() {
        return authority;
      }

      …..
    }
```

Now, if the `UserDetails` data matches the incoming message's username/password, it returns a response; otherwise, it returns a SOAP fault message.

Same as the 7.1 project, setting `digestPassword` to `true`/`false` in `securityPolicy.xml` on the server/client-side causes the password to be transmitted in plain text or in the digested format.

 In real time, we never configure the plain password option. This is a good option for hackers to enable and disable. We never need such an option in real time. Passwords are always transmitted in encrypted format, irrespective of any type of system or application configuration.

See also...

The recipes *Authenticating a Web-Service call using Spring security to authenticate a username token with plain/digested password, Authenticating a Web-Service call using JAAS service to authenticate a username token*, and *Authenticating a Web-Service call using X509 certificate*, discussed in this chapter.

Authenticating a Web-Service call using a JAAS service to authenticate a username token

We make use of the same authentication task with a plain username token, as used in the first recipe. The only difference here is that Java Authentication and Authorization Service (JAAS) is used here for authentication and authorization. Since the JAAS framework is beyond the scope of this book, it is not described here. However, you can read more about JAAS in the reference documentation (`http://download.oracle.com/javase/6/docs/technotes/guides/security/jaas/JAASRefGuide.html`).

`JaasPlainTextPasswordValidationCallbackHandler` from the `xwss` package is the API that calls the `Login` module that is configured inside the JAAS configuration file.

Getting ready

In this recipe, the project's name is `LiveRestaurant_R-7.3` (for the server-side Web-Service) and has the following Maven dependencies:

- `spring-ws-security-2.0.1.RELEASE.jar`
- `spring-expression-3.0.5.RELEASE.jar`
- `log4j-1.2.9.jar`

`LiveRestaurant_R-7.3-Client` (for the client-side Web-Service) has the following Maven dependencies:

- `spring-ws-security-2.0.1.RELEASE.jar`
- `spring-ws-test-2.0.0.RELEASE.jar`
- `spring-expression-3.0.5.RELEASE.jar`
- `log4j-1.2.9.jar`
- `junit-4.7.jar`

How to do it...

In this recipe, all the steps are the same as in the previous recipe, *Authenticating a Web-Service call using username token with plain/digested password*, except that the server-side application context file (`spring-ws.servlet.xml`) callback handler changes and uses the JAAS framework as an authentication and authorization service:

1. Register the JAAS `callbackHandler` (`JaasPlainTextPasswordValidationCallbackHandler`) in the server-side application context file (`spring-ws.servlet.xml`).

2. Add the JAAS framework's required classes (`RdbmsPrincipal`, `RdbmsCredential`, and `RdbmsPlainTextLoginModule`) and the configuration file (`jaas.config`).

3. Run the following command from `Liverestaurant_R-7.3`:

   ```
   mvn clean package tomcat:run  -Djava.security.auth.login.
   config="src/main/resources/jaas.config"
   ```

4. Run the following command from `Liverestaurant_R-7.3-Client`:

   ```
   mvn clean package
   ```

   The following is the client-side output:

   ```
   INFO: ==== Sending Message Start ====
   ....
   <SOAP-ENV:Envelope ....">
   <SOAP-ENV:Header>
   <wsse:Security ....>
   <wsu:Timestamp ...>
   <wsu:Created>2011-11-06T11:59:09.712Z</wsu:Created>
   <wsu:Expires>2011-11-06T12:04:09.712Z</wsu:Expires>
   </wsu:Timestamp>
   <wsse:UsernameToken ...>
   ```

```
<wsse:Username>clinetUser</wsse:Username>

<wsse:Password ....#PasswordText">****</wsse:Password>

<wsse:Nonce ...0#Base64Binary">...</wsse:Nonce>

<wsu:Created>2011-11-06T11:59:09.774Z</wsu:Created>

</wsse:UsernameToken>

</wsse:Security>

</SOAP-ENV:Header>

<SOAP-ENV:Body>

<tns:placeOrderRequest...>

.....

</tns:placeOrderRequest>

</SOAP-ENV:Body>

</SOAP-ENV:Envelope>

==== Sending Message End  ====

...

INFO: ==== Received Message Start ====

...

<SOAP-ENV:Envelope ...>

<SOAP-ENV:Header>

<wsse:Security ...>

<wsu:Timestamp ....>

<wsu:Created>2011-11-06T11:59:11.630Z</wsu:Created>

<wsu:Expires>2011-11-06T12:04:11.630Z</wsu:Expires>

</wsu:Timestamp>

</wsse:Security>

</SOAP-ENV:Header>

<SOAP-ENV:Body>

<tns:placeOrderResponse ...>

<tns:refNumber>order-John_Smith_1234</tns:refNumber>

</tns:placeOrderResponse>

</SOAP-ENV:Body>

</SOAP-ENV:Envelope>

==== Received Message End  ====
```

How it works...

In the `Liverestaurant_R-7.3` project, everything about security for the client and server is almost the same as the `Liverestaurant_R-7.1` project that we used in the recipe *Authenticating a Web-Service call using a username with plain/digested password token* except for validating a user on the server side. A JAAS framework is responsible for validating the user and password by comparison of incoming message's username/password with fetched data from a data source (database here).

The client sends a request SOAP message that contains the username token in plain text. The server receives this message and uses the JAAS framework to compare an incoming message username/password with what is fetched from the DAO layer by JAAS. If it matches, it returns a normal response; otherwise, it returns a failure message.

In `spring-ws-servlet.xml`, `JaasPlainTextPasswordValidationCallbackHandler` is registered as a callback handler that uses `RdbmsPlainText` as a pluggable JAAS login module for the username/password authentication:

```
<sws:interceptors>
    ......
    <bean class="org.springframework.ws.soap.security.xwss.
XwsSecurityInterceptor">
      <property name="policyConfiguration" value="/WEB-INF/
securityPolicy.xml" />
      <property name="callbackHandlers">
        <list>
          <ref bean="jaasValidationHandler" />
        </list>
      </property>
    </bean>
  </sws:interceptors>
  <bean id="jaasValidationHandler"  class="org.
springframework.ws.soap.security.xwss.callback.jaas.
JaasPlainTextPasswordValidationCallbackHandler">
      <property name="loginContextName" value="RdbmsPlainText" />
  </bean>
```

When the server side is being run using `mvn -Djava.security.auth.login.config="src/main/resources/jaas.config"`, it uses the `jaas.config` file to locate the JAAS login module (`RdbmsPlainTextLoginModule`) that is registered in the server-side application context as `RdbmsPlainText`:

```
RdbmsPlainText {
    com.packtpub.liverestaurant.service.security.
RdbmsPlainTextLoginModule Required;
};
```

The `login` method from `RdbmsPlainTextLoginModule.java` will be called to fetch the user password and credentials from the DAO layer. If the fetched password matches the incoming message's password, then it sets credential and returns `true`; otherwise, it throws an exception that leads the server to send back a fault message to the client:

```java
public class RdbmsPlainTextLoginModule implements LoginModule {
    private Subject subject;
    private CallbackHandler callbackHandler;
    private boolean success;
    private List<RdbmsPrincipal> principals = new
ArrayList<RdbmsPrincipal>();
    private List<RdbmsCredential> credentials = new
ArrayList<RdbmsCredential>();

  @Override
  public void initialize(Subject subject, CallbackHandler
callbackHandler,
      Map<String, ?> sharedState, Map<String, ?> options) {
      …..
  }
  @Override
  public boolean login() throws LoginException {
    ….. .
  }
    private List<String> getAllPermission(String username) {
      ….. .
  }
  private boolean  authenticate(String username,String password)
      {
….

      }

  public boolean commit() throws LoginException {
    ….. .
    }
  @Override
  public boolean logout() throws LoginException {
    ….. .
  }
}
```

In important applications, even the username is encrypted. This provides more security and competitors can't guess which users are coming from which location using ISP-level filtering. Hackers guess or track a username and send duplicate requests to load servers with unnecessary data. In this recipe, since the password is being transmitted in plain-text format, using an SSL connection is recommended. Spring-WS also supports JaasCertificateValidationCallbackHandler, which uses a certificate for authentication. This handler is not used here. However, you can find out more about it at the following URL:

http://static.springsource.org/spring-ws/site/apidocs/
org/springframework/ws/soap/security/xwss/callback/
jaas/JaasCertificateValidationCallbackHandler.html.

See also...

The recipes *Authenticating a Web-Service call using username token with plain/digested password*, *Authenticating a Web-Service call using Spring Security to authenticate a username token with plain/digested password*, and *Authenticating a Web-Service call using X509 certificate*, discussed in this chapter.

Preparing pair and symmetric keystores

In order to add more security measures for a Web-Service call, we do need some extra operations such as signing and verifying the signature of Web-Service messages, encryption/decryption, and authentication using certificates. XWSS provides these operations using keystores. The java.security.KeyStore class provides a memory container for the cryptographic keys and certificates. This class can include three types of entries:

▶ Private key entry, which contains a private key and a public key certificate (note that the public key here is wrapped within the X.509 certificate—a combination of a private key and a public key certificate is known as a **key pair**)

▶ Secret key entry, which contains a symmetric key

▶ Trusted certificate entry, which contains a trusted certificate (this certificate is the other party certificate, imported as a trusted certificate, which means the owner keys store the public key within the other party's certificate that belongs to the third party)

A keystore may contain one to many entries. Aliases in a keystore are for distinguishing entries from one another. The private key and certificate are referred to by one alias while any other trusted certificates or secret key entries are referred to by different individual aliases within a keystore.

Earlier in this chapter, authentication of a Web-Service call using the username token was presented. A Web-Service call can be authenticated by using a certificate. Later in this chapter, in the recipe *Authenticating a Web-Service call using X509 certificate*, authentication using a certificate will be presented. In addition, these certificates can be used for certificate validation, signature verification, and encryption.

Java keytool is a tool that generates and stores the keys and certificates in a keystore file. This keystore is protected by a keystore password. In addition, there is another password that protects the private key.

In this recipe, using the keytool to generate keystores with symmetric key entries, private key entries (private keys and public key certificates), and trusted certificate entries is presented. These keys will be used later in this chapter and in *Chapter 8, Securing SOAP Web-Services using WSS4J Library*, for signing and verifying the signature of Web-Service messages, encryption/decryption, and authentication using certificates.

Getting ready

Installation of Java, as described in the first recipe.

How to do it...

To generate a keystore with a secret key entry with the alias *symmetric*, run the following command (this keystore is to be used later for symmetric encryption/decryption):

```
keytool -genseckey -alias 'symmetric' -keyalg 'DESede' -keystore
symmetricStore.jks -storepass 'symmetricPassword' -keypass 'keyPassword'
-storetype "JCEKS"
```

To generate a keystore with a private key entry or a key pair (that contains private key and public certificate pairs) follow next steps:

1. To generate a receiver (server side here) keystore, run the following command and follow the command prompt:

   ```
   keytool -genkey -alias server -keyalg RSA -keystore serverStore.
   jks -validity 3653

   Enter keystore password:serverPassword

   Re-enter new password:serverPassword

   What is your first and last name?
      [Unknown]:  MyFirstName MyLastName
   What is the name of your organizational unit?
      [Unknown]:  Software
   ```

```
What is the name of your organization?
  [Unknown]:  MyCompany
What is the name of your City or Locality?
  [Unknown]:  MyCity
What is the name of your State or Province?
  [Unknown]:  MyProvince
What is the two-letter country code for this unit?
  [Unknown]:  ME
Is CN=MyFirstName MyLastName, OU=Software, O=MyCompany, L=MyCity,
ST=MyProvince, C=ME correct?
  [no]:  yes
Enter key password for <server>
        (RETURN if same as keystore password):serPkPassword
Re-enter new password:serPkPassword
```

2. To generate a sender (client side here) keystore, run the following command and follow the command prompt:

```
keytool -genkey -alias client  -keyalg RSA -keystore clientStore.
jks -validity 3653
Enter keystore password:clientPassword
Re-enter new password:clientPassword


What is your first and last name?
  [Unknown]:  MyFirstName MyLastName
What is the name of your organizational unit?
  [Unknown]:  Software
What is the name of your organization?
  [Unknown]:  MyCompany
What is the name of your City or Locality?
  [Unknown]:  MyCity
What is the name of your State or Province?
  [Unknown]:  MyProvince
What is the two-letter country code for this unit?
  [Unknown]:  ME
Is CN=MyFirstName MyLastName, OU=Software, O=MyCompany, L=MyCity,
ST=MyProvince, C=ME correct?
  [no]:  yes
```

```
Enter key password for <server>
        (RETURN if same as keystore password):cliPkPassword
Re-enter new password:cliPkPassword
```

3. To see the generated private key entry in a keystore, run the following command (please note `privateKeyEntry` within the underlined text):

```
keytool -list -v -keystore serverStore.jks -storepass
serverPassword

Keystore type: JKS

Keystore provider: SUN


Your keystore contains 1 entry


Alias name: server

Creation date: 26-Jul-2011

Entry type: PrivateKeyEntry

Certificate chain length: 1

Certificate[1]:

Owner: CN=MyFirstName MyLastName, OU=Software, O=MyCompany,
L=MyCity, ST=MyProvince, C=ME

Issuer: CN=MyFirstName MyLastName, OU=Software, O=MyCompany,
L=MyCity, ST=MyProvince, C=ME

Serial number: 4e2ebd0c

Valid from: Tue Jul 26 17:11:40 GST 2011 until: Mon Jul 26
17:11:40 GST 2021

Certificate fingerprints:

        MD5:  9E:DF:5E:18:F5:F6:52:4A:B6:9F:67:04:39:C9:57:66

        SHA1: C5:0B:8C:E6:B6:02:BD:38:56:CD:BB:50:CC:C6:BA:74:86:
27:6C:C7

        Signature algorithm name: SHA1withRSA

        Version: 3
```

4. To generate a certificate (public key) from a keystore with a private key entry, run the following command for the client/server-side keystore:

```
keytool -export -file clientStore.cert -keystore clientStore.jks
-storepass clientPassword  -alias client

keytool -export -file serverStore.cert -keystore serverStore.jks
-storepass serverPassword  -alias server
```

5. To import the sender (client) public key certificate into the receiver (server) keystore, run the following command for the server-side keystore (this certificate will be stored as a trusted certificate entry in the keystore with the alias *client*):

```
keytool -import -file clientStore.cert -keystore serverStore.jks
-storepass serverPassword -alias client

Owner: CN=MyFirstName MyLastName, OU=Software, O=MyCompany,
L=MyCity, ST=MyProvince, C=ME

Issuer: CN=MyFirstName MyLastName, OU=Software, O=MyCompany,
L=MyCity, ST=MyProvince, C=ME

Serial number: 4e2ebf1e

Valid from: Tue Jul 26 17:20:30 GST 2011 until: Mon Jul 26
17:20:30 GST 2021

Certificate fingerprints:

        MD5:  FD:BE:98:72:F0:C8:50:D5:4B:10:B0:80:3F:D4:43:E8

        SHA1: 91:FB:9D:1B:69:E9:5F:0B:97:8C:E2:FE:49:0E:D8:CD:25:
FB:D8:18

        Signature algorithm name: SHA1withRSA

        Version: 3

Trust this certificate? [no]:  yes

Certificate was added to keystore
```

6. To import the receiver (server) public key certificate into the sender (client) keystore, run the following command for the sender (client side) keystore (this certificate will be stored as a trusted certificate entry in the keystore with the alias *server*):

```
keytool -import -file serverStore.cert -keystore clientStore.jks
-storepass clientPassword -alias server

Owner: CN=MyFirstName MyLastName, OU=Software, O=MyCompany,
L=MyCity, ST=MyProvince, C=ME

Issuer: CN=MyFirstName MyLastName, OU=Software, O=MyCompany,
L=MyCity, ST=MyProvince, C=ME

Serial number: 4e2ebf1e

Valid from: Tue Jul 26 17:20:30 GST 2011 until: Mon Jul 26
17:20:30 GST 2021

Certificate fingerprints:

        MD5:  FD:BE:98:72:F0:C8:50:D5:4B:10:B0:80:3F:D4:43:E8

        SHA1: 91:FB:9D:1B:69:E9:5F:0B:97:8C:E2:FE:49:0E:D8:CD:25:
FB:D8:18

        Signature algorithm name: SHA1withRSA

        Version: 3

Trust this certificate? [no]:  yes

Certificate was added to keystore
```

7. To see the server's private key entry and trusted certificate entry in the keystore, run the following command (please note `trustedCertEntry` and privateKeyEntry within the underlined text):

```
keytool -list -v -keystore serverStore.jks -storepass
serverPassword
Keystore type: JKS
Keystore provider: SUN


Your keystore contains 2 entries


Alias name: client
Creation date: 26-Jul-2011
Entry type: trustedCertEntry


Owner: CN=MyFirstName MyLastName, OU=Software, O=MyCompany,
L=MyCity, ST=MyProvince, C=ME
Issuer: CN=MyFirstName MyLastName, OU=Software, O=MyCompany,
L=MyCity, ST=MyProvince, C=ME
Serial number: 4e2ebf1e
Valid from: Tue Jul 26 17:20:30 GST 2011 until: Mon Jul 26
17:20:30 GST 2021
Certificate fingerprints:
         MD5:  FD:BE:98:72:F0:C8:50:D5:4B:10:B0:80:3F:D4:43:E8
         SHA1: 91:FB:9D:1B:69:E9:5F:0B:97:8C:E2:FE:49:0E:D8:CD:25:
FB:D8:18
         Signature algorithm name: SHA1withRSA
         Version: 3
*****************************************
*****************************************
Alias name: server
Creation date: 26-Jul-2011
Entry type: PrivateKeyEntry
Certificate chain length: 1
Certificate[1]:
Owner: CN=MyFirstName MyLastName, OU=Software, O=MyCompany,
L=MyCity, ST=MyProvince, C=ME
Issuer: CN=MyFirstName MyLastName, OU=Software, O=MyCompany,
L=MyCity, ST=MyProvince, C=ME
```

```
Serial number: 4e2ebd0c

Valid from: Tue Jul 26 17:11:40 GST 2011 until: Mon Jul 26
17:11:40 GST 2021

Certificate fingerprints:

        MD5:   9E:DF:5E:18:F5:F6:52:4A:B6:9F:67:04:39:C9:57:66

        SHA1: C5:0B:8C:E6:B6:02:BD:38:56:CD:BB:50:CC:C6:BA:74:86:
27:6C:C7

        Signature algorithm name: SHA1withRSA

        Version: 3

********************************************

********************************************
```

8. To see the client's private key entry and trusted certificate entry in the keystore, run
   the following command:

```
keytool -list -v -keystore clientStore.jks -storepass
clientPassword


Keystore type: JKS

Keystore provider: SUN


Your keystore contains 2 entries


Alias name: client

Creation date: 26-Jul-2011

Entry type: PrivateKeyEntry

Certificate chain length: 1

Certificate[1]:

Owner: CN=MyFirstName MyLastName, OU=Software, O=MyCompany,
L=MyCity, ST=MyProvince, C=ME

Issuer: CN=MyFirstName MyLastName, OU=Software, O=MyCompany,
L=MyCity, ST=MyProvince, C=ME

Serial number: 4e2ebf1e

Valid from: Tue Jul 26 17:20:30 GST 2011 until: Mon Jul 26
17:20:30 GST 2021

Certificate fingerprints:

        MD5:   FD:BE:98:72:F0:C8:50:D5:4B:10:B0:80:3F:D4:43:E8

        SHA1: 91:FB:9D:1B:69:E9:5F:0B:97:8C:E2:FE:49:0E:D8:CD:25:
FB:D8:18
```

```
        Signature algorithm name: SHA1withRSA

        Version: 3

****************************************

****************************************

Alias name: server

Creation date: 26-Jul-2011

Entry type: trustedCertEntry


Owner: CN=MyFirstName MyLastName, OU=Software, O=MyCompany,
L=MyCity, ST=MyProvince, C=ME

Issuer: CN=MyFirstName MyLastName, OU=Software, O=MyCompany,
L=MyCity, ST=MyProvince, C=ME

Serial number: 4e2ebd0c

Valid from: Tue Jul 26 17:11:40 GST 2011 until: Mon Jul 26
17:11:40 GST 2021

Certificate fingerprints:

        MD5:  9E:DF:5E:18:F5:F6:52:4A:B6:9F:67:04:39:C9:57:66

        SHA1: C5:0B:8C:E6:B6:02:BD:38:56:CD:BB:50:CC:C6:BA:74:86:
27:6C:C7

        Signature algorithm name: SHA1withRSA

        Version: 3


****************************************

****************************************
```

How it works...

In the beginning, a symmetric key store is generated that can be shared by a client and a server for encryption and decryption. This command generates the symmetric key store:

```
keytool -genseckey -alias 'symmetric' -keyalg 'DESede' -keystore
symmetricStore.jks -storepass 'symmetricPassword' -keypass
'keyPassword' -storetype "JCEKS"
```

To generate a keystore with a private key entry and a trusted certificate entry, first a key pair (private key and public certificate) keystore for both the client and server side should be generated.

Then the public key certificate should be exported from the client/server keystore. Finally, the client certificate should be imported into the server keystore and the server certificate should be imported into the client keystore (this imported certificate will be called **trusted certificate**).

```
keytool -genkey -alias aliasName  -keyalg RSA -keystore
keyStoreFileName.jks -validity 3653
```

The preceding command generates a keystore with a private key entry for which `aliasName` is an identifier of the keystore. Validity is the number of days that this key is valid.

```
keytool -export -file clientStore.cert -keystore clientStore.jks
-storepass clientPassword  -alias client
```

The preceding command exports the public key certificate that is embedded inside the private key entry in a keystore.

```
keytool -import -file clientStore.cert -keystore serverStore.jks
-storepass serverPassword -alias client
```

The preceding command imports the generated public key certificate from the client keystore into the server keystore (this imported certificate will be called trusted certificate).

More information about cryptography and keystores can be found at the following URLs:

```
http://docs.oracle.com/javase/1.5.0/docs/api/java/security/KeyStore.
html.
```

```
http://en.wikipedia.org/wiki/Category:Public-key_cryptography.
```

See also...

The recipes *Securing SOAP messages using digital signature, Authenticating a Web-Service call using X509 certificate,* and *Encrypting/Decrypting of SOAP messages*, discussed in this chapter.

Securing SOAP messages using digital signature

The purpose of **digital signature** is to verify whether a received message is altered to prove the sender is who he/she claims to be (authentication) and to prove the action from a specific sender. Digital signing of a message means adding hash data, that is, a piece of information (token) added to the SOAP envelop. The receiver needs to regenerate its own hash from the incoming message and compare it with the sender's one. If the receiver's hash matches the sender's one, the data integrity is achieved and the receiver will proceed; otherwise it returns a SOAP fault message to the sender.

In order to authenticate the sender, the sender should encrypt the signature token using his/her own private key. The receiver should have the sender's public-key certificate in the receiver keystore (the certificate is called a trusted certificate and comes under the trusted certificate entry) to decrypt the sender's signature token and repeat the already-explained step to check the message integrity. Now if the message integrity is achieved, the authentication of the sender is proved (since only the sender's certificate embedded in the receiver keystore could decrypt the encrypted signature of the sender). In addition, the action of sending the message by the sender also is proved (since successful decryption of the signature on the receiver's side shows that the sender has encrypted it by its own private key).

In this recipe, the sender (client) signs a message and uses its own private key (within the client keystore) for encryption of signature. On the receiver side (server), the client public key certificate in the server keystore (the certificate is called trusted certificate and comes under the trusted certificate entry within the keystore) will be used for decryption of the signature of the token; then the server verifies the signature token.

Getting ready

In this recipe, the project's name is `LiveRestaurant_R-7.4` (for the server-side Web-Service) with the following Maven dependencies:

- `spring-ws-security-2.0.1.RELEASE.jar`
- `spring-expression-3.0.5.RELEASE.jar`
- `log4j-1.2.9.jar`

`LiveRestaurant_R-7.4-Client` (for the client-side Web-Service) has the following Maven dependencies:

- `spring-ws-security-2.0.1.RELEASE.jar`
- `spring-ws-test-2.0.0.RELEASE.jar`
- `spring-expression-3.0.5.RELEASE.jar`
- `log4j-1.2.9.jar`
- `junit-4.7.jar`

How to do it...

1. Copy `serverStore.jks` to the server and `clientStore.jks` to the client (these keystores are already generated in the recipe *Preparing pair and symmetric keystores* discussed in this chapter.

2. Configure the security policy file (`securityPolicy.xml`) on the server side to expect a signature token along with the incoming message on the client side to sign outgoing messages.

3. Register `keyStoreHAndler` (`KeyStoreCallbackHandler`) and `trustStore` (`KeyStoreFactoryBean`) in the server-side application context file.

4. Register `keyStoreHAndler` (`KeyStoreCallbackHandler`) and `keyStore` (`KeyStoreFactoryBean`) in the client-side application context file.

5. Run the following command from `Liverestaurant_R-7.4`:

   `mvn clean package tomcat:run`

6. Run the following command from `Liverestaurant_R-7.4-Client`:

   `mvn clean package`

   The following is the client-side output (note the tag `ds:Signature`) within the underlined text:

   ```
   INFO: ==== Sending Message Start ====
   ....
   <SOAP-ENV:Envelope.....>
   <SOAP-ENV:Header>
   <wsse:Security ....>
   ...
   <ds:Signature ....>
   <ds:SignedInfo>
   .....
   </ds:SignedInfo>
   <ds:SignatureValue>....</ds:SignatureValue>
   <ds:KeyInfo>
   <wsse:SecurityTokenReference .........>
   <wsse:Reference ..../>
   </wsse:SecurityTokenReference>
   </ds:KeyInfo>
   </ds:Signature>
   </wsse:Security>
   </SOAP-ENV:Header>
   <SOAP-ENV:Body....>
   <tns:placeOrderRequest ...>
   ......
   </tns:placeOrderRequest>
   </SOAP-ENV:Body>
   </SOAP-ENV:Envelope>
   ```

```
==== Sending Message End  ====....
<SOAP-ENV:Header/>
<SOAP-ENV:Body>
<tns:placeOrderResponse ....>
<tns:refNumber>order-John_Smith_1234</tns:refNumber>
</tns:placeOrderResponse>
</SOAP-ENV:Body>
</SOAP-ENV:Envelope>
==== Received Message End  ====
```

How it works...

Security policy on the server side requires the client to include a binary signature token in the message. Settings in the client-side policy file include the signature token in the outgoing messages. A client uses its own private key included in the client-side keystore to encrypt the signature token of the message. On the server side, the client public key certificate, included in the server keystore (the certificate is called trusted certificate and comes under the trusted certificate entry within the keystore), will be used for decrypting the incoming signature token. Then the server proceeds towards the verification of the signature.

The following server-side security configuration in the policy files causes the server to expect a security token from the incoming message (for verification of incoming messages):

```
    <xwss:RequireSignature requireTimestamp="false" />
</xwss:SecurityConfiguration>
```

On the client side, however, this security configuration in the policy files causes the client to include a security token inside the SOAP message in the outgoing message:

```
    <xwss:Sign includeTimestamp="false">

</xwss:Sign>
```

The following setting in the client-side application context causes the client to use the private key inside `clientStore.jks` to encrypt the signature token of the message. The private key's password is `cliPkPassword`, the alias of the private key entry is `client`, and the keystore bean is generated by reading the keystore `clientStore.jks` with the keystore password `clientPassword`:

```
    <bean id="keyStore"    class="org.springframework.ws.soap.security.
support.KeyStoreFactoryBean">
    <property name="password" value="clientPassword" />
    <property name="location" value="/clientStore.jks" />
    </bean>
```

```
<bean id="keyStoreHandler"    class="org.springframework.ws.soap.
security.xwss.callback.KeyStoreCallbackHandler">
    <property name="keyStore" ref="keyStore" />
    <property name="privateKeyPassword" value="cliPkPassword" />
    <property name="defaultAlias" value="client" />
</bean>
```

On the server side, the following setting in the server configuration file causes the server to first decrypt the signature token using a client certificate in the server keystore (the certificate is called a trusted certificate). It then verifies the signature of the incoming messages (to see whether the original message is altered):

```
<bean id="keyStoreHandler"    class="org.springframework.
ws.soap.security.xwss.callback.KeyStoreCallbackHandler">
    <property name="trustStore" ref="trustStore"/>

</bean>
<bean id="trustStore"    class="org.springframework.ws.soap.security.
support.KeyStoreFactoryBean">
    <property name="location" value="/WEB-INF/serverStore.jks" />
    <property name="password" value="serverPassword" />
</bean>
```

See also...

The recipes *Preparing pair and symmetric key stores* and *Authenticating a Web-Service call using X509 certificate*, discussed in this chapter.

Authenticating a Web-Service call using X509 certificate

In the previous recipe, *Securing SOAP messages using digital signature*, by changing the sender (client) security policy file, the sender can include the client's certificate along with the outgoing messages. Then on the receiver side (server), before the verification of signatures, the server tries to authenticate the sender by comparing the client's certificate along with incoming message with client certificate embedded in the server keystore (trusted certificate). Additionally in this recipe, the client certificate is included in the sender's outgoing message and to extract data included in the certificate for authentication and authorization purposes, on the receiver side.

`SpringCertificateValidationCallbackHandler`, from the XWSS package, can extract the certificate data (such as `CN=MyFirstName MyLastName`) and this data could be for authentication as well as authorization.

In this recipe, we make use of the *Securing SOAP messages using digital signature* recipe for the signing and verification of signatures. Then `SpringCertificateValidationCallbackHandler` is used for authentication, using data fetching from the DAO layer as well as authorization for that Web-Service call.

Getting ready

In this recipe, the project's name is `LiveRestaurant_R-7.5` (for the server-side Web-Service) and it has the following Maven dependencies:

- `spring-ws-security-2.0.1.RELEASE.jar`
- `spring-expression-3.0.5.RELEASE.jar`
- `log4j-1.2.9.jar`

`LiveRestaurant_R-7.5-Client` (for the client-side Web-Service) has the following Maven dependencies:

- `spring-ws-security-2.0.1.RELEASE.jar`
- `spring-ws-test-2.0.0.RELEASE.jar`
- `spring-expression-3.0.5.RELEASE.jar`
- `log4j-1.2.9.jar`
- `junit-4.7.jar`

How to do it...

In this recipe, all the steps are the same as in the previous recipe, *Securing SOAP messages using a digital signature*, except for modifying the client's policy file, as that changes to include the client certificate along with the outgoing message and the server-side application context file (`spring-ws.servlet.xml`) changes, and it uses the DAO layer to fetch data:

1. Register `springSecurityCertificateHandler` in the server-side application context file (`spring-ws-servlet.xml`).
2. Modify the client-side security policy file to include the client certificate along with the outgoing messages.
3. Add the DAO layer classes to fetch data.

   The following is the client-side output (note the X509 client certification) within the underlined text:

   ```
   INFO: ==== Sending Message Start ====
   <?xml...>
   <SOAP-ENV:Header>
   <wsse:Security ...>
   ```

```
<wsse:BinarySecurityToken...wss-x509-token-...>.....</
wsse:BinarySecurityToken>

<ds:Signature .....>

<ds:SignedInfo>

......

</ds:SignedInfo>

<ds:SignatureValue>.....</ds:SignatureValue>

<ds:KeyInfo>

<wsse:SecurityTokenReference...>

<wsse:Reference ...wss-x509-token-profile-1.0.../>

</wsse:SecurityTokenReference>

</ds:KeyInfo>

</ds:Signature>

</wsse:Security>

</SOAP-ENV:Header>

<SOAP-ENV:Body ....>

<tns:placeOrderRequest ...>

.....

</tns:placeOrderRequest>

</SOAP-ENV:Body>

</SOAP-ENV:Envelope>

==== Sending Message End  ====

INFO: ==== Received Message Start ====

<?xml version="1.0" ....>

<SOAP-ENV:Header/>

<SOAP-ENV:Body>

<tns:placeOrderResponse xmlns:tns="http://www.packtpub.com/
liverestaurant/OrderService/schema">

<tns:refNumber>order-John_Smith_1234</tns:refNumber>

</tns:placeOrderResponse>

</SOAP-ENV:Body>

</SOAP-ENV:Envelope>

==== Received Message End  ====
```

How it works...

Everything about signatures is the same as described in the recipe *Securing SOAP messages using a digital signature*. In addition, the client-side certificate is included in the outgoing messages and extracting a client's certificate data on the server side for some processing operations.

Once the client's certificate is extracted (that is, embedded within the incoming message), authentication can be done by retrieving the username or other information.

Including the following section in the client-side policy file causes the client to include its own public key certificate in the outgoing messages:

```
<xwss:X509Token certificateAlias="client" />
```

Embedding a client certificate in a caller message while signing the message causes the server to validate this certificate with the one included in the server keystore (sender trusted certificate entry) before signature validation. This validation confirms that the caller is the person he/she claims to be. However, if activation/locking of account needs to be checked or authorization of the caller to access specific resources is required, then `springSecurityCertificateHandler`, configured in the server configuration file, handles these tasks:

```
<bean class="org.springframework.ws.soap.security.xwss.
XwsSecurityInterceptor">
        <property name="policyConfiguration" value="/WEB-INF/
securityPolicy.xml"/>
        <property name="secureResponse" value="false" />
        <property name="callbackHandlers">
            <list>
                <ref bean="keyStoreHandler"/>
                <ref bean="springSecurityCertificateHandler"/>
            </list>
        </property>
    </bean>
</sws:interceptors>

  <bean id="springSecurityCertificateHandler"
     class="org.springframework.ws.soap.security.xwss.callback.
SpringCertificateValidationCallbackHandler">
      <property name="authenticationManager"
ref="authenticationManager"/>
    </bean>

    <bean id="authenticationManager"
```

```
              class="org.springframework.security.authentication.
    ProviderManager">
          <property name="providers">
              <bean class="org.springframework.ws.soap.security.x509.
    X509AuthenticationProvider">
                  <property name="x509AuthoritiesPopulator">
                      <bean class="org.springframework.ws.soap.security.
    x509.populator.DaoX509AuthoritiesPopulator">
                          <property name="userDetailsService"
    ref="userDetailsService"/>
                      </bean>
                  </property>
              </bean>
          </property>
      </bean>

      <bean id="userDetailsService" class="com.packtpub.liverestaurant.
    service.dao.MyUserDetailService" />
```

This handler uses the authentication manager that calls `DaoX509AuthoritiesPopulator`, which applies the customized service class `MyUserDetailService` for authentication and extracts the user credentials for authorization purposes:

```
public class MyUserDetailService implements UserDetailsService {

   @Override
   public UserDetails loadUserByUsername(String username)
      throws UsernameNotFoundException, DataAccessException {
    return findUserDetailFromDAO(username);
   }
   private UserDetails  findUserDetailFromDAO(String userName)throws
UsernameNotFoundException{
    MyUserDetail mydetail=null;

    /**
      *Real scenario: Find user-name from  DAO layer, if user
found,  get data from the DAO and set MyUserDetail otherwise throw
UsernameNotFoundException.
     */
    if(! userName.equals("MyFirstName MyLastName")){
      throw new UsernameNotFoundException("User name not found");
    }
      mydetail=new MyUserDetail(userName,"fetchedPassword",true,true,t
rue,true,new GrantedAuthorityImpl("ROLE_GENERAL_OPERATOR"));
    return mydetail;
   }
}
```

See also...

The recipes _Securing SOAP messages using a digital signature_ and _Preparing pair and symmetric keystores_, discussed in this chapter.

Encrypting/decrypting of SOAP messages

Encryption is the process of converting readable or plain text data format into an un-readable encrypted format or cipher text using specific algorithms. These algorithms, known as encryption algorithms, require an encryption key. Decryption is just the reverse operation of encryption; it converts back the cipher text into readable or plain text data format using a decryption key. The encryption and decryption keys could be the same or different. If encryption and decryption keys are the same and the sender and receiver share the key, then this key is known as **symmetric** or **secret key**. The encryption and decryption keys could be different, and in this case, the key is called **asymmetric** or **public key**.

The following diagram presents the usage of a symmetric key for encryption/decryption. The sender and receiver can share the same key, which is known as symmetric key. Those having this key can decrypt/encrypt messages. For example, a symmetric key is used for encryption by the sender and decryption by the receiver:

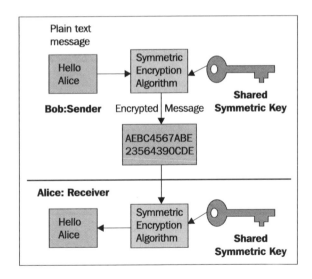

The following diagram presents the usage of the public/private key for encryption/decryption. Bob, as a sender, gets Alice's public key, encrypts a message, and sends it to Alice. Since only she is the holder of her own private key, she can decrypt the message:

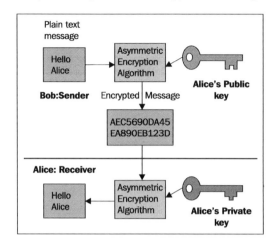

In this recipe, the sender (client here) encrypts a message and sends it to a receiver (server here) in three different cases. In the first case, a symmetric key (which is in a store with the secret key entry that is the same for the client and server) is used for encryption on the client side and for decryption on the server side. Then, in the second case, the receiver's (server) public key certificate on the sender's (client) keystore (within the receiver trusted certificate entry) is used for data encryption and the receiver's (server) private key on the server-side keystore is used for decryption.

Since encryption of the whole payload in the `annotation` endpoint mappings (`PayloadRootAnnotationMethodEndpointMapping`) makes routing information (for example, `localPart = "placeOrderRequest"`, `namespace = "http://www.packtpub.com/liverestaurant/OrderService/schema"`, which is included in payload) encrypted along with whole payload, and the `annotation` endpoint mapping cannot be used. Instead, the `SoapActionAnnotationMethodEndpointMapping` addressing style is used for endpoint mapping. In this case, routing data is included in the SOAP header whereas it is included in payload in the annotation endpoint mapping. Although encryption of a part of the payload can work with the payload annotation endpoint mapping, however for consistency, `SoapActionAnnotationMethodEndpointMapping` addressing style is used for whole of the recipe.

For more information about endpoint mapping, refer to the recipes *Setting up an endpoint by annotating the payload-root* and *Setting up a transport-neutral WS-Addressing endpoint*, discussed in *Chapter 1, Building SOAP Web-Services*.

In the first two cases, the whole payload is used for encryption/decryption. The XWSS policy configuration file makes it possible to encrypt/decrypt the payload part. In the third case, only a part of the payload is set as the target for encryption/decryption.

Getting ready

In this recipe, the project's name is `LiveRestaurant_R-7.6` (for the server-side Web-Service) and has the following Maven dependencies:

- `spring-ws-security-2.0.1.RELEASE.jar`
- `spring-expression-3.0.5.RELEASE.jar`
- `log4j-1.2.9.jar`
- `mail-1.4.1.jar`
- `saaj-api-1.3.jar`
- `saaj-impl-1.3.2.jar`

`LiveRestaurant_R-7.6-Client` (for the client-side Web-Service) has the following Maven dependencies:

- `spring-ws-security-2.0.1.RELEASE.jar`
- `spring-ws-test-2.0.0.RELEASE.jar`
- `spring-expression-3.0.5.RELEASE.jar`
- `log4j-1.2.9.jar`
- `junit-4.7.jar`

How to do it...

The following steps implement encryption/decryption using a shared symmetric key (`symmetricStore.jks`):

1. Register `keyStoreHandler` and `symmetricStore` in the server/client application context. Copy the symmetric keystore (`symmetricStore.jks`) to the server/client folder (this keystore is already generated in the recipe *Preparing pair and symmetric keystores* discussed in this chapter).

2. Configure the security policy file (`securityPolicy.xml`) on the server side to expect encryption of messages from its client and on the client side to encrypt the outgoing messages.

3. Run the following command from `Liverestaurant_R-7.6`:

   mvn clean package tomcat:run

4. Run the following command from `Liverestaurant_R-7.6-Client`:

   mvn clean package

The following is the client-side output (note the underlined part in the output):

```
INFO: ==== Received Message Start ====
....
<SOAP-ENV:Envelope ....>
<SOAP-ENV:Header>
<wsse:Security ....>
.......
</wsse:Security>
</SOAP-ENV:Header>
<SOAP-ENV:Body>
<xenc:EncryptedData.....">
<xenc:EncryptionMethod ....>
<ds:KeyInfo ...xmldsig#">
<ds:KeyName>symmetric</ds:KeyName>
</ds:KeyInfo>
<xenc:CipherData>
<xenc:CipherValue>
3esI76ANNDEIZ5RWJt.....
</xenc:CipherValue>
</xenc:CipherData>
</xenc:EncryptedData>
</SOAP-ENV:Body>
</SOAP-ENV:Envelope>
==== Received Message End  ====


Nov 7, 2011 11:48:46 PM com.sun.xml.wss.impl.filter.DumpFilter
process
INFO: ==== Sending Message Start ====
<?xml version="1.0" ...
><SOAP-ENV:Envelope ...>
<SOAP-ENV:Header/>
<SOAP-ENV:Body>
<tns:placeOrderResponse xmlns:tns="http://www.packtpub.com/
liverestaurant/OrderService/schema">
<tns:refNumber>order-John_Smith_1234</tns:refNumber>
```

```
</tns:placeOrderResponse>

</SOAP-ENV:Body>

</SOAP-ENV:Envelope>

==== Sending Message End   ====
```

The following steps implement encryption using a server-trusted certificate (or public key) on the client-side keystore (`clientStore.jks`) and decryption on the server private key on the server-side keystore (`serverStore.jks`):

1. Modify `securityPolicy.xml` for encryption of messages using a server-trusted certificate on the client side (included in `clientStore.jks`) and decryption on the server side by the server private key (included in `serverStore.jks`).

2. Register `keyStoreHandler` and `keyStore` on the server side and `keyStoreHandler` and `trustStore` on the client-side application context. Copy `clientStore.jks` to the client and `serverStore.jks` to the server folder (this keystore is already generated in the recipe *Preparing pair and symmetric Keystores* discussed in this chapter).

3. Configure the security policy file (`securityPolicy.xml`) on the server side to expect encryption of messages from its client and on the client side to encrypt the outgoing messages.

4. Run the following command from `Liverestaurant_R-7.6`:

   ```
   mvn clean package tomcat:run
   ```

5. Run the following command from `Liverestaurant_R-7.6-Client`:

   ```
   mvn clean package
   ```

   The following is the client-side output (note the underlined part in the output):

   ```
   INFO: ==== Sending Message Start ====

   ...

   <SOAP-ENV:Envelope ....>

   <SOAP-ENV:Header>

   <wsse:Security ...>

   ........

   </wsse:Security>

   </SOAP-ENV:Header>

   <SOAP-ENV:Body>

   <xenc:EncryptedData....>

   <xenc:EncryptionMethod .../>

   <ds:KeyInfo xmlns:ds="http://www.w3.org/2000/09/xmldsig#">

   <wsse:SecurityTokenReference...>
   ```

```
<wsse:Reference ..../>
</wsse:SecurityTokenReference>
</ds:KeyInfo>
<xenc:CipherData>
...
</xenc:CipherValue>
</xenc:CipherData>
</xenc:EncryptedData>
</SOAP-ENV:Body>
</SOAP-ENV:Envelope>
==== Sending Message End  ====


Nov 8, 2011 12:12:11 AM com.sun.xml.wss.impl.filter.DumpFilter
process
INFO: ==== Received Message Start ====
<SOAP-ENV:Envelope ....>
<SOAP-ENV:Header/>
<SOAP-ENV:Body>
<tns:placeOrderResponse xmlns:tns="http://www.packtpub.com/
liverestaurant/OrderService/schema">
<tns:refNumber>order-John_Smith_1234</tns:refNumber>
</tns:placeOrderResponse>
</SOAP-ENV:Body>
</SOAP-ENV:Envelope>
==== Received Message End  ====
```

The following steps implement encryption/decryption for a part of the payload:

1. Modify `securityPolicy.xml` on client side/server side to set the target of the encryption.

2. Run the following command from `Liverestaurant_R-7.6`:

   ```
   mvn clean package tomcat:run
   ```

3. Run the following command from `Liverestaurant_R-7.6-Client`:

   ```
   mvn clean package
   ```

The following is the client-side output (note underlined part in the output):

```
INFO: ==== Sending Message Start ====
...
<SOAP-ENV:Envelope ....>
<SOAP-ENV:Header>
<wsse:Security ....>
........
</wsse:Security>
</SOAP-ENV:Header>
<SOAP-ENV:Body>
<tns:placeOrderRequest ...>
<xenc:EncryptedData …..>
….......
<xenc:CipherData>
<xenc:CipherValue>NEeTuduV....
….......
</xenc:CipherValue>
</xenc:CipherData>
</xenc:EncryptedData>
</tns:placeOrderRequest>
</SOAP-ENV:Body>
</SOAP-ENV:Envelope>
==== Sending Message End  ====


Nov 8, 2011 12:18:39 AM com.sun.xml.wss.impl.filter.DumpFilter
process
INFO: ==== Received Message Start ====
....
<SOAP-ENV:Envelope ...>
<SOAP-ENV:Header/>
<SOAP-ENV:Body>
<tns:placeOrderResponse ....>
<tns:refNumber>order-John_Smith_1234</tns:refNumber>
</tns:placeOrderResponse>
</SOAP-ENV:Body>
</SOAP-ENV:Envelope>
==== Received Message End  ====
```

How it works...

In the first case, both the client and the server share the symmetric key. The client encrypts the whole payload using a symmetric key and sends it to the server. On the server side, the same key will be used to decrypt the payload. However, in the second and third cases, the server certificate embedded in the client store is used for encryption of the payload and the server-side private key of the server store will be used for decryption.

The `RequireEncryption/Encrypt` tag in the server/client policy files causes the client to encrypt a message and the server to decrypt it. The `keyAlias` is the alias name that is set at the time of symmetric keystore generation. The following sections in the client- and server-side policy files target the part of a message envelop that is to be encrypted/decrypted. `qname:` `{http://schemas.xmlsoap.org/soap/envelope/}Body` causes only the body part of a SOAP envelop to be used for encryption/decryption.

```
---server policy file
  <xwss:RequireEncryption>
    <xwss:SymmetricKey keyAlias="symmetric" />

    <xwss:EncryptionTarget type="qname"  value="{http://schemas.
xmlsoap.org/soap/envelope/}Body" enforce="true"
       contentOnly="true" />
  </xwss:RequireEncryption>

---client policy file
<xwss:Encrypt>
    <xwss:SymmetricKey keyAlias="symmetric" />
    <xwss:Target type="qname">{http://schemas.xmlsoap.org/soap/
envelope/}Body
    </xwss:Target>
  </xwss:Encrypt>
```

This part in the server and client configuration files causes a symmetric store to be used for cryptography. The `callbackHandler` (`keyStoreHandlerBean`) uses a symmetric keystore (`symmetricStore` bean) with the key password as `keyPassword`. The `KeyStore` bean will be generated by reading from a keystore location (`symmetricStore.jks`) with the keystore password as `symmetricPassword` and the type set to JCEKS (passwords and the type are set at the time of symmetric keystore generation).

```
            <bean id="keyStoreHandler"    class="org.springframework.
ws.soap.security.xwss.callback.KeyStoreCallbackHandler">
    <property name="symmetricStore" ref="symmetricStore" />
    <property name="symmetricKeyPassword" value="keyPassword" />
  </bean>
  <bean id="symmetricStore"
```

```
      class="org.springframework.ws.soap.security.support.
  KeyStoreFactoryBean">
      <property name="password" value="symmetricPassword" />
      <property name="location" value="/WEB-INF/symmetricStore.jks" />
      <property name="type" value="JCEKS" />
  </bean>
```

In the second case, almost all the settings are the same, except that the client is using the server public key for encrypting and the server is using the server store private key for decryption. The following section in the server-side configuration file causes the server to use a server private key in the server-side keystore for decryption. The private key password is `serPkPasswords` and the alias of the private key entry in the keystore is *server*. The `KeyStore` bean will be generated by reading from the keystore file (`serverStore.jks`) with the password `serverPassword` (passwords and the alias are set at the time of keystore generation).

```
  ---server configuration
      <bean id="keyStoreHandler"
      class="org.springframework.ws.soap.security.xwss.callback.
  KeyStoreCallbackHandler">
      <property name="keyStore" ref="keyStore" />

      <property name="privateKeyPassword" value="serPkPassword" />

      <property name="defaultAlias" value="server" />
  </bean>

  <bean id="keyStore"
      class="org.springframework.ws.soap.security.support.
  KeyStoreFactoryBean">
      <property name="location" value="/WEB-INF/serverStore.jks" />
      <property name="password" value="serverPassword" />
  </bean>
```

This section in the client-side configuration file causes the client to use the server certificate (public key) in the client-side trust store for encryption. The `KeyStore` (trust store here) bean will be generated by reading from `clientStore.jks` with the password `clientPAssword`.

```
  ---client configuration
      <bean id="keyStoreHandler"
      class="org.springframework.ws.soap.security.xwss.callback.
  KeyStoreCallbackHandler">
      <property name="trustStore" ref="trustStore"/>

  </bean>
```

```
<bean id="trustStore"
   class="org.springframework.ws.soap.security.support.
KeyStoreFactoryBean">
   <property name="location" value="/clientStore.jks" />
   <property name="password" value="clientPassword" />
</bean>
```

In the policy file for the client and server side, the following line causes the server public key to be used for encrypting in the client and the private key in the server store to be used for decryption.

```
<xwss:X509Token certificateAlias="server"/>
```

In the third case, the following section in the policy files for the server and client causes only a part of the payload to be encrypted:

```
<xwss:Target  type="qname">{http://www.packtpub.com/LiveRestaurant/
placeOrderService/schema}OrderRequest</xwss:Target>
```

When encrypting the whole of the payload, use WS-Addressing because routing information will be included in the header.

Keystore, key management, frequent updates to keys, and certificates are separate areas and are not a part of this book. Choosing the best option needs more study, and this is part of architecture-related work.

See also...

The recipes *Securing SOAP messages using a digital signature* and *Preparing pair and symmetric keystores*, discussed in this chapter.

The recipe *Creating Web-Service client for WS-Addressing endpoint*, discussed in *Chapter 2, Building Clients for SOAP Web Services.*

8

Securing SOAP
Web-Services using
WSS4J Library

In this chapter, we will cover:

- ▶ Authenticating a Web-Service call using a username token with a plain/digest password
- ▶ Authenticating a Web-Service call using Spring security to authenticate a username token with a plain/digest password
- ▶ Securing SOAP messages using a digital signature
- ▶ Authenticating a Web-Service call using an X509 certificate
- ▶ Encrypting/decrypting SOAP Messages

Introduction

In the previous chapter, the usage of SUN's implementation (**XWSS**): OASIS **Web-Services Security** (**WS-Security** or **WSS**) specification in Spring-WS (that uses `XwsSecurityInterceptor` to perform security operations) is explained. In this chapter, Spring-WS's support for Apache's implementation (WSS4J) of OASIS WS-Security specification will be explained. Even though both of these implementation of WS-Security are capable of performing the required security operations (authentication, signing messages, and encryption/decryption), WSS4J performs faster than XWSS.

Spring-WS supports WSS4J using `Wss4jSecurityInterceptor`, which is an `EndpointInterceptor` that performs security operations on request messages before calling the `Endpoint`.

While XWSS uses the external configuration policy file, WSS4J (and `Wss4jSecurityInterceptor` accordingly) requires no external configuration file and is entirely configurable by properties. The **validation** (receiver-side) and **securement** (sender-side) actions applied by this interceptor are specified through `validationActions` and `securementActions` properties. Multiple actions can be set as space-separated strings. Here is an example configuration on the receiver side (server-side in this chapter):

```
<!--In receiver side(server-side in this chapter)-->
<bean id="wss4jSecurityInterceptor"
  <property name="validationActions" value="UsernameToken Encrypt" />
  ..
  <!--In sender side(client-side in this chapter)-->
  <property name="securementActions" value="UsernameToken Encrypt" />
  ..
</bean>
```

The `validationActions` is an operations list made up of space-separated strings. When a sender sends a message, the `validationActions` (on receiver-side) will be executed.

The `securementActions` is an operations list made of space-separated strings. These actions will be executed when the sender sends a message to a receiver.

> ▸ **Validation actions**: `UsernameToken`, `Timestamp`, `Encrypt`, `signature`, and `NoSecurity`.

> ▸ **Securement actions**: `UsernameToken`, `UsernameTokenSignature`, `Timestamp`, `Encrypt`, `Signature`, and `NoSecurity`.

The order of the actions is important and is applied by the `Wss4jSecurityInterceptor`. This interceptor will return a fault message if the incoming SOAP message `securementActions` (in sender-side) was sent in a different way than the one configured by `validationActions` (in receiver-side).

For the operations, such as encryption/decryption or signatures, WSS4J needs to read data from a key store (`store.jks`):

```
<bean class="org.springframework.
  ws.soap.security.wss4j.support.CryptoFactoryBean">
  <property name="key storePassword" value="storePassword" />
  <property name="key storeLocation" value="/WEB-INF/store.jks" />
</bean>
```

Security concepts such as authentication, signatures, decryption, and encryption were already detailed in the previous chapter. In this chapter, we will discuss how to implement these features using WSS4J.

For simplification, for most of the recipes in this chapter, use the projects in *How to integrate test using Spring-JUnit support, Chapter 3, Testing and Monitoring Web-Services*, to set up a server and to send and receive messages by the client. However, in the last recipe, projects from *Chapter 2, Creating Web-Service client for WS-Addressing endpoint*, are used for the server and client side.

Authenticating a Web-Service call using a username token with a plain/digest password

Authentication simply means to check whether callers of a service are who they claim to be. One way of checking the authentication of a caller is to check its password (if we consider a username as a person, the password is similar to the signature of the person). Spring-WS uses `Wss4jSecurityInterceptor` to send/receive the username token with the password along with SOAP messages, and to compare it (in the receiver-side) with what is set as a pre-defined username/password in the property format. This property setting of the Interceptor force tells the sender of messages that a username token with the password should be included in the sender messages, and in the receiver side, the receiver expects to receive this username token with a password for authentication.

Transmitting a plain password makes a SOAP message unsecure. `Wss4jSecurityInterceptor` provides configuration properties (in the property format) to include the digest of the password along with sender message. On the receiver's side, the digested password included in the incoming message will be compared with the digested password, calculated from what is set in the property format.

This recipe presents how to authenticate a Web-Service call using the username token. Here, the client acts as a sender and the server acts as the receiver. This recipe contains two cases. In the first case, the password will be transmitted in plain text format. In the second case, by changing the property, the password will be transmitted in digest format.

Getting ready

In this recipe, we have the following two projects:

1. `LiveRestaurant_R-8.1` (for a server-side Web-Service), with the following Maven dependencies:

   - `spring-ws-security-2.0.1.RELEASE.jar`
   - `spring-expression-3.0.5.RELEASE.jar`
   - `log4j-1.2.9.jar`

2. `LiveRestaurant_R-8.1-Client` (for client-side), with the following Maven dependencies:

   - `spring-ws-security-2.0.1.RELEASE.jar`
   - `spring-ws-test-2.0.0.RELEASE.jar`
   - `spring-expression-3.0.5.RELEASE.jar`
   - `log4j-1.2.9.jar`
   - `junit-4.7.jar`

How to do it...

Follow these steps to implement authentication using a plain username token with a plain-text password:

1. Register `Wss4jSecurityInterceptor` in the server-side application context (`spring-ws-servlet.xml`), set the validation action to `UsernameToken`, and configure the `callbackHandler` (`….wss4j.callback.SimplePasswordValidationCallbackHandler`) within this interceptor.

2. Register `Wss4jSecurityInterceptor` in the client-side application context (`applicationContext.xml`), set the `securement` action to `UsernameToken`, and set the `username`, `password`, and `password type` (in `text` format here).

3. Run the following command on `Liverestaurant_R-8.1`:

   `mvn clean package tomcat:run`

4. Run the following command on `Liverestaurant_R-8.1-Client`:

   `mvn clean package`

   Here is the output of the client side (note the `UsernameToken` with the plain password tags that is highlighted within the `Header` of the SOAP's `Envelope`):

   ```
   Sent request .....
   [<SOAP-ENV:Envelope>
   <SOAP-ENV:Header>
     <wsse:Security ...>
       <wsse:UsernameToken ...>
         <wsse:Username>admin</wsse:Username>
         <wsse:Password #PasswordText">password</wsse:Password>
       </wsse:UsernameToken>
     </wsse:Security>
   </SOAP-ENV:Header>

   ....
   ```

```
<tns:placeOrderRequest ...>

  ....

  </tns:order>

</tns:placeOrderRequest>

... Received response ....

<tns:placeOrderResponse ...">

  <tns:refNumber>order-John_Smith_1234</tns:refNumber>

</tns:placeOrderResponse>

  ...
```

Follow these steps to implement authentication using the username token with the digest password:

1. Modify the client-side application context (`applicationContext.xml`) to set the password's type to the digest format (note that no change in the server side is required).

2. Run the following command on `Liverestaurant_R-8.1`:

   ```
   mvn clean package tomcat:run
   ```

3. Run the following command on `Liverestaurant_R-8.1-Client`:

   ```
   mvn clean package
   ```

   Here is the client-side output (note the `UsernameToken` with the digest password tags that is highlighted within the `Header` of the SOAP's `Envelope`):

   ```
   Sent request .....
   [<SOAP-ENV:Envelope>
     <SOAP-ENV:Header>
       <wsse:Security ...>
         <wsse:UsernameToken ...>
           <wsse:Username>admin</wsse:Username>
           <wsse:Password #PasswordDigest">
             VstlXUXOwyKCIxYh29bNWaSKsRI=
           </wsse:Password>
         </wsse:UsernameToken>
       </wsse:Security>
     </SOAP-ENV:Header>
     ....
     <tns:placeOrderRequest ...>
       ....
   ```

```
        </tns:order>
      </tns:placeOrderRequest>
      ... Received response ....
      <tns:placeOrderResponse ...">
        <tns:refNumber>order-John_Smith_1234</tns:refNumber>
      </tns:placeOrderResponse>
      ...
```

How it works...

The `Liverestaurant_R-8.1` project is a server-side Web-Service that requires its client to send a SOAP envelope that contains a username with a password.

The `Liverestaurant_R-8.1-Client` project is a client-side test project that sends SOAP envelopes to the server that contains a username token with a password.

On the server side, `Wss4jSecurityInterceptor` forces the server for a username token validation for all the incoming messages:

```
<sws:interceptors>
  ....
  <bean id="wss4jSecurityInterceptor"        class="org.
      springframework.
      ws.soap.security.wss4j.Wss4jSecurityInterceptor">
    <property name=
        "validationCallbackHandler" ref="callbackHandler" />
    <property name="validationActions" value="UsernameToken" />
  </bean>
</sws:interceptors>
```

The interceptor uses a `validationCallbackHandler`
(`SimplePasswordValidationCallbackHandler`) to compare the incoming message's username/password with the included username/password (admin/password).

```
<bean id="callbackHandler" class="org.springframework.aws.soap.
  security.wss4j.callback.SimplePasswordValidationCallbackHandler">
  <property name="users">
    <props>
      <prop key="admin">password</prop>
    </props>
  </property>
</bean>
```

On the client side, `wss4jSecurityInterceptor` includes the username (admin/password) token in all outgoing messages:

```
<bean id="wss4jSecurityInterceptor" class="org.springframework.ws.
  soap.security.wss4j.Wss4jSecurityInterceptor">
  <property name="securementActions" value="UsernameToken" />
  <property name="securementUsername" value="admin" />
  <property name="securementPassword" value="password" />
  <property name="securementPasswordType" value="PasswordText" />
</bean>
```

In this case, authenticate using a plain username token, since the client includes a plain password (`<property name="securementPasswordType" value="PasswordText"/>`) in the ongoing messages:

```
<wsse:UsernameToke......>
  <wsse:Username>admin</wsse:Username>
  <wsse:Password ...#PasswordText">password</wsse:Password>
</wsse:UsernameToken>
```

However, in the second case, authenticate using the digest username token, since the password digest (`<property name="securementPasswordType" value="PasswordDigest">`) is included in the username token:

```
<wsse:UsernameToken...>
  <wsse:Username>admin</wsse:Username>
  <wsse:Password ...#PasswordDigest">
    VstlXUXOwyKCIxYh29bNWaSKsRI=
  </wsse:Password>
  ...
</wsse:UsernameToken>
```

In this case, the server compares an incoming SOAP message digest password with the calculated digested password set inside `spring-ws-servlet.xml`. In this way, the communication will be more secure by comparison with the first case on which the password was transmitted in plain text.

See also...

In this chapter:

▸ *Authenticating a Web-Service call using Spring security, to authenticate a username token with a plain/digest password*

▸ *Authenticating a Web-Service call using an X509 certificate*

Authenticating a Web-Service call using Spring security to authenticate a username token with a plain/digest password

Here we have the authentication task using the username token with the digest/plain password, as we did in the first recipe of this chapter. The only difference here is that the Spring security framework is used for authentication (SpringPlainTextPasswordValidationCallbackHandler and SpringDigestPasswordValidationCallbackHandler). Since the Spring security framework is beyond the scope of this book, it is not described here. However, you can read more about it in the *Spring security reference* documentation, available at the following website: http://www.springsource.org/security.

Just like the first recipe of this chapter, this recipe also contains two cases. In the first case, the password will be transmitted in a plain-text format. In the second case, by changing the configuration, the password will be transmitted in a digest format.

Getting ready

In this recipe, we have the following two projects:

1. LiveRestaurant_R-8.2 (for a server-side Web-Service), with the following Maven dependencies:

    ❑   spring-ws-security-2.0.1.RELEASE.jar

    ❑   spring-expression-3.0.5.RELEASE.jar

    ❑   log4j-1.2.9.jar

2. LiveRestaurant_R-8.2-Client (for client-side), with the following Maven dependencies:

    ❑   spring-ws-security-2.0.1.RELEASE.jar

    ❑   spring-ws-test-2.0.0.RELEASE.jar

    ❑   spring-expression-3.0.5.RELEASE.jar

    ❑   log4j-1.2.9.jar

    ❑   junit-4.7.jar

How to do it...

Follow these steps to implement the authentication of a Web-Service call, using Spring security to authenticate a username token with a plain-text password:

1. Register `Wss4jSecurityInterceptor` in the server-side application context (`spring-ws-servlet.xml`), set the validation action to `UsernameToken`, and configure the `validationCallbackHandler` (`....wss4j.callback. SpringPlainTextPasswordValidationCallbackHandler`) within this interceptor.

2. Register `Wss4jSecurityInterceptor` in the client-side application context (`applicationContext.xml`), set securement action to `UsernameToken`, and set the username, password, and password type (`text` format here).

3. Run the following command on `Liverestaurant_R-8.2`:

```
mvn clean package tomcat:run
```

4. Run the following command on `Liverestaurant_R-8.2-Client`:

```
mvn clean package
```

   Here is the output of the client side (note the `UsernameToken` with the digest password tags that is highlighted within the `Header` of the SOAP's `Envelop`):

```
Sent request .....
[<SOAP-ENV:Envelope>
<SOAP-ENV:Header>
  <wsse:Security ...>
    <wsse:UsernameToken ...>
      <wsse:Username>admin</wsse:Username>
      <wsse:Password #PasswordText">password</wsse:Password>
    </wsse:UsernameToken>
  </wsse:Security>
</SOAP-ENV:Header>
....
<tns:placeOrderRequest ...>
  ....
  </tns:order>
</tns:placeOrderRequest>
... Received response ....
<tns:placeOrderResponse ...">
  <tns:refNumber>order-John_Smith_1234</tns:refNumber>
</tns:placeOrderResponse>
....
```

Follow these steps to implement the authentication of a Web-Service call using Spring security to authenticate a username token with a digested password:

1. Modify `Wss4jSecurityInterceptor` in the server-side application context (`spring-ws-servlet.xml`) and configure the `validationCallbackHandler` (`….ws.soap.security.wss4j.callback.SpringDigestPasswordValidationCallbackHandler`) within this interceptor.

2. Modify `Wss4jSecurityInterceptor` in the client-side application context (`applicationContext.xml`) to set the password type (`digest` format here).

3. Run the following command on `Liverestaurant_R-8.2`:

    ```
    mvn clean package tomcat:run
    ```

4. Run the following command on `Liverestaurant_R-8.2-Client`:

    ```
    mvn clean package
    ```

    Here is the output of the client side (note the `UsernameToken` with the digest password tags that is highlighted within `Header` of the SOAP's `Envelop`):

    ```
    Sent request .....
    [<SOAP-ENV:Envelope>
    <SOAP-ENV:Header>
      <wsse:Security ...>
        <wsse:UsernameToken ...>
          <wsse:Username>admin</wsse:Username>
          <wsse:Password #PasswordDigest">
            VstlXUXOwyKCIxYh29bNWaSKsRI=</wsse:Password>
        </wsse:UsernameToken>
      </wsse:Security>
    </SOAP-ENV:Header>
    ....
    <tns:placeOrderRequest ...>
       ....
    </tns:order>
    </tns:placeOrderRequest>
    ... Received response ....
    <tns:placeOrderResponse ...">
      <tns:refNumber>order-John_Smith_1234</tns:refNumber>
    </tns:placeOrderResponse>
    ...
    ```

How it works...

In the `Liverestaurant_R-8.2` project, security for client and server is almost the same as `Liverestaurant_R-8.1` (as shown in the first recipe of this chapter), except for the validation of the username token on the server side. A Spring security class is responsible for validating the username and the password, by comparison with the incoming message's username/password with the fetch data from a DAO layer (instead of hardcoding the username/password in `spring-ws-servlet.xml`). In addition, other data related to the successfully authenticated user can be fetched from the DAO layer and returned for authorization to check some account data.

In the first case, the `CallbackHandler` `SpringPlainTextPasswordValidationCallbackHandler` uses an `authenticationManager`, which uses `DaoAuthenticationProvider`.

```
<bean id="springSecurityHandler"
  class="org.springframework.ws.soap.security.
  wss4j.callback.SpringPlainTextPasswordValidationCallbackHandler">
  <property name="authenticationManager"
    ref="authenticationManager"/>
</bean>

<bean id="authenticationManager" class=
  "org.springframework.security.authentication.ProviderManager">
  <property name="providers">
    <bean class="org.springframework.
      security.authentication.dao.DaoAuthenticationProvider">
      <property name="userDetailsService" ref="userDetailsService"/>
    </bean>
  </property>
</bean>
```

This provider calls a customized user information service (`MyUserDetailService.java`) that gets a username from the provider and internally fetches all the information for that user from a DAO layer (for example, password, roles, is expired, and so on). This service finally returns the populated data in the `UserDetails` type class (`MyUserDetails.java`). Now, if the `UserDetails` data matches the incoming message's username/password, it returns a response; otherwise, it returns a SOAP fault message:

```
public class MyUserDetailService implements UserDetailsService {

@Override
public UserDetails loadUserByUsername(String username)
throws UsernameNotFoundException, DataAccessException {
```

```
    return getUserDataFromDao(username);
}

private MyUserDetail getUserDataFromDao(String username) {

 /**
  *Real scenario: find user data from a DAO layer  by userName,
  * if this user name found, populate  MyUserDetail with its
    data(username, password,Role, ....).
  */
  MyUserDetail mydetail=new MyUserDetail(
    username,"pass",true,true,true,true);
  mydetail.getAuthorities().add(
    new GrantedAuthorityImpl("ROLE_GENERAL_OPERATOR"));

    return mydetail;

}
```

In the second case, however, the `CallbackHandler` is
`SpringDigestPasswordValidationCallbackHandler`, which compares the digest
password included in the SOAP incoming message with the digested password that is fetched
from the DAO layer (note that the DAO layer could fetch data from different data-sources, such
as the database, LDAP, XML file, and so on):

```
<bean  id="springSecurityHandler"
  class="org.springframework.ws.soap.security.wss4j.callback.
  SpringDigestPasswordValidationCallbackHandler">
  <property name="userDetailsService" ref="userDetailsService"/>
</bean>
```

Same as the first recipe in this chapter, setting `<property
name="securementPasswordType" value="PasswordText">` to `PasswordDigest` in
the client application context causes the password to be transmitted into a digested format.

See also...

In this chapter:

- ▶ *Authenticating a Web-Service call, using a username token with a plain/digest password*
- ▶ *Authenticating a Web-Service call using an X509 certificate*

Securing SOAP messages using a digital signature

The purpose of a signature in the security term is to verify whether a received message is altered. Signature covers two main tasks in WS-Security, namely, signing and verifying signatures of messages. All concepts involved in a message signature are detailed in the previous chapter, in the *Securing SOAP messages using digital signature* recipe. In this recipe, signing and verification of a signature using WSS4J is presented.

Spring-WS's `Wss4jSecurityInterceptor` is capable of signing and verification of signatures based on the WS-Security standard.

Setting this interceptor's `securementActions` property to `Signature` causes the sender to sign outgoing messages. To encrypt the signature token, the sender's private key is required. Properties of a key store are needed to be configured in the application context file. The alias and the password of the private key (inside key store) for use are specified by the `securementUsername` and `securementPassword` properties. The `securementSignatureCrypto` should specify the key store containing the private key.

Setting `validationActions` to `value="Signature"` causes the receiver of the message to expect and validate the incoming message signatures (as described at beginning). The `validationSignatureCrypto` bean should specify the key store that contains the public key certificates (trusted certificate) of the sender.

`org.springframework.ws.soap.security.wss4j.support.CryptoFactoryBean` from the `wss4j` package can extract the key store data (such as the certificate and other key store information), and this data could be used for authentication.

In this recipe, the client store private key is used for encryption of the client's signature of a message. On the server-side, the client's public key certificate, included in the server key store (within a trusted certificate entry), will be used for decryption of the message signature token. Then the server does the verification of the signature (as described in the beginning). Key store used in *Chapter 7*, in the recipe *Preparing pair and symmetric Key stores*.

Getting ready

In this recipe, we have the following two projects:

1. `LiveRestaurant_R-8.3` (for a server-side Web-Service), with the following Maven dependencies:

    - `spring-ws-security-2.0.1.RELEASE.jar`
    - `spring-expression-3.0.5.RELEASE.jar`
    - `log4j-1.2.9.jar`

2. `LiveRestaurant_R-8.3-Client` (for the client-side), with the following Maven dependencies:

- `spring-ws-security-2.0.1.RELEASE.jar`
- `spring-ws-test-2.0.0.RELEASE.jar`
- `spring-expression-3.0.5.RELEASE.jar`
- `log4j-1.2.9.jar`
- `junit-4.7.jar`

How to do it...

1. Register `Wss4jSecurityInterceptor` in the server-side application context (`spring-ws-servlet.xml`), set the validation action to `Signature`, and set the property `validationSignatureCrypto` to `CryptoFactoryBean` (configure the server-side key store location and its password) within this interceptor.

2. Register `Wss4jSecurityInterceptor` in the client-side application context (`applicationContext.xml`), set the securement action to `Signature`, and set the property `securementSignatureCrypto` to `CryptoFactoryBean` (configure the client-side key store location and its password) within this interceptor.

3. Run the following command on `Liverestaurant_R-8.3`:

```
mvn clean package tomcat:run
```

4. Run the following command on `Liverestaurant_R-8.3-Client`:

```
mvn clean package
```

Here is the output of the client side (please note highlighted text):

```
Sent request ....
<SOAP-ENV:Header>
  <wsse:Security...>
    <ds:Signature ...>
      <ds:SignedInfo>
        .....
      </ds:SignedInfo>
      <ds:SignatureValue>
        IYSEHmk+.....
      </ds:SignatureValue>
      <ds:KeyInfo ..>
        <wsse:SecurityTokenReference ...>
          <ds:X509Data>
            <ds:X509IssuerSerial>
```

```
            <ds:X509IssuerName>
                CN=MyFirstName MyLastName,OU=Software,O=MyCompany,
        L=MyCity,ST=MyProvince,C=ME
            </ds:X509IssuerName>
            <ds:X509SerialNumber>1311686430</
        ds:X509SerialNumber>
            </ds:X509IssuerSerial>
            </ds:X509Data>
            </wsse:SecurityTokenReference>
            </ds:KeyInfo>
            </ds:Signature>
        </wsse:Security>
    </SOAP-ENV:Header>
    <SOAP-ENV:Body ...>
        <tns:placeOrderRequest ...>
            .....
            </tns:order>
    </tns:placeOrderRequest>
    .. Received response
    .....<tns:placeOrderResponse....>
        <tns:refNumber>order-John_Smith_1234</tns:refNumber>
    </tns:placeOrderResponse>
```

How it works...

Security configuration on the server side requires the client to include a binary signature token in the message. Settings in the client-side configuration file include the signature token in the outgoing messages. A client uses its own private key, included in client-side key store, to encrypt the signature of a message (calculated based on the message's content). On the server-side, the client certificate from the server-side (trusted certificate) key store is used for decrypting of a signature token. Then the verification of the signature from the binary signature token (as described at the beginning of this recipe) will be done.

Setting `validationActions` to `Signature` on the server-side causes it to expect a signature from the client configuration, and setting the key store causes the client-side public-key certificate (trusted certificate) in the server-side key store to be used for the decryption of the signature. Then the server does a verification of the signature:

```
<sws:interceptors>
    <bean class="org.springframework.ws.soap.server.endpoint.
        interceptor.PayloadValidatingInterceptor">
```

```xml
            <property name="schema" value="/WEB-INF/orderService.xsd" />
            <property name="validateRequest" value="true" />
            <property name="validateResponse" value="true" />
        </bean>
        <bean class="org.springframework.ws.soap.server.endpoint.
            interceptor.SoapEnvelopeLoggingInterceptor"/>
        <bean id="wsSecurityInterceptor" class="org.springframework.ws.
            soap.security.wss4j.Wss4jSecurityInterceptor">
          <property name="validationActions" value="Signature" />
          <property name="validationSignatureCrypto">
            <bean class="org.springframework.ws.soap.security.
              wss4j.support.CryptoFactoryBean">
              <property name="key storePassword" value="serverPassword"
                  />
              <property name="key storeLocation"
                value="/WEB-INF/serverStore.jks" />
            </bean>
          </property>
        </bean>
    </sws:interceptors>
```

The code statement `<property name="securementActions"`
`value="Signature" />`, and setting the key store on the client-side configuration causes
the client to send the encrypted signature (using the client's private key with the alias
`client`, and the client encrypts a hash (signature) generated from the message) and
is sent along with the message:

```xml
    <bean id="wss4jSecurityInterceptor" class="org.springframework.ws.
        soap.security.wss4j.Wss4jSecurityInterceptor">
      <property name="securementActions" value="Signature" />
      <property name="securementUsername" value="client" />
      <property name="securementPassword" value="cliPkPassword" />
      <property name="securementSignatureCrypto">
        <bean class="org.springframework.ws.soap.security.
            wss4j.support.CryptoFactoryBean">
          <property name="key storePassword" value="clientPassword" />
            <property name="key storeLocation"
              value="classpath:/clientStore.jks" />
        </bean>
      </property>
    </bean>
```

See also...

In this chapter:

> ▸ _Authenticating a Web-Service call using an X509 certificate_

Chapter 7, Securing SOAP Web Services using XWSS Library:

> ▸ _Preparing pair and symmetric Key stores_

Authenticating a Web-Service call using an X509 certificate

Earlier in this chapter, how to use a username token for authentication of an incoming message is presented. The client's certificate, which came along with an incoming message, could be used to authenticate as an alternative for the username's token for authentication.

To make sure that all incoming SOAP messages carry a client's certificate, the configuration file on the sender's side should sign and the receiver should require signatures on all messages. In other words, the client should sign the message, and include the X509 certificate in the outgoing message, and the server, first compares the incoming certificate with the trusted certificate, which is embedded within server key store, and then it goes into the steps to verify the signature of the incoming message.

Getting ready

In this recipe, we have the following two projects:

1. `LiveRestaurant_R-8.4` (for a server-side Web-Service), with the following Maven dependencies:
    - `spring-ws-security-2.0.1.RELEASE.jar`
    - `spring-expression-3.0.5.RELEASE.jar`
    - `log4j-1.2.9.jar`

2. `LiveRestaurant_R-8.4-Client` (for the client-side), with the following Maven dependencies:
    - `spring-ws-security-2.0.1.RELEASE.jar`
    - `spring-ws-test-2.0.0.RELEASE.jar`
    - `spring-expression-3.0.5.RELEASE.jar`
    - `log4j-1.2.9.jar`
    - `junit-4.7.jar`

How to do it...

1. Register `Wss4jSecurityInterceptor` on the server-side application context (`spring-ws-servlet.xml`), set the validation action to `Signature`, and set the property `validationSignatureCrypto` to `CryptoFactoryBean` (configure the server-side key store location and its password) within this interceptor.

2. Register `Wss4jSecurityInterceptor` in the client-side application context (`applicationContext.xml`), set the securement action to `Signature`, set a property (`securementSignatureKeyIdentifier`) to include a binary `X509` token, and set the property `securementSignatureCrypto` to `CryptoFactoryBean` (configure the client-side key store location and its password) within this interceptor.

Here is the output of the client side (please note highlighted text):

```
Sent request ....
<SOAP-ENV:Header>
  <wsse:Security ...>
    <wsse:BinarySecurityToken....wss-x509-token-profile-
      1.0#X509v3" ...>
      MIICbTCCAdagAwIBAgIETi6/HjANBgkqhki...
    </wsse:BinarySecurityToken>
    <ds:Signature ....>
      .....
      ....
    </ds:Signature>....
```

How it works...

Signing and verification of signature is the same as the *Securing SOAP messages using a digital signature* recipe from this chapter. The difference is the following part of the configuration to generate a `BinarySecurityToken` element containing the X509 certificate, and to include it in the outgoing message on the sender's side:

```
<property name="securementSignatureKeyIdentifier"
  value="DirectReference" />
```

Embedding the client certificate in the caller message while signing the message causes the server to validate this certificate with the one included in the key store (trusted certificate entry). This validation confirms whether the caller is the person he/she claims to be.

See also...

In this chapter:

> ▸ *Securing Soap messages using a digital signature*

Chapter 7, Securing SOAP Web Services using XWSS Library:

> ▸ *Preparing pair and symmetric Key stores*

Encrypting/decrypting SOAP messages

The concepts of encryption and decryption of SOAP messages are the same as described in *Encrypting/Decrypting of SOAP Messages* from *Chapter 7.* Spring-WS's `Wss4jSecurityInterceptor` provides decryption of the incoming SOAP messages by including the setting property `validationActions` to `Encrypt` on the receiver's-side (server-side here). On the sender's side (the client side here), setting the property `securementActions` causes the sender to `encrypt` outgoing messages.

`Wss4jSecurityInterceptor` needs to access the key store for encryption/decryption. In the case of using a symmetric key, `Key storeCallbackHandler` is responsible for accessing (by setting the properties of `location` and `password`) and reading from a symmetric key store, and passing it to the interceptor. However, in the case of using a private/public key pair store, `CryptoFactoryBean` will do the same job.

In this recipe, in the first case, a symmetric key, which is shared by the client and server, is used for encryption on the client-side and decryption on the server-side. Then, in the second case, the server public key certificate in the client-side key store (trusted certificate) is used for data encryption and the server private key in the server-side key store is used for decryption.

In the first two cases, the whole payload is used in Encryption/Decryption. By setting one property, it is possible to Encrypt/Decrypt part of the payload. In the third case, only part of the payload is set as the target of Encryption/Decryption.

Getting ready

In this recipe, we have the following two projects:

1. `LiveRestaurant_R-8.5` (for a server-side Web-Service), with the following Maven dependencies:
    - ❑ `spring-ws-security-2.0.1.RELEASE.jar`
    - ❑ `spring-expression-3.0.5.RELEASE.jar`
    - ❑ `log4j-1.2.9.jar`

2. `LiveRestaurant_R-8.5-Client` (for the client-side), with the following Maven dependencies:

   ❑ `spring-ws-security-2.0.1.RELEASE.jar`
   ❑ `spring-ws-test-2.0.0.RELEASE.jar`
   ❑ `spring-expression-3.0.5.RELEASE.jar`
   ❑ `log4j-1.2.9.jar`
   ❑ `junit-4.7.jar`

How to do it...

Follow these steps to implement encryption/decryption using a symmetric key:

1. Register `Wss4jSecurityInterceptor` on the server-side application context (`spring-ws-servlet.xml`), set the validation action to `Encrypt`, and configure `Key storeCallbackHandler` to read from the symmetric key store (configure the server-side symmetric key store location and its password) within this interceptor.

2. Register `Wss4jSecurityInterceptor` on the client-side application context (`applicationContext.xml`), set the securement action to `Encrypt`, and configure the `Key storeCallbackHandler` to read from the symmetric key store (configure the client-side symmetric key store location and its password) within this interceptor.

3. Run the following command on `Liverestaurant_R-8.5`:

   `mvn clean package tomcat:run`

4. Run the following command on `Liverestaurant_R-8.5-Client`:

   `mvn clean package`

   Here is the output of the client side (note highlighted text):

   `Sent request...`

   `<SOAP-ENV:Header>`

     `<wsse:Security...>`

       `<xenc:ReferenceList><xenc:DataReference../>`
       `</xenc:ReferenceList>`

     `</wsse:Security>`

   `</SOAP-ENV:Header>`

   `<SOAP-ENV:Body>`

     `<xenc:EncryptedData ...>`

       `<xenc:EncryptionMethod..tripledes-cbc"/>`

       `<ds:KeyInfo...>`

```
            <ds:KeyName>symmetric</ds:KeyName>
        </ds:KeyInfo>
        <xenc:CipherData><xenc:CipherValue>
            3a2tx9zTnVTK17E+Q6wm...
        </xenc:CipherValue></xenc:CipherData>
    </xenc:EncryptedData>
    </SOAP-ENV:Body>
</SOAP-ENV:Envelope>
```

Follow these steps to implement encryption, using a server-trusted certificate on the client-side key store (in `clientStore.jsk`), and decryption on the server-side private key (in `serverStore.jks`):

1. Register `Wss4jSecurityInterceptor` on the server-side application context (`spring-ws-servlet.xml`), set the validation action to `Encrypt`, and set the property `validationSignatureCrypto` to `CryptoFactoryBean` (configure the server-side key store location and its password) within this interceptor.

2. Register the `Wss4jSecurityInterceptor` in the client-side application context (`applicationContext.xml`), set the securement action to `Encrypt`, and set `securementSignatureCrypto` to `CryptoFactoryBean` (configure the client-side key store location and its password) within this interceptor.

Here is the output of the server side (note highlighted text):

```
<SOAP-ENV:Header>
  <wsse:Security...>
    <xenc:EncryptionMethod ..">
      <wsse:SecurityTokenReference ...>
        <ds:X509Data>
          <ds:X509IssuerSerial>
            <ds:X509IssuerName>
              CN=MyFirstName MyLastName,OU=Software,O=MyCompany,
                L=MyCity,ST=MyProvince,C=ME
            </ds:X509IssuerName>
            <ds:X509SerialNumber>1311685900</ds:X509SerialNumber>
          </ds:X509IssuerSerial>
        </ds:X509Data>
      </wsse:SecurityTokenReference>
    </ds:KeyInfo>
    <xenc:CipherData>
      <xenc:CipherValue>dn0lokNhtmZ9...</xenc:CipherValue>
      </xenc:CipherData><xenc:ReferenceList>
```

```
    . . . .
    </wsse:Security>
    </SOAP-ENV:Header><SOAP-ENV:Body>
    <xenc:EncryptedData .../>
    <ds:KeyInfo ...xmldsig#">
    <wsse:SecurityTokenReference ...>
    <wsse:Reference .../>
    </wsse:SecurityTokenReference>
    </ds:KeyInfo>
    <xenc:CipherData><xenc:CipherValue>
    UDO872y+r....</xenc:CipherValue>
    </xenc:CipherData></xenc:EncryptedData>
    </SOAP-ENV:Body>
```

Follow these steps to implement encryption/decryption on the payload:

1. Modify case 2, set the property `securementEncryptionParts` to a specific part of the payload in `Wss4jSecurityInterceptor` on the server side/client side.

2. Run the following command on `Liverestaurant_R-8.5`:

   ```
   mvn clean package tomcat:run
   ```

3. Run the following command on `Liverestaurant_R-8.5-Client`:

   ```
   mvn clean package
   ```

   Here is the output of the client side (note highlighted text):

```
.........
<SOAP-ENV:Body>
<tns:placeOrderRequest...>
<xenc:EncryptedData...>
<xenc:EncryptionMethod .../>
<ds:KeyInfo..xmldsig#">
<wsse:SecurityTokenReference ...>
<wsse:Reference.../></wsse:SecurityTokenReference>
</ds:KeyInfo><xenc:CipherData>
<xenc:CipherValue>
pGzc3/j5GX......
</xenc:CipherValue>
</xenc:CipherData>
</xenc:EncryptedData>
</tns:placeOrderRequest>
......
```

How it works...

In the first case, the client and the server both share the symmetric key. The client encrypts the entire payload using a symmetric key, and sends it to the server. On the server side, the same key will be used to decrypt the payload.

However, in the second and third cases, the client-side server certificate, embedded in the client store, is used for encryption of the payload, and on the server side, the private key of the server store will be used for decryption. The difference between the second and the third case is that the second case encrypts/decrypts the whole payload, but in the third case, only part of the payload will be the target of encryption/decryption.

In the first case, the setting `validationActions` to `Encrypt` on server-side causes the server to decrypt the incoming messages using a symmetric key. The interceptor uses the `ValidationCallbackHandler` for decryption, using a symmetric key store, set in the `location` property. The property `type` sets the store type of the key, and `password` sets the key store password of the symmetric key:

```
<bean class="org.springframework.ws.soap.
  security.wss4j.Wss4jSecurityInterceptor">
  <property name="validationActions" value="Encrypt"/>

  <property name="validationCallbackHandler">
    <bean class="org.springframework.ws.soap.security.
      wss4j.callback.Key storeCallbackHandler">
      <property name="key store">
        <bean class="org.springframework.ws.soap.security.
          support.Key storeFactoryBean">
          <property name="location" value="/WEB-
            INF/symmetricStore.jks"/>
          <property name="type" value="JCEKS"/>
          <property name="password" value="symmetricPassword"/>
        </bean>
      </property>
      <property name="symmetricKeyPassword" value="keyPassword"/>
    </bean>
  </property>
</bean>
```

On the client-side, the setting property `securementActions` to `Encrypt` causes the client to encrypt all outgoing messages. Encryption is customized by setting `securementEncryptionKeyIdentifier` to `EmbeddedKeyName`. When the `EmbeddedKeyName` type is chosen, the secret key to encryption is mandatory. The symmetric key alias (symmetric here) is set by the `securementEncryptionUser`.

By default, the ds:KeyName element in the SOAP header takes
the value of the securementEncryptionUser property.
securementEncryptionEmbeddedKeyName could be used to indicate a different value.
The securementEncryptionKeyTransportAlgorithm property defines which algorithm
to use to encrypt the generated symmetric key. securementCallbackHandler is provided
with Key storeCallbackHandler, which points to the appropriate key store, that is, a
symmetric key store, as described in the server-side configuration:

```
<bean        class="org.springframework.ws.soap.
  security.wss4j.Wss4jSecurityInterceptor">
  <property name="securementActions" value="Encrypt" />
  <property name="securementEncryptionKeyIdentifier"
    value="EmbeddedKeyName"/>
  <property name="securementEncryptionUser" value="symmetric"/>
  <property name="securementEncryptionEmbeddedKeyName"
    value="symmetric"/>
  <property name="SecurementEncryptionSymAlgorithm"
    value="http://www.w3.org/2001/04/xmlenc#tripledes-cbc"/>

  <property name="securementCallbackHandler">
    <bean class="org.springframework.ws.soap.security.
      wss4j.callback.Key storeCallbackHandler">
      <property name="symmetricKeyPassword" value="keyPassword"/>
      <property name="key store">
        <bean class="org.springframework.ws.soap.security.
          support.Key storeFactoryBean">
          <property name="location" value="/symmetricStore.jks"/>
          <property name="type" value="JCEKS"/>
          <property name="password" value="symmetricPassword"/>
        </bean>
      </property>
    </bean>
  </property>
</bean>
```

In the second and the third case, the validationDecryptionCrypto, configured on the
server side is almost the same as the first case for decrypting data:

```
<bean class="org.springframework.ws.soap.security.
  wss4j.Wss4jSecurityInterceptor">
  <property name="validationActions" value="Encrypt" />

  <property name="validationDecryptionCrypto">

    <bean class="org.springframework.ws.soap.security.
      wss4j.support.CryptoFactoryBean">
```

```
        <property name="key storePassword" value="serverPassword" />
        <property name="key storeLocation" value="/WEB-
          INF/serverStore.jks" />
      </bean>
    </property>
    <property name="validationCallbackHandler">
      <bean class="org.springframework.ws.soap.security.
        wss4j.callback.Key storeCallbackHandler">
        <property name="privateKeyPassword" value="serPkPassword" />
      </bean>
    </property>
  </bean>
```

On the client-side, setting `value="Encrypt"` of `securementActions` causes the client to encrypt all outgoing messages. `securementEncryptionCrypto` is for setting the key store location and the password. `SecurementEncryptionUser` is for setting the alias of the server certificate to reside on the client key store:

```
<bean class="org.springframework.ws.soap.security.
  wss4j.Wss4jSecurityInterceptor">
  <property name="securementActions" value="Encrypt" />
  <property name="securementEncryptionUser" value="server" />

  <property name="securementEncryptionCrypto">
    <bean class="org.springframework.ws.soap.security.
      wss4j.support.CryptoFactoryBean">
      <property name="key storePassword" value="clientPassword" />
      <property name="key storeLocation" value="/clientStore.jks" />
    </bean>
  </property>
</bean>
```

The difference between *case 2* and *3* is that the following the configuration setting on the client-side/server-side configuration causes only a part of the payload to be encrypted/decrypted.

```
---client/server configuration file
<property name="securementEncryptionParts"value="{Content}
  {http://www.packtpub.com/LiveRestaurant/OrderService/schema}
  placeOrderRequest"/>
```

See also...

In this chapter:

> ▸ *Securing SOAP messages using a digital signature*

Chapter 2, Building Clients for SOAP Web-Services

> ▸ *Creating Web-Service client for WS-Addressing endpoint*

Chapter 7, Securing SOAP Web Services using XWSS Library

> ▸ *Preparing a pair and symmetric key stores*

9

RESTful Web-Services

In this chapter, we will cover:

- ▶ Setting up a Spring RESTful Web-Service, using RESTful features in Spring MVC
- ▶ Using the RESTClient tool to access a Spring RESTful Web-Service
- ▶ Setting up a Spring RESTful Web-Service using HTTP message conversion
- ▶ Creating a WS client for the Spring RESTful Web-Service using Spring template classes

Introduction

Simple Object Access Protocol (**SOAP**) allows applications to communicate with one another using XML as the communication format (SOAP is well understood), but because it is XML-based, it tends to be verbose, even for very simple Web-Service scenarios.

Representational State Transfer (**REST**), published as a doctoral dissertation by Roy Fielding in 2000, aimed at simplifying the usage of Web-Service.

While SOAP uses a lot of XML (that looks very complex) to communicate, REST uses very lightweight and human-readable data (for example, the request URI `http://localhost:8080/LiveRestaurant/customerAccount/234` returns `123-3456`. Compare this simple request and response with SOAP request/response envelop, already presented in the earlier chapters of this book. Since REST Web-Service implementation is very flexible and could be very easy, it requires no toolkit. However, SOAP-based Web-Services need tools for simplification (for example, to call a SOAP Web-Service, you would use tools to generate client-side proxy classes for a contract-last Web-Service class, or use tools to generate domain classes from a schema in a contract-first Web-Service). In the earlier chapters, you will have realized how strict a contract-first Web-Service is with the `request/response` format (it must match the contract). The REST Web-Service `request/response` format is all up to developers, and could be designed as easily as possible. While using SOAP Web-Services, using JavaScript is not easy (it needs a lot of code). REST usage is simplified using AJAX technologies and the JSON format.

Here are some of REST's demerits: REST only works over HTTP;calling a RESTful Web-Service is limited by HTTP verbs: GET, POST, PUT, and DELETE.

RESTful was built on the principles of REST, in which HTTP's methods are used based on their concepts. For example, HTTP's `GET`, `POST`, `PUT`, and `DELETE` are all used in a RESTful architecture that match their meaning in the same fashion as with HTTP.

RESTful Web-Services expose the state of its resources. In this chapter, for example, a RESTful service is exposed to get the list of available order items and the order object, when an order is placed in an online restaurant. To get a list of the available order items, the `GET` method is used, and for placing an order, the `POST` method is used. The method `PUT` could be used to add/update an entry, and `DELETE` could be used to delete an entry.

Here is the sample URL to make a RESTful Web-Service call and to get the list of available order items:

```
http://localhost:8080/LiveRestaurant/orderItems.
```

The following is the return response (response format is not necessarily in XML format; it could be in JSON, plain-text, or any format):

```
<list>
  <orderItem>
    <name>Burger</name>
    <id>0</id>
  </orderItem>
  <orderItem>
    <name>Pizza</name>
    <id>1</id>
  </orderItem>
  <orderItem>
    <name>Sushi</name><id>2</id>
  </orderItem>
  <orderItem>
    <name>Salad</name>
  <id>3</id>
  </orderItem>
</list>
```

There are several implementations of the RESTful Web-Service such as `Restlet`, `RestEasy`, and `Jersey`. `Jersey`, the most significant one in this group, is the implementation of JAX-RS (JSR 311).

Spring, being a widely-used framework of Java EE, introduced support for RESTful Web-Services in release 3. RESTful has been integrated into Spring's MVC layer that allows applications to build on Spring using RESTful features. The most significant of these features includes:

▶ **Annotations**, such as `@RequestMapping` and `@PathVariable`, used for URI mappings and passing parameters.

▶ `ContentNegotiatingViewResolver`, which allows the usage of different MIME types (such as `text/xml`, `text/json`, and `text/plain`)

▶ `HttpMessageConverter`, which allows the production of multiple representations, based on the client requests (such as ATOM, XML, and JSON).

Setting up a Spring RESTful Web-Service using RESTful features in Spring MVC

Spring 3.0 supports RESTful Web-Services based on Spring MVC. Spring uses annotations to set up a RESTful Web-Service and needs to be configured (within the Spring application context file) to scan for annotation. A spring MVC controller is required to set up a RESTful Web-Service. The `@Controller` annotation tags a class as the MVC controller (`http://static.springsource.org/spring/docs/current/spring-framework-reference/html/mvc.html`). The `@RequestMapping` annotation maps incoming requests to an appropriate Java method in the controller class. Using this annotation, you can define the URI and the HTTP method that is mapped to a Java class method. For example, in the following example, the method `loadOrderItems` will be called if the request URI is followed by `/orderItems`, and `@PathVariable` is for injecting the value of the request parameters (`{cayegoryId}`) variable into a method parameter (`String cayegoryId`):

```
@RequestMapping( value="/orderItem/{cayegoryId}",
   method=RequestMethod.GET )
public ModelAndView loadOrderItems(@PathVariable String cayegoryId)
{...}
```

In this recipe, implementing a RESTful Web-Service using Spring 3 MVC is presented. The client project of this Web-Service is implemented here, but it will be detailed in the last recipe of this chapter: *Creating a WS client for Spring RESTful Web-Service using Spring template classes*.

Getting ready

In this recipe, the project's name is `LiveRestaurant_R-9.1` (the `LiveRestaurant_R-9.1-Client` project is included in the code for testing purposes) with the following Maven dependencies:

- ▸ `com.springsource.javax.servlet-2.5.0.jar`
- ▸ `spring-oxm-3.0.5.RELEASE.jar`
- ▸ `spring-web-3.0.5.RELEASE.jar`
- ▸ `spring-webmvc-3.0.5.RELEASE.jar`
- ▸ `xstream-1.3.1.jar`
- ▸ `commons-logging-1.1.1.jar`

`spring-oxm` is the Spring support for Object/XML mapping, `spring-web` and `spring-webmvc` are the support for Seb and MVC support, and `xstream` is for the Object/XML mapping framework.

How to do it...

1. Configure `MessageDispatcherServlet` inside the `web.xml` file (URL:`http://<host>:<port>/<appcontext>/*` is to be forwarded to this servlet).

2. Define the controller file (`OrderController.java`).

3. Define the domain POJOs (`Order.java`, `OrderItem.java`) and services (`OrderService`, `OrderServiceImpl`).

4. Configure the server-side application context-file (`order-servlet.xml`).

5. Run the following command on `Liverestaurant_R-9.1`:

   `mvn clean package tomcat:run`

6. Run the following command on `Liverestaurant_R-9.1-Client`:

   `mvn clean package`

   Here is client-side output:

   ```
   .... Created POST request for
     "http://localhost:8080/LiveRestaurant/order/1"
   .....Setting request Accept header to [application/xml, text/xml,
     application/*+xml]
   .... POST request for "http://localhost:8080/LiveRestaurant/
   order/1"
     resulted in 200 (OK)
   .....Reading [com.packtpub.liverestaurant.domain.Order] as
     "application/xml;charset=ISO-8859-1"
   ```

```
.....
.....Created GET request for
  "http://localhost:8080/LiveRestaurant/orderItems"
.....Setting request Accept header to [application/xml, text/xml,
  application/*+xml]
.....GET request for "http://localhost:8080/LiveRestaurant/
orderItems"
  resulted in 200 (OK)
```

7. Browse to this link: `http://localhost:8080/LiveRestaurant/orderItems`, and you will be provided with the following response:

```
<list>
  <orderItem>
    <name>Burger</name>
    <id>0</id>
  </orderItem>
  <orderItem>
  <name>Pizza</name>
    <id>1</id>
  </orderItem>
  <orderItem>
    <name>Sushi</name><id>2</id>
  </orderItem>
  <orderItem>
    <name>Salad</name>
    <id>3</id>
  </orderItem>
</list>
```

How it works...

The application is an MVC web project, in which a controller returns Spring's `Model` and `View` objects. Spring's `MarshallingView` marshalls the model object into XML, using a `marshaller` (`XStreamMarshaller`), and the XML will be sent back to the client.

All requests will come to `DispatcherServlet`, which will be forwarded to the controller - `OrderController`, and based on the request URI, an appropriate method will be called that will return a response back to the caller. The following configuration in `web.xml` forwards all the requests to the `DispatcherServlet`:

```
<servlet>
  <servlet-name>order</servlet-name>
  <servlet-class>
    org.springframework.web.servlet.DispatcherServlet
  </servlet-class>
  <load-on-startup>1</load-on-startup>
</servlet>

<servlet-mapping>
  <servlet-name>order</servlet-name>
  <url-pattern>/*</url-pattern>
</servlet-mapping>
```

The following setting in `order-context.xml` causes Spring to detect all annotations in the package (this includes `OrderService` and `OrderController`). The `BeanNameViewResolver` is for mapping a name (`orderXmlView` in `OrderController`) to a view (the bean `orderXmlView`), which is an instance of `org.springframework. web.servlet.view.xml.MarshallingView`:

```
<context:component-scan base-package=
  "com.packtpub.liverestaurant.orderservice" />
<bean class=
  "org.springframework.web.servlet.view.BeanNameViewResolver" />
<bean id="orderXmlView" class=
  "org.springframework.web.servlet.view.xml.MarshallingView">
...
</bean>
```

`@Controller` tags the class `OrderController` as the controller in an MVC pattern. All caller requests will be forwarded to this class, and based on the request URI, an appropriate method will be called. For example, the method `placeOrder` will be called if any URI similar to `http://<host>:<port>/<appcontext>/order/1` with an HTTP `POST` method comes from a caller request.

```
@RequestMapping(value = "/order/{orderId}", method = RequestMethod.
POST)
public ModelAndView placeOrder(@PathVariable String orderId) {..}
```

`@PathVariable` causes the `orderId` parameter from the URI to be injected and passed to the `placeOrder` method.

The body of the method, `placeOrder`, calls a method from the `OrderService` interface and returns the `Order` object:

```
Order order = orderService.placeOrder(orderId);
ModelAndView mav = new ModelAndView("orderXmlView",
  BindingResult.MODEL_KEY_PREFIX + "order", order);
return mav;
```

Then, it builds a view based on marshalling the `Order` object into the XML format, using the `Marshallingview` bean (`MarshallingView`, which is the view in MVC, uses `XStreamMarshaller` to marshall the model object into XML format), and returns it to the caller of the service.

```
<bean id="orderXmlView" class=
  "org.springframework.web.servlet.view.xml.MarshallingView">
  <constructor-arg>
    <bean class="org.springframework.oxm.xstream.XStreamMarshaller">
      <property name="autodetectAnnotations" value="true"/>
    </bean>
  </constructor-arg>
</bean>
```

The `loadOrderItems` method works in the same way, except that the URI should be similar to the following pattern: `http://<host>:<port>/<appcontext>/orderItems`, with an HTTP `GET`:

```
@RequestMapping(value = "/orderItems", method = RequestMethod.GET)
public ModelAndView loadOrderItems() {
  List<OrderItem> orderItems = orderService.listOrderItems();
  ModelAndView modelAndView = new ModelAndView("orderXmlView",
    BindingResult.MODEL_KEY_PREFIX + "orderItem", orderItems);
  return modelAndView;
}
```

In this recipe, the database activities are not implemented. However, in a real application, the HTTP method `DELETE` could be used to delete an entity (for example, `orderItem`) from the database, and the `PUT` method could be used to update a record (for example, `order`).

See also...

In this book:

Chapter 6, Marshalling and Object-XML Mapping (OXM):

Marshalling with XStream

Using the REST Client tool to access Spring RESTful Web-Service

REST Client is an application to call and test RESTful Web-Services. REST Client is provided as a Firefox/Flock add-on. The Firefox REST Client supports all HTTP methods, **RFC2616** (**HTTP/1.1**), and **RFC2518** (**WebDAV**). Using this add-on, you can build your own customized URI, add a header, send it to RESTful Web-Services, and get the response back.

In this recipe, we will learn how to use Firefox REST Client to test how a RESTful Web-Service is presented. This recipe uses the first recipe of this chapter, *Setting up a Spring RESTful Web-Service using RESTful features in Spring MVC*, as RESTful Web-Services.

Getting ready

Download and install the following add-on for Firefox:

`https://addons.mozilla.org/en-US/firefox/addon/restclient/`.

How to do it...

1. Run `LiveRestaurant_R-9.1` from this chapter.

2. Open the Firefox browser and go to **Tools | Rest Client**.

3. Change the **Method** to **GET** and enter the URL: `http://localhost:8080/ LiveRestaurant/orderItems`, and click on **Send**:

Here is the result:

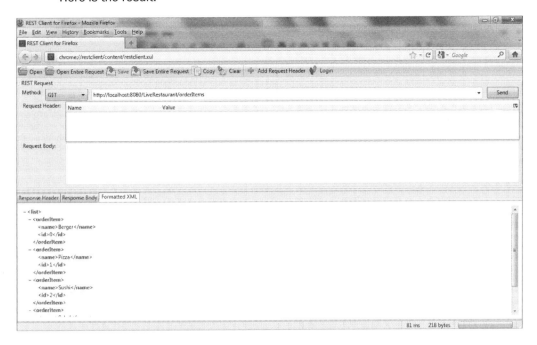

4. Change **Method** to **POST**, enter the URL: `http://localhost:8080/LiveRestaurant/order/1`, and click on **Send**:

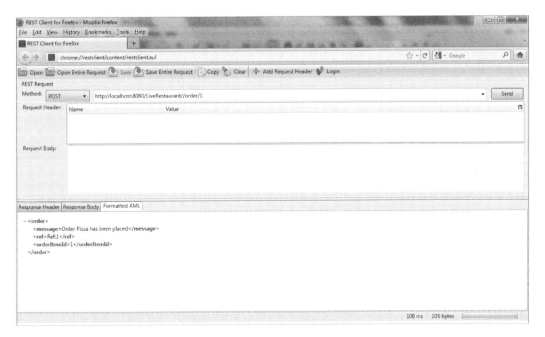

See also...

In this chapter:

Setting up a Spring RESTful Web-Service using RESTful features in Spring MVC

Setting up a Spring RESTful Web-Service using HTTP message conversion

The client and server on the HTTP protocol exchange data using text format. Eventually, there are requirements to accept different request formats and covert the text format into a meaningful format, such as an Object or the JSON format. Spring provides features to provide multiple requests/presentations to/from the same text format.

Spring 3 introduced `ContentNegotiatingViewResolver`, which can select various views from the same URI and can provide multiple presentations.

The alternate way of doing the same task is using the `HttpMessageConverter` interface and the `@ResponseBody` annotation. Implementation of the `HttpMessageConverter` interface from Spring converts HTTP messages into several formats. Its widely used implementations include:

- `StringHttpMessageConverter` implementation reads/writes text from the HTTP request/response. This is the default converter.

- `MarshallingHttpMessageConverter` implementation marshalls/unmarshalls objects from the text HTTP request/response. It gets a constructor argument to specify the type of Marshaller (such as `Jaxb`, `XStream`, and so on).

- `MappingJacksonHttpMessageConverter` implementation converts text into the JSON data format or vice-versa.

In this recipe, message conversion using `MarshallingHttpMessageConverter`, `MappingJacksonHttpMessageConverter`, and `AtomFeedHttpMessageConverter` is presented. Since this project is similar to the first recipe of this chapter, *Setting up a Spring RESTful Web-Service using RESTful features in Spring MVC*, it is reused as a template for the project. The difference in this recipe is in the controller implementation and the application context configuration.

The client project of this Web-Service is implemented here, but it will be detailed in the last recipe of this chapter, *Creating a WS client for Spring RESTful Web-Service using Spring template classes*.

Getting ready

In this recipe, the project's name is `LiveRestaurant_R-9.2` (`LiveRestaurant_R-9.2-Client` is included in the code for testing purposes in this recipe. However, it will be explained in the last recipe), and it has the following Maven dependencies:

- `com.springsource.javax.servlet-2.5.0.jar`
- `spring-oxm-3.0.5.RELEASE.jar`
- `spring-web-3.0.5.RELEASE.jar`
- `spring-webmvc-3.0.5.RELEASE.jar`
- `xstream-1.3.1.jar`
- `commons-logging-1.1.1.jar`
- `jackson-core-asl-1.7.5.jar`
- `jackson-mapper-asl-1.7.5.jar`
- `rome-1.0.jar`

`jackson-core` and `jackson-mapper` support the JSON format and the others support the ATOM format.

How to do it...

1. Configure the `DispatcherServlet` inside the `web.xml` file (URL:`http://<host>:<port>/<appcontext>/*` is to be forwarded to this servlet).

2. Define the controller file (`OrderController.java`).

3. Define domain POJOs (`Order.java`, `OrderItem.java`) and services (`OrderService`, `OrderServiceImpl`)

4. Configure the server-side application context-file (`order-servlet.xml`) and register the converters.

5. Change the **Method** to **POST** and add a **Request Header: Name** - accept, **Value** - application/json. Enter the URL http://localhost:8080/ LiveRestaurant/orderJson/1 and click on **Send**:

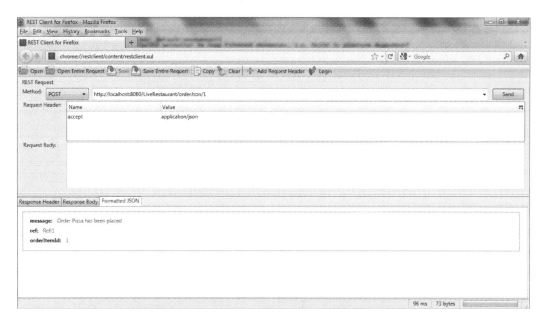

6. Change the **Method** to **GET**, and add **Request Header**: **Name** - accept, **Value** - application/atom+xml. Enter the URL http://localhost:8080/ LiveRestaurant/orderItemsFeed and click on **Send**:

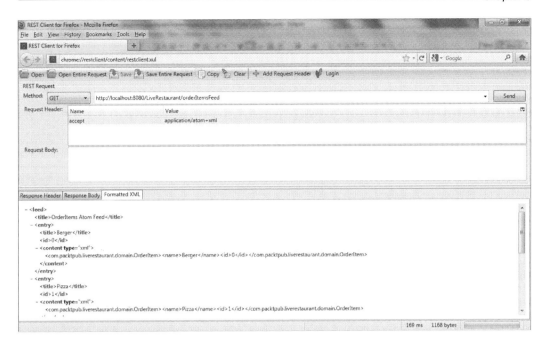

How it works...

This recipe is almost the same as the first recipe of this chapter, except that it uses the message converter and @ResponseBody to provide multiple presentations.

In the first recipe, MarshallingView was responsible for converting the response to the selected XML type of the view (using XstreamMarshaller). However, here, the message converters are responsible for rendering data models into a selected format, MarshallingHttpMessageConverter is responsible for converting the List<OrderItem> to the application/xml format (using XstreamMarshaller), and MappingJacksonHttpMessageConverter is used to convert an order into the application/json format. AtomFeedHttpMessageConverter is used to convert Feed (that wraps XML content generated from List<OrderItem> using XStreamMarshaller into the application/atom+xml format:

```
<context:component-scan base-package=
  "com.packtpub.liverestaurant.orderservice" />
<bean id="xStreamMarshaller" class=
  "org.springframework.oxm.xstream.XStreamMarshaller"/>
<bean class="org.springframework.
  web.servlet.mvc.annotation.DefaultAnnotationHandlerMapping" />
<bean class="org.springframework.
  web.servlet.mvc.annotation.AnnotationMethodHandlerAdapter">
  <property name="messageConverters">
```

```xml
        <list>
          <ref bean="marshallingConverter" />
          <ref bean="jsonConverter" />
          <ref bean="atomConverter" />
        </list>
      </property>
  </bean>

  <bean id="marshallingConverter" class="org.springframework.
    http.converter.xml.MarshallingHttpMessageConverter">
    <constructor-arg>
      <bean class="org.springframework.oxm.xstream.XStreamMarshaller">
        <property name="autodetectAnnotations" value="true"/>
      </bean>
    </constructor-arg>
  <property name="supportedMediaTypes" value="application/xml"/>
  </bean>
  <bean id="jsonConverter" class="org.springframework.
    http.converter.json.MappingJacksonHttpMessageConverter">
    <property name="supportedMediaTypes" value="application/json" />
  </bean>
  <bean id="atomConverter"class="org.springframework.
    http.converter.feed.AtomFeedHttpMessageConverter">
    <property name="supportedMediaTypes" value="application/atom+xml" />
  </bean>
```

In the controller, the following code causes the controller's method to accept the request URI method's POST format—json:

```java
@RequestMapping(method=RequestMethod.POST, value="/orderJson/
{orderId}",
  headers="Accept=application/json")
public @ResponseBody Order placeOrderJson(@PathVariable String
orderId) {
  Order order=orderService.placeOrder(orderId);
  return order;
}
```

And it returns the Order object in JSON format (using @ResponseBody and MappingJacksonHttpMessageConverter, configured in order-context.xml):

```json
{"message":"Order Pizza has been
  placed","ref":"Ref:1","orderItemId":"1"}
```

The following code causes the controller's method to accept the request URI method's GET format—atom:

```
@RequestMapping(method=RequestMethod.GET, value="/orderItemsFeed",
  headers="Accept=application/atom+xml")
public @ResponseBody Feed loadOrderItemsAtom() {
  Feed feed = null;
  try {
    feed= getOrderItemsFeed(orderService.listOrderItems());
  } catch (Exception e) {
    throw new RuntimeException(e);
  }
  return feed;
}
```

It also returns the List<OrderItem> object in Atom format (using @ResponseBody and AtomFeedHttpMessageConverter, configured in order-context.xml):

```
<?xml version="1.0" encoding="UTF-8"?>
<feed xmlns="http://www.w3.org/2005/Atom">
  <title>OrderItems Atom Feed</title>
  <entry>
    <title>Burger</title>
    <id>0</id>
    <content type="xml">
      &lt;com.packtpub.liverestaurant.domain.OrderItem&gt;&lt;name&gt;
        Burger&lt;/name&gt;&lt;id&gt;0&lt;/id&gt;&lt;/com.packtpub.
        liverestaurant.domain.OrderItem&gt;
    </content>
  </entry>
  <entry>
    <title>Pizza</title>
    <id>1</id>
    <content type="xml">&lt;com.packtpub.liverestaurant.domain.
      OrderItem&gt;&lt;name&gt;Pizza&lt;/name&gt;&lt;id&gt;1&lt;
        /id&gt;&lt;/com.packtpub.liverestaurant.domain.OrderItem&gt;
    </content>
  </entry>
  ...
```

See also...

In this chapter:

Setting up a Spring RESTful Web-Service using RESTful features in Spring MVC

Creating a WS Client for the Spring RESTful Web-Service using Spring template classes

Spring provides varieties of template classes that simplify many complexities using different technologies. For example, `WebServiceTemplate` is for calling a SOAP-based Web-Service, and `JmsTemplate` is for sending/receiving JMS messages. Spring also has the `RestTemplate` to simplify the interaction with RESTful Web-Services.

To use `RestTemplate`:

▶ Create an instance of `RestTemplate` (can be done using the `@Autowired` feature)

▶ Configure one-to-many message converters (as described in the previous recipe)

▶ Call methods of `RestTemplate` to call a RESTful Web-Service and get a response back

In this recipe, we will learn to consume a RESTful Web-Service using the `RestTemplate`. This recipe uses the third recipe of this chapter, *Setting up a Spring RESTful Web-Service using HTTP Message Conversion*, as the RESTful Web-Service.

Getting ready

In this recipe, the project's name is `LiveRestaurant_R-9.2-Client` (`LiveRestaurant_R-9.2` is included in this recipe to set up a RESTful server, as explained earlier in the recipe *Setting up a Spring RESTful Web-Service using HTTP Message Conversion*) with the following Maven dependencies:

▶ `spring-oxm-3.0.5.RELEASE.jar`

▶ `spring-web-3.0.5.RELEASE.jar`

▶ `xstream-1.3.1.jar`

▶ `commons-logging-1.1.1.jar`

▶ `jackson-core-asl-1.7.5.jar`

▶ `jackson-mapper-asl-1.7.5.jar`

▶ `rome-1.0.jar`

▶ `junit-4.6.jar`

▶ `spring-test-3.0.5.RELEASE.jar`

How to do it...

1. Define domain POJOs (`Order.java`, `OrderItem.java`) and services (`OrderService`, `OrderServiceImpl`).

2. Configure the client-side application context-file (`order-servlet.xml`) and register the converters.

3. Create a helper class (`OrderClient`) that wraps calling the RESTful Web-Service using the `RestTemplate`.

4. Run the following command on `Liverestaurant_R-9.2`:

   ```
   mvn clean package tomcat:run
   ```

5. Run the following command on `Liverestaurant_R-9.2-Client`:

   ```
   mvn clean package
   ```

   Here is the client-side output:

   ```
   ....
   .. Created GET request for
      "http://localhost:8080/LiveRestaurant/orderItems"
   .. Setting request Accept header to [application/xml, text/xml,
      application/*+xml, application/json]
   .. GET request for "http://localhost:8080/LiveRestaurant/
   orderItems"
      resulted in 200 (OK)
   .. Reading [java.util.List] as "application/xml" using ....
   .. Created POST request for
      "http://localhost:8080/LiveRestaurant/orderJson/1"
   .. Setting request Accept header to [application/xml, text/xml,
      application/*+xml, application/json]
   .. POST request for "http://localhost:8080/LiveRestaurant/
   orderJson/1"
      resulted in 200 (OK)
   .. Reading [com.packtpub.liverestaurant.domain.Order] as
      "application/xml" using ...
   ...Created GET request for
      "http://localhost:8080/LiveRestaurant/orderItemsFeed"
   .. Setting request Accept header to [application/xml, text/xml,
      application/*+xml, application/json, application/atom+xml]
   .. GET request for "http://localhost:8080/LiveRestaurant/
   orderItemsFeed"
      resulted in 200 (OK)
   .. Reading [com.sun.syndication.feed.atom.Feed] as "application/
   xml"
      using ...
   ```

How it works...

Application context loaded by `OrderServiceClientTest`, loads, instantiates, and injects `RestTemplate` into `OrderClient`. This class calls the controller's method using `RestTemplate` and returns a value back to the test suite class (`OrderServiceClientTest`).

In the suite class test methods, the response will be compared with the desired values.

The `applicationContext.xml` defines the `restTemplate` bean and sets a list of message converters:

```
......
<bean id="restTemplate"
  class="org.springframework.web.client.RestTemplate">
  <property name="messageConverters">
    <list>
      <ref bean="xmlMarshallingHttpMessageConverter" />
      <ref bean="jsonConverter" />
      <ref bean="atomConverter" />
    </list>
  </property>
</bean>

<bean id="xmlMarshallingHttpMessageConverter" class="org.
springframework.
  http.converter.xml.MarshallingHttpMessageConverter">
  <constructor-arg>
    <ref bean="xStreamMarshaller" />
  </constructor-arg>
</bean>

<bean id="xStreamMarshaller"
  class="org.springframework.oxm.xstream.XStreamMarshaller">
  <property name="annotatedClasses">
    <list>
      <value>com.packtpub.liverestaurant.domain.Order</value>
      <value>com.packtpub.liverestaurant.domain.OrderItem</value>
    </list>
  </property>
</bean>

<bean id="atomConverter" class="org.springframework.
  http.converter.feed.AtomFeedHttpMessageConverter">
```

```
    <property name="supportedMediaTypes" value="application/atom+xml" />
  </bean>
  <bean id="jsonConverter" class="org.springframework.
    http.converter.json.MappingJacksonHttpMessageConverter">
    <property name="supportedMediaTypes" value="application/json" />
  </bean>
```

Converters set inside the `messageConverters` are responsible for converting requests/responses in different formats (XML, JSON, ATOM) back to `object` type. `XstreamMarshaller` gets the list of recognized POJOs (`Order`, `OrderItem`), using the annotation tags in those classes.

`OrderClient.java` is a helper class that wraps calling RESTful Web-Services, using `RestTemplate`:

```
  protected RestTemplate restTemplate;
  private final static String serviceUrl =
    "http://localhost:8080/LiveRestaurant/";
  @SuppressWarnings("unchecked")
  public List<OrderItem> loadOrderItemsXML() {
    HttpEntity<String> entity = getHttpEntity(MediaType.APPLICATION_
  XML);
    ResponseEntity<List> response = restTemplate.exchange(serviceUrl
      + "orderItems", HttpMethod.GET, entity, List.class);
    return response.getBody();
  }
  .....
  ...
  public String loadOrderItemsAtom() {
    HttpEntity<String> httpEntity =
      getHttpEntity(MediaType.APPLICATION_ATOM_XML);
    String outputStr = null;
    ResponseEntity<Feed> responseEntity = restTemplate.
  exchange(serviceUrl
      + "orderItemsFeed", HttpMethod.GET, httpEntity, Feed.class);
    WireFeed wireFeed = responseEntity.getBody();
    WireFeedOutput wireFeedOutput = new WireFeedOutput();
    try {
      outputStr = wireFeedOutput.outputString(wireFeed);
    } catch (Exception e) {
      throw new RuntimeException(e);
    }
    return outputStr;
  }
  private HttpEntity<String> getHttpEntity(MediaType mediaType) {
```

```
HttpHeaders httpHeaders = new HttpHeaders();
httpHeaders.setContentType(mediaType);
HttpEntity<String> httpEntity = new HttpEntity<String>(httpHeaders);
return httpEntity;
}
```

There's more

This recipe uses only two methods of the RestTemplate (exchange and postForEntity). However, RestTemplate supports several caller methods:

► exchange: It calls specific HTTP (GET, POST, PUT, and DELETE) methods and converts the HTTP response

► getForObject: It calls the HTTP GET method and converts the HTTP response into an object

► postForObject: It calls the HTTP POST method and converts the HTTP response into an object

See also...

In this chapter:

► *Setting up a Spring RESTful Web-Service using RESTful features in Spring MVC*

► *Setting up a Spring RESTful Web-Service using HTTP message conversion*

The book, *RESTful Java Web Services*, at http://www.packtpub.com/restful-java-web-services/book.

10
Spring Remoting

In this chapter, we will cover:

- ▸ Setting up Web-Services using RMI
- ▸ Setting up servlet-based Web-Services using Hessian/Burlap, exposing business beans
- ▸ Setting up Web-Services using JAX-WS
- ▸ Exposing servlet-based Web-Services using Apache CXF
- ▸ Exposing Web-Services using JMS as the underlying communication protocol

Introduction

Spring-WS project is a contract-first approach to build a Web-Service. This approach is already detailed in the first eight chapters. However, sometimes the requirement is to expose the existing business Spring beans as a Web-Service, which is called **contract-last** approach, to set up a Web-Service.

Spring's remoting supports communication with several remoting technologies. Spring remoting allows you to expose existing Spring beans on server side as a Web-Service. On the client side, Spring remoting allows the client application to call a remote Spring bean (which is exposed as a Web-Service) through a local interface. In this chapter, Spring's features for the following remoting technologies are detailed:

- ▸ **RMI**: Spring's `RmiServiceExporter` allows you to expose local business services on **Remote Method Invocation** (**RMI**) on the server side, and Spring's `RmiProxyFactoryBean` is the client-side proxy bean to call the Web-Service.

- ▸ **Hessian**: Spring's `HessianServiceExporter` allows you to expose local business services on lightweight HTTP-based protocol, introduced by Caucho technology (`http://hessian.caucho.com`) on the server side, and `HessianProxyFactoryBean` is the client-side proxy bean to call the Web-Service.

- ▸ **Burlap**: This is an XML alternative of Hessian by Caucho Technology. Spring provides support classes using two of Spring's beans, namely, `BurlapProxyFactoryBean` and `BurlapServiceExporter`.

- ▸ **JAX-RPC**: Spring's support to set up Web-Services is based on a Remote Procedure Call that uses J2EE 1.4's JAX-RPC Web-Service API

- ▸ **JAX-WS**: Spring's support to set up Web-Services using Java EE 5+ JAX-WS API that allows message-oriented as well as Remote Procedure Call Web-Service development.

- ▸ **JMS**: Spring exposes/consumes Web-Services using JMS as the underlying communication protocol using `JmsInvokerServiceExporter` and `JmsInvokerProxyFactoryBean` classes.

Since JAX-WS is the successor of JAX-RPC, JAX-RPC is not included in this chapter. Instead, Apache CXF will be detailed in this chapter, as it can use JAX-WS to set up Web-Services, even though it is not part of Spring's remoting.

For simplification, in this chapter, the following local business service is to be exposed as a Web-Service (the domain model is the one described in the *Introduction* section of *Chapter 1, Building SOAP Web-Services*).

```
public interface OrderService  {
   placeOrderResponse placeOrder(PlaceOrderRequest placeOrderRequest);
}
```

And this is the interface implementation:

```
public class OrderServiceImpl implements OrderService{

   public PlaceOrderResponse placeOrder(PlaceOrderRequest
     placeOrderRequest) {
     PlaceOrderResponse response=new PlaceOrderResponse();
     response.setRefNumber(getRandomOrderRefNo());
     return response;
   }
...
```

Setting up Web-Services using RMI

RMI, a part of J2SE, allows calling a method on different **Java Virtual Machines** (**JVMs**). RMI's goal is to expose objects in separate JVM's, as if they are like local objects. The client that calls the remote object through RMI doesn't know whether an object is remote or local, and calling methods on the remote object has the same syntax as a method invocation on a local object.

Spring's remoting provides features to expose/access Web-Services, based on RMI technology. On the server side, Spring's `RmiServiceExporter` bean exposes server-side Spring business bean as a Web-Service. On the client-side, Spring's `RmiProxyFactoryBean` presents the Web-Service's methods as a local interface.

In this recipe, we will learn to set up a Web-Service using RMI, and learn how the call to Web-Service through RMI is presented.

Getting ready

In this recipe, we have the following two projects:

1. `LiveRestaurant_R-10.1` (for a server-side Web-Service), with the following Maven dependencies:
    - `spring-context-3.0.5.RELEASE.jar`
    - `log4j-1.2.9.jar`

2. `LiveRestaurant_R-10.1-Client` (for the client-side), with the following Maven dependencies:
    - `spring-context-3.0.5.RELEASE.jar`
    - `spring-ws-test-2.0.0.RELEASE.jar`
    - `log4j-1.2.9.jar`
    - `junit-4.7.jar`
    - `xmlunit-1.1.jar`

How to do it...

1. Register the server-side service implementation within Spring's `RmiServiceExporter` in the server-side application context (`applicationContext.xml`) and set the port and service name.

2. Register the local interface (same as server-side) within Spring's `RmiProxyFactoryBean` in the client-side application context (`applicationContext.xml`) and set the service's URL.

3. Add a Java class to load the server-side application context-file (in the class's `main` method) to set up the server.

4. Add a JUnit test case class on the client side that calls a Web-Service using the local interface.

5. Run the following command on `Liverestaurant_R-10.1`:

    `mvn clean package exec:java`

6. Run the following command on `Liverestaurant_R-10.1-Client`:

```
mvn clean package
```

7. Here is the client-side output:

```
......
... - Located RMI stub with URL [rmi://localhost:1199/
OrderService]
....- RMI stub [rmi://localhost:1199/OrderService] is an RMI
invoker
 ......
Tests run: 1, Failures: 0, Errors: 0, Skipped: 0, Time elapsed:
0.78 sec
...
Tests run: 1, Failures: 0, Errors: 0, Skipped: 0
......
[INFO] BUILD SUCCESS
```

How it works...

`OrderServiceSetUp` is the class that loads the server-side application context and sets up the server to expose the server-side business service as a Web-Service. `OrderServiceClientTest` is the client-side test class that loads the client-side application context and calls the Web-Service methods through a client-side local interface that represents a remote business service.

The `OrderServiceImpl` is the service to be exposed through a Web-Service. In the server-side's application context, within `org.springframework.remoting.rmi.RmiServiceExporter` Bean, `OrderService` is the name of the service that will be registered with the RMI registry. The service property is for passing the `RmiServiceExporter` and the bean instance. `serviceInterface` is the interface that represents the local business service remotely. Only those methods that are defined in this interface can be called remotely:

```xml
<bean id="orderService"
  class="com.packtpub.liverestaurant.service.OrderServiceImpl" />

  <bean class="org.springframework.remoting.rmi.RmiServiceExporter">
  <property name="serviceName" value="OrderService" />
  <property name="service" ref="orderService" />
  <property name="serviceInterface"
    value="com.packtpub.liverestaurant.service.OrderService" />
  <property name="registryPort" value="1199" />
</bean>
```

On the client side's configuration file, `serviceUrl` is the URL address of the Web-Service and `serviceInterface` in the local interface that enables client calls to the server-side methods remotely:

```
<bean id="orderService"
  class="org.springframework.remoting.rmi.RmiProxyFactoryBean">
  <property name="serviceUrl" value="
    rmi://localhost:1199/OrderService" />
  <property name="serviceInterface"
    value="com.packtpub.liverestaurant.service.OrderService" />
</bean>
```

`OrderServiceClientTest` is the JUnit test case class that loads the application context and calls remote methods through the local interface:

```
@RunWith(SpringJUnit4ClassRunner.class)
@ContextConfiguration("/applicationContext.xml")
public class OrderServiceClientTest {
  @Autowired
  OrderService  orderService;
  @Autowired
  private GenericApplicationContext applicationContext;
  @Before
  @After
  public  void setUpAfter() {
    applicationContext.close();
  }

  @Test
  public  final void testPlaceOrder() throws Exception {
    PlaceOrderRequest orderRequest = new PlaceOrderRequest();
    orderRequest.setOrder(getDummyOrder());
    PlaceOrderResponse orderResponse =
      orderService.placeOrder(orderRequest);
    Assert.assertTrue(orderResponse.getRefNumber().indexOf("1234")>0);
  }

  private Order getDummyOrder() {
    Order order=new Order();
    order.setRefNumber("123");
    List<FoodItem> items=new ArrayList<FoodItem>();
    FoodItem item1=new FoodItem();
    item1.setType(FoodItemType.BEVERAGES);
    item1.setName("beverage");
    item1.setQuantity(1.0);
......
  }
........
}
```

Setting up a servlet-based Web-Service using Hessian/Burlap, exposing business beans

Hessian and Burlap, developed by Caucho (`http://hessian.caucho.com`), are lightweight HTTP-based remoting technologies. Even though both of them use the HTTP protocol to communicate, Hessian communicates using binary messages, while Burlap communicates using XML messages.

Spring's remoting provides features to expose/access Web-Services based on these technologies. On the server side, Spring's `ServiceExporter` bean exposes the server-side Spring business bean (`OrderServiceImpl`) as a Web-Service:

```
<bean id="orderService"
  class="com.packtpub.liverestaurant.service.OrderServiceImpl" />


<bean name="/OrderService"
  class="....ServiceExporter">
  <property name="service" ref="orderService" />
  </bean>
```

On the client-side, Spring's `ProxyFactory` bean exposes remote interface through local client-side interface (`OrderService`):

```
<bean id="orderService"
  class="....ProxyFactoryBean">
  <property name="serviceUrl"
    value="http://localhost:8080/LiveRestaurant/services/OrderService"
/>
  <property name="serviceInterface"
    value="com.packtpub.liverestaurant.service.OrderService"  />
```

Getting ready

In this recipe, we have the following two projects:

1. `LiveRestaurant_R-10.2` (for the server-side Web-Service), with the following Maven dependencies:

    - `spring-webmvc-3.0.5.RELEASE.jar`
    - `log4j-1.2.9.jar`
    - `hessian-3.1.5.jar`

2. `LiveRestaurant_R-10.2-Client` (for the client-side), with the following Maven dependencies:

   - `spring-web-3.0.5.RELEASE.jar`
   - `spring-test-3.0.5.RELEASE.jar`
   - `log4j-1.2.9.jar`
   - `junit-4.7.jar`
   - `hessian-3.1.5.jar`

How to do it...

Follow these steps to set up a servlet-based Web-Service using the Hessian service:

1. Configure `DispatcherServlet` inside the `web.xml` file (URL: `http://<host>:<port>/<appcontext>/services` to be forwarded to this servlet).

2. Register the server-side service interface within Spring's `HessianServiceExporter` in the server-side application context (`applicationContext.xml`), and set service name and service interface.

3. Register the local interface (same as the server side) within Spring's `HessianProxyFactoryBean` in the client-side application context (`applicationContext.xml`), and set service's URL.

4. Add a JUnit test case class in the client side that calls a Web-Service using the local interface

5. Run the following command on `Liverestaurant_R-10.2`:

   `mvn clean package tomcat:run`

6. Run the following command on `Liverestaurant_R-10.2-Client`:

   `mvn clean package`

   In the client-side output, you will be able to see the success message of running the test case, as follows:

   ```
   text.annotation.internalCommonAnnotationProcessor]; root of
   factory
     hierarchy
   Tests run: 1, Failures: 0, Errors: 0, Skipped: 0, Time elapsed:
   0.71 sec

   Results :

   Tests run: 1, Failures: 0, Errors: 0, Skipped: 0

   [INFO]
   ```

Follow these steps to set up a servlet-based Web-Service using the Burlap service:

1. Modify the server-side service interface to Spring's `BurlapServiceExporter` in the server-side application context (`applicationContext.xml`).

2. Modify the client-side application context (`applicationContext.xml`) to Spring's `BurlapProxyFactoryBean`.

3. Run the following command on `Liverestaurant_R-10.2`:

   ```
   mvn clean package tomcat:run
   ```

4. Run the following command on `Liverestaurant_R-10.2-Client`:

   ```
   mvn clean package
   ```

   In the client-side output, you will be able to see the success message of a running test case, as follows:

   ```
   text.annotation.internalCommonAnnotationProcessor]; root of
   factory
      hierarchy
   Tests run: 1, Failures: 0, Errors: 0, Skipped: 0, Time elapsed:
   0.849
      sec


   Results :


   Tests run: 1, Failures: 0, Errors: 0, Skipped: 0


   [INFO]
   [INFO] --- maven-jar-plugin:2.3.1:jar ..
   [INFO] Building jar: ...
   [INFO] --------------------------------------------------------------
   -------------
   [INFO] BUILD SUCCESS
   ```

How it works...

The `Liverestaurant_R-10.2` project is a server-side Web-Service that sets up a servlet-based Web-Service, using the burlap/hessian exporter from Spring's remoting.

The `Liverestaurant_R-10.2-Client` project is a client-side test project that calls the burlap/hessian Web-Service, using the burlap/hessian client proxy from Spring's remoting.

On the server side, `DiapatcherServlet` will forward all the requests using the URL pattern to `BurlapServiceExporter/ HessianServiceExporter` (`http://<hostaddress>/< context>/<services>`):

```
<servlet>
  <servlet-name>order</servlet-name>
  <servlet-class>
    org.springframework.web.servlet.DispatcherServlet
  </servlet-class>
  <load-on-startup>1</load-on-startup>
</servlet>

<servlet-mapping>
  <servlet-name>order</servlet-name>
  <url-pattern>/services/*</url-pattern>
</servlet-mapping>
```

These exporters expose the internal local service implementation (`OrderServiceImpl`) as a Web-Service:

```
<bean name="/OrderService"
    class="org.springframework.remoting.caucho.BurlapServiceExporter">
  <property name="service" ref="orderService" />
  <property name="serviceInterface"
    value="com.packtpub.liverestaurant.service.OrderService" />
</bean>
```

On the client-side, `BurlapProxyFactoryBean/HessianProxyFactoryBean` is responsible for exposing remote methods to the client, using a local client-side service interface (`OrderService`):

```
<bean id="orderService"
  class="org.springframework.remoting.caucho.BurlapProxyFactoryBean">
  <property name="serviceUrl"
    value="http://localhost:8080/LiveRestaurant/services/OrderService"
/>
  <property name="serviceInterface"
    value="com.packtpub.liverestaurant.service.OrderService" />
</bean>
```

The `OrderServiceClientTest` implementation is the same as described in the recipe *Setting up Web-Services using RMI*.

See also...

In this chapter:

Setting up a Web-Services using RMI

Setting up Web-Services using JAX-WS

JAX-RPC was a standard that came with Java EE 1.4 to develop Web-Services, and has become less and less popular in recent years. JAX-WS 2.0 was introduced with Java EE 5 and is more flexible and annotation-based than JAX-RPC in biding concept. Here are some of the advantages of JAX-WS over JAX-RPC:

▶ JAX-WS supports both message-oriented as well as **Remote Procedure Call** (**RPC**) Web-Services, while JAX-RPC supports only RPC

▶ JAX-WS supports SOAP 1.2 and SOAP 1.1, but JAX-RPC supports SOAP 1.1

▶ JAX-WS relies on the rich features of Java 5.0, while JAX-RPC works with Java 1.4

▶ JAX-WS uses the very powerful XML for Object mapping framework (uses JAXB) while JAX-RPC uses its own framework that appeared weak on complex data models

Spring remoting provides feature to set up a JAX-WS Web-Service using java 1.5+ features. For example here, the annotation `@WebService` causes Spring to detect and expose this service as a Web-Service, and `@WebMethod` causes the following method: `public OrderResponse placeOrder(..)`, to be called as a Web-Service method (`placeOrder`):

```
@Service("OrderServiceImpl")
@WebService(serviceName = "OrderService",endpointInterface =
  "com.packtpub.liverestaurant.service.OrderService")
public class OrderServiceImpl  implements OrderService {
  @WebMethod(operationName = "placeOrder")
  public PlaceOrderResponse placeOrder(PlaceOrderRequest
    placeOrderRequest) {
```

In this recipe, JDK's built-in HTTP server is used to set up the Web-Service (since Sun's JDK `1.6.0_04`, JAX-WS can be integrated with the JDK's built-in HTTP server).

Getting ready

Install Java and Maven (SE runtime environment (build `jdk1.6.0_29`)).

In this recipe, we have the following two projects:

1. `LiveRestaurant_R-10.3` (for the server-side Web-Service), with the following Maven dependencies:

   ❑ `spring-web-3.0.5.RELEASE.jar`

   ❑ `log4j-1.2.9.jar`

2. `LiveRestaurant_R-10.3-Client` (for the client-side), with the following Maven dependencies:

- ❑ `spring-web-3.0.5.RELEASE.jar`
- ❑ `log4j-1.2.9.jar`
- ❑ `junit-4.7.jar`

How to do it...

1. Annotate the business service class and its methods.

2. Register the service in the application context file (`applicationContext.xml`), then configure the `SimpleJaxWsServiceExporter` bean, and create a class to load the server-side application context (this sets up the server).

3. Register the local interface (in the same way as you did for the server-side interface) within Spring's `.JaxWsPortProxyFactoryBean` in the client-side application context (`applicationContext.xml`), and set the service's URL.

4. Add a JUnit test case class in the client-side that calls the Web-Service using the local interface.

5. Run the following command on `Liverestaurant_R-10.3` and browse to see the WSDL file located at `http://localhost:9999/OrderService?wsdl`:

   `mvn clean package exec:java`

6. Run the following command on `Liverestaurant_R-10.3-Client`:

   `mvn clean package`

   In the client-side output, you will be able to see the success message of a running test case, as follows:

   ```
   .....

   Dynamically creating request wrapper Class com.packtpub.
   liverestaurant.service.jaxws.PlaceOrder

   Nov 14, 2011 11:34:13 PM com.sun.xml.internal.ws.model.
   RuntimeModeler getResponseWrapperClass

   INFO: Dynamically creating response wrapper bean Class com.
   packtpub.liverestaurant.service.jaxws.PlaceOrderResponse

    ......

   Results :


   Tests run: 1, Failures: 0, Errors: 0, Skipped: 0
   ```

How it works...

The `Liverestaurant_R-10.3` project is a server-side Web-Service (by Spring remoting's exporter bean) that sets up a JAX-WS using DK's built-in HTTP server.

The `Liverestaurant_R-10.3-Client` project is a client-side test project that calls JAX-WS Web-Service using the client proxy from Spring remoting.

On the server-side, `applicationContext.xml` scans and detects annotating tags in `OrderServiceImpl`. Then `SimpleJaxWsServiceExporter` exposes this business service as a Web-Service:

```
<context:annotation-config/>

<context:component-scan base-package=
  "com.packtpub.liverestaurant.service"/>
<bean class=
  "org.springframework.remoting.jaxws.SimpleJaxWsServiceExporter">
  <property name="baseAddress" value="http://localhost:9999/" />
</bean>
```

In the service class, the annotations `@WebService` and `@WebMethod` cause Spring detects(by scanning), and expose(by `SimpleJaxWsServiceExporter`) this service class as a Web-Service and its method (`placeOrder`) as a Web-Service method:

```
@Service("orderServiceImpl")
@WebService(serviceName = "OrderService")
public class OrderServiceImpl  implements OrderService {
  @WebMethod(operationName = "placeOrder")
  public PlaceOrderResponse placeOrder(PlaceOrderRequest
    placeOrderRequest) {
    PlaceOrderResponse response=new PlaceOrderResponse();
    response.setRefNumber(getRandomOrderRefNo());
    return response;
  }
  .......
}
```

On the client side, `JaxWsPortProxyFactoryBean` is responsible for exposing remote methods to the client, using a local client-side interface. `WsdlDocumentUrl` is the Web-Service WSDL address, `portName` is the `portName` value in WSDL, `namespaceUri` is the `targetNameSpace` in WSDL, and `serviceInterface` is the local client-side service interface:

```
<bean id="orderService" class=
  "org.springframework.remoting.jaxws.JaxWsPortProxyFactoryBean">
  <property name="serviceInterface" value=
```

```
      "com.packtpub.liverestaurant.service.OrderService"/>
    <property name="wsdlDocumentUrl" value=
      "http://localhost:9999/OrderService?wsdl"/>
    <property name="namespaceUri" value=
      "http://service.liverestaurant.packtpub.com/"/>
    <property name="serviceName" value="OrderService"/>
    <property name="portName" value="OrderServiceImplPort"/>
  </bean>
```

The `OrderServiceClientTest` implementation is the same as described in the recipe named *Setting up a Web-Services using RMI*.

See also...

In this chapter:

Setting up a Web-Services using RMI

In this book:

Chapter 2, Building Clients for SOAP Web Services

Creating a Web-Service client on HTTP transport

Exposing servlet-based Web-Services using Apache CXF

Apache CXF originated from a combination of the projects, namely: **Celtix (IONA Technologies)** and **XFire (Codehaus)**, which are integrated into the **Apache software foundation**. CXF, by name, implies that it originates from the **Celtix** and **XFire** project names.

Apache CXF provides features to build and deploy Web-Services. The Apache CXF's recommended Web-Service configuration method (frontend or API) is JAX-WS 2.x. Apache CXF, which is not part of Spring's remoting, however, since it can use JAX-WS as its frontend, will be explained in this recipe.

Getting ready

Install Java and Maven (SE Runtime Environment (build `jdk1.6.0_29`)).

In this recipe, we have the following two projects:

1. `LiveRestaurant_R-10.4` (for the server-side Web-Service), with the following Maven dependencies:

    ❑   `cxf-rt-frontend-jaxws-2.2.6.jar`

    ❑   `cxf-rt-transports-http-2.2.6.jar`

❑   `spring-web-3.0.5.RELEASE.jar`

❑   `commons-logging-1.1.1.jar`

2.   `LiveRestaurant_R-10.4-Client` (for the client side), with the following Maven dependencies:

     ❑   `cxf-rt-frontend-jaxws-2.2.6.jar`

     ❑   `cxf-rt-transports-http-2.2.6.jar`

     ❑   `spring-web-3.0.5.RELEASE.jar`

     ❑   `log4j-1.2.9.jar`

     ❑   `junit-4.7.jar`

How to do it...

1. Annotate the business service class and methods (in the same way as you did for JAX-WS).

2. Register the service in the application context file (`applicationContext.xml`) and configure `CXFServlet` inside the `web.xml` file (URL:`http://<host>:<port>/` is to be forwarded to this servlet).

3. Register the local interface (in the same way as you did for the server side) within Spring's `.JaxWsPortProxyFactoryBean`, in the client-side application context (`applicationContext.xml`), and set the service's URL.

4. Add a JUnit test case class in the client side, which calls the Web-Service using the local interface.

How it works...

The `Liverestaurant_R-10.4` project is a server-side Web-Service that set up a CXF, using the JAX-WS API.

The `Liverestaurant_R-10.4-Client` project is a client-side test project that calls JAX-WS Web-Service, using the client proxy from Spring's remoting.

On the server side, the configuration in `applicationContext.xml` detects annotating tags in `OrderServiceImpl`. Then `jaxws:endpoint` exposes this business service as a Web-Service:

```
<!-- Service Implementation -->
<bean id="orderServiceImpl" class=
  "com.packtpub.liverestaurant.service.OrderServiceImpl" />

<!-- JAX-WS  Endpoint -->
<jaxws:endpoint id="orderService" implementor="#orderServiceImpl"
  address="/OrderService" />
```

The `OrderServiceImpl` explanation is the same as described in the recipe *Setting up Web-Services using JAX-WS*.

On the client side, `JaxWsProxyFactoryBean` is responsible for exposing remote methods to the client using a local client-side interface. `address` is the Web-Service service address and `serviceInterface` is the local client-side service interface:

```
<bean id="client" class=
    "com.packtpub.liverestaurant.service.OrderService"
    factory-bean="clientFactory" factory-method="create"/>

<bean id="clientFactory"
    class="org.apache.cxf.jaxws.JaxWsProxyFactoryBean">
    <property name="serviceClass"
        value="com.packtpub.liverestaurant.service.OrderService"/>
    <property name="address"
        value="http://localhost:8080/LiveRestaurant/OrderService"/>
</bean>
```

The `OrderServiceClientTest` implementation is the same as described in the recipe *Setting up Web-Services using RMI*.

See also...

In this chapter:

Setting up Web-Services using RMI

Exposing Web-Services using JMS as the underlying communication protocol

Java Message Service (**JMS**) introduced by Java 2 and J2EE was founded by Sun Microsystems in 1999. Systems using JMS are able to communicate in a synchronous or asynchronous mode, and are based on the point-to-point and publish-subscribe models.

Spring remoting provides the facility to expose Web-Services using JMS as the underlying communication protocol. Spring's JMS remoting sends and receives messages on the same thread in the single-threaded and non-transactional session.

However, for multi-threaded and transactional support for Web-Service on JMS, you can use Spring-WS on JMS protocol, which is based on Spring's JMS-based messaging.

In this recipe, `apache-activemq-5.4.2` is used to set up a JMS server, and default objects, created by this JMS server (`queue`, broker), are used by the projects.

Getting ready

Install Java and Maven (SE Runtime Environment (build `jdk1.6.0_29`)).

Install `apache-activemq-5.4.2`.

In this recipe, we have the following two projects:

1. `LiveRestaurant_R-10.5` (for the server-side Web-Service), with the following Maven dependencies:

   - `activemq-all-5.2.0.jar`
   - `spring-jms-3.0.5.RELEASE.jar`

2. `LiveRestaurant_R-10.5-Client` (for the client side), with the following Maven dependencies:

   - `activemq-all-5.2.0.jar`
   - `spring-jms-3.0.5.RELEASE.jar`
   - `junit-4.7.jar`
   - `spring-test-3.0.5.RELEASE.jar`
   - `xmlunit-1.1.jar`

How to do it...

Register the business service within the `JmsInvokerServiceExporter` bean and register `SimpleMessageListenerContainer` using the `activemq` default objects (`broker`, `destination`) in the server-side application context file.

1. Create a Java class to load the application context and set up the server.
2. Register `JmsInvokerProxyFactoryBean` in the client-side application context file using the `activemq` default objects (`broker`, `destination`)
3. Add a JUnit test case class in the client side that calls the Web-Service using the local interface.
4. Run `apache-activemq-5.4.2` (to set up the JMS server).
5. Run the following command on `Liverestaurant_R-10.5` and browse to see the WSDL file located at `http://localhost:9999/OrderService?wsdl`:

   mvn clean package exec:java

6. Run the following command on `Liverestaurant_R-10.5-Client`:

   mvn clean package

In the client-side output, you will be able to see a success message of a running test case.

```
T E S T S
----------------------------------------------------
Running com.packtpub.liverestaurant.service.client.
OrderServiceClientTest
log4j:WARN No appenders could be found for logger (org.
springframework.test.context.junit4.SpringJUnit4ClassRunner).
log4j:WARN Please initialize the log4j system properly.
Tests run: 1, Failures: 0, Errors: 0, Skipped: 0, Time elapsed:
1.138 sec


Results :


Tests run: 1, Failures: 0, Errors: 0, Skipped: 0
```

How it works...

The `Liverestaurant_R-10.5` project is a server-side Web-Service that sets up a Web-Service by listening on a JMS queue.

The `Liverestaurant_R-10.5-Client` project is a client-side test project that sends JMS messages to a JMS queue.

On the server side, the class `OrderServiceSetUp` loads `applicationContext.xml` and creates a `messageListener` in a container (using `SimpleMessageListenerContainer`) that waits to listen for a message at a specific destination (`requestQueue`). As soon as a message arrives, it calls the method on the business class (`OrderServiceImpl`) through Spring's remoting class (`JmsInvokerServiceExporter`):

```xml
<bean id="orderService"
  class="com.packtpub.liverestaurant.service.OrderServiceImpl"/>
<bean id="listener"
  class="org.springframework.jms.remoting.JmsInvokerServiceExporter">
  <property name="service" ref="orderService"/>
  <property name="serviceInterface"
    value="com.packtpub.liverestaurant.service.OrderService"/>
</bean>
<bean id="container" class=
  "org.springframework.jms.listener.SimpleMessageListenerContainer">
  <property name="connectionFactory" ref="connectionFactory"/>
  <property name="messageListener" ref="listener"/>
  <property name="destination" ref="requestQueue"/>
</bean>
```

On the client side, `JmsInvokerProxyFactory` is responsible for exposing remote methods to the client, using a local client-side interface (`OrderService`). When the client calls the method `OrderService`, `JmsInvokerProxyFactory` send a JMS message to the queue (`requestQueue`), which is the queue the server is listening to:

```xml
<bean id="orderService" class=
   "org.springframework.jms.remoting.JmsInvokerProxyFactoryBean">
   <property name="connectionFactory" ref="connectionFactory"/>
   <property name="queue" ref="requestQueue"/>
   <property name="serviceInterface"
      value="com.packtpub.liverestaurant.service.OrderService"/>
</bean>
```

Index

Thank you for buying
Spring Web Services 2 Cookbook

About Packt Publishing

Packt, pronounced 'packed', published its first book "*Mastering phpMyAdmin for Effective MySQL Management*" in April 2004 and subsequently continued to specialize in publishing highly focused books on specific technologies and solutions.

Our books and publications share the experiences of your fellow IT professionals in adapting and customizing today's systems, applications, and frameworks. Our solution based books give you the knowledge and power to customize the software and technologies you're using to get the job done. Packt books are more specific and less general than the IT books you have seen in the past. Our unique business model allows us to bring you more focused information, giving you more of what you need to know, and less of what you don't.

Packt is a modern, yet unique publishing company, which focuses on producing quality, cutting-edge books for communities of developers, administrators, and newbies alike. For more information, please visit our website: www.packtpub.com.

About Packt Open Source

In 2010, Packt launched two new brands, Packt Open Source and Packt Enterprise, in order to continue its focus on specialization. This book is part of the Packt Open Source brand, home to books published on software built around Open Source licences, and offering information to anybody from advanced developers to budding web designers. The Open Source brand also runs Packt's Open Source Royalty Scheme, by which Packt gives a royalty to each Open Source project about whose software a book is sold.

Writing for Packt

We welcome all inquiries from people who are interested in authoring. Book proposals should be sent to author@packtpub.com. If your book idea is still at an early stage and you would like to discuss it first before writing a formal book proposal, contact us; one of our commissioning editors will get in touch with you.

We're not just looking for published authors; if you have strong technical skills but no writing experience, our experienced editors can help you develop a writing career, or simply get some additional reward for your expertise.

Apache Axis2 Web Services, 2nd Edition

ISBN: 978-1-84951-156-8   Paperback: 308 pages

Create secure, reliable, and easy-to-use web services using Apache Axis2

1. Extensive and detailed coverage of the enterprise ready Apache Axis2 Web Services / SOAP / WSDL engine.

2. Attain a more flexible and extensible framework with the world class Axis2 architecture.

3. Learn all about AXIOM - the complete XML processing framework, which you also can use outside Axis2.

4. Covers advanced topics like security, messaging, REST and asynchronous web services.

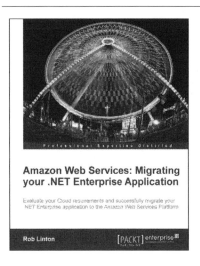

Amazon Web Services: Migrating your .NET Enterprise Application

ISBN: 978-1-84968-194-0   Paperback: 336 pages

Evaluate your Cloud requirements and successfully migrate your .NET Enterprise application to the Amazon Web Services Platform

1. Get to grips with Amazon Web Services from a Microsoft Enterprise .NET viewpoint

2. Fully understand all of the AWS products including EC2, EBS, and S3

3. Quickly set up your account and manage application security

4. Learn through an easy-to-follow sample application with step-by-step instructions

Please check **www.PacktPub.com** for information on our titles

Made in the USA
Lexington, KY
18 December 2013